Relational Grammar

Croom Helm Linguistic Theory Guides
General editor Dick Hudson

Relational Grammar

Barry J. Blake

Routledge
London and New York

First published 1990
by Routledge
11 New Fetter Lane, London EC4P 4EE

Simultaneously published in the USA and Canada
by Routledge
a division of Routledge, Chapman and Hall, Inc.
29 West 35th Street, New York, NY 10001

Typeset in 10 on 11pt Linotron Times by
Hope Services (Abingdon) Ltd
Printed in Great Britain by
T. J. Press (Padstow) Cornwall

British Library Cataloguing in Publication Data
Blake, Barry J.
Relational grammar. – (Croom Helm linguistic theory guides)
1. Syntax. Theories
I. Title
415
ISBN 0 415 01023 3

Library of Congress Cataloging in Publication Data
Blake, Barry J.
  Relational grammar / Barry Blake.
    p. cm. – (Croom Helm linguistic theory guides)
  Bibliography: p.
  Includes indexes.
  ISBN 0 415 01023 3
  1. Relational grammar. I. Title. II. Series.
P158.6.B54 1989   415–dc20   89–10374

Contents

Contents

Contents

Series editor's preface

The Croom Helm Linguistic Theory guides have been commissioned with a rather special readership in mind – the typical linguist, who knows a good deal about a small number of theories in his or her area of specialism, but is baffled by the problem of keeping up with other theories even in that area, to say nothing of other areas. There just aren't enough hours in the day to read more widely, and even if there were it wouldn't help much because so much of the literature is simply incomprehensible except to the initiated. The result is that most of us cultivate our own garden reasonably conscientiously, but have very little idea of what is happening in other people's gardens.

This theoretical narrowing is a practical problem if you are expected to teach on a broad front – say, to give a course of lectures on syntactic theory – when you only know one theory of syntax. Honesty demands that one should tell students about alternative approaches, but how can you when you have at best a hazy idea of what most theories have to say? Another practical problem is the danger of missing pearls of wisdom which might be vitally important in one's research, because they happen to have been formulated in terms of some unfamiliar theory. There can be very few linguists who have not rediscovered some wheel in their area of specialism, out of ignorance about work in other theories.

However, there is an even more serious problem at the research level, because one of the main goals of our joint research effort is to work towards the best possible theory (or set of theories), and this can only be done if we constantly compare and evaluate all the available theories. From this perspective, it is simply pointless to spend one's life developing one theory, or some part of it, if it is already outclassed by some other theory. It is true that evaluation of theories is quite a subjective matter, and is far too complex for any kind of absolute certainty to be arrived at. All we can do is to make a reasonably dispassionate, though subjective, assessment of the strengths and weaknesses of the alternatives, in the full expectation that our colleagues may disagree radically with our verdict. Total ignorance of the alternative theories is clearly not a good basis for evaluating them – though it is arguably better than the misinformation that can be used to bolster one's confidence in one's favourite theory.

It is with these problems in mind, then, that we have planned the Linguistic Theory guides. Each book in the series will focus on one theory that is currently prominent in the literature (or in a few special cases, on a range of such theories). The list of titles is open-ended, and new titles will be added as new theories come into prominence. The aim will be both to inform and to evaluate – to provide enough information to enable the reader to appreciate whatever literature presupposes the theory concerned, and to highlight its strengths and weaknesses. The intention is emphatically not to sell the theory, though the evaluation will naturally be sufficiently positive to explain why the theory is worth considering seriously. Several of the theories are already well provided with textbooks which say a great deal about their strengths and very little about their weaknesses. We assume that our typical reader finds such books irritating at best. What they want is clear exposition at the right level of sophistication (i.e. well above first-year undergraduate level), and wise evaluation, both internally and in relation to other theories.

It is not easy to write a book with these qualities, and we have selected our authors with great care. What we have looked for in each case is essentially someone who is a sympathetic outsider, rather than a devotee of the theory – someone who has experience of working within other theories, but who is well-disposed to the theory concerned, and reasonably well-informed about it. We hope that this recipe will produce books which will be acceptably non-partisan in tone, but we have also taken steps to make them factually reliable as descriptions of the theories concerned. Each book has benefited from detailed comment by at least one prominent devotee (a term which we do not apply disparagingly – without their devotees theories would not come into being, still less develop, and there would be no theoretical linguistics), as well as by an outside reader. Needless to say, the authors have been allowed to stick to their evaluations if the protests of their devotee readers have failed to change their minds.

It is our sincere hope that these books will make a significant contribution to the growth and development of our subject, as well as being helpful to those who read them.

Dick Hudson

Preface

Relational Grammar was developed by David Perlmutter and Paul Postal in the early 1970s and first presented to a large audience at the 1974 Linguistic Society of America Summer Institute in Amherst. The first publications began appearing around this time and by the end of 1987 about 150 linguists had written in this framework, contributing between them over 300 papers, over 40 theses (honours, MA, and PhD), and more than a dozen anthologies and published monographs. However, until now there has been no general book-length treatment of the theory, though a useful booklet by Donald Frantz outlining typical Relational Grammar analyses was put out by the Indiana University Linguistics Club (Frantz 1981).

The present text describes the basic ideas, evaluates them, and compares them with other approaches in other theories. The treatment is straightforward and should be comprehensible to anyone conversant with traditional grammatical terminology. All the unfamiliar terms and conventions of Relational Grammar are explained and illustrated.

The book is aimed primarily at readers interested in modern theories of grammar, but it should also be of relevance to those who are interested in surface-based, function-oriented, comparative linguistics. It contains a wealth of data on morphology and syntax and it also includes comparisons of Relational Grammar analyses with those of 'non-aligned' linguists who are working with much the same data (see section 8.2).

My own background is in Australian Aboriginal languages and this is reflected in the sentences from Kalkatungu and Yalarnnga sprinkled among the examples that are quoted from the Relational Grammar literature. This background has also given me an interest in ergativity and has prompted a section on Relational Grammar's treatment of ergative languages, among which I include many Philippines-type languages like Tagalog, which I claim have been seriously misrepresented in the literature.

Barry Blake
December 1988

x

Acknowledgements

I would first of all like to thank all the Relational Grammarians who have sent me copies of their work: Judith Aissen, Albert Bickford, Bill Davies, Matthew Dryer, Stan Dubinsky, Donna Gerdts, Jeanne Gibson, Nora Gonzales, Alice Harris, Terry Klokeid, Carol Rosen, and Monty Wilkinson. I would particularly like to thank Carol Rosen for sending me kilos of theses, preprints, and offprints of her own work and the work of others.

To the readers of my manuscript I am most grateful for their insightful comments: Matthew Dryer, Anna Siewierska, Jae Jung Song, Stan Starosta, and Nigel Vincent; Dick Hudson, who read in his capacity as editor; Bernard Comrie, who read as the referee; and Bill Davies, who read the draft from the point of view of Relational Grammar.

Various scholars lent me books and procured obscure references. I remember Peter Austin, Edith Bavin, Alice Blake, Kate Burridge, Hilary Chappell, Mark Durie, Bruce Hooley, Graham Mallinson, and Monty Wilkinson and I hope I haven't forgotten any others.

My 'Current Issues' class of 1988 deserve a mention for asking numerous awkward questions: Ketut Artawa, Sandra Cootes, Jane Foley, Harry Klomp, Aveline Perez, and Yvonne Ware.

Ketut Artawa and Rabin Hardjadibrata helped me with the Indonesian examples, and Peter Paul with the German.

On the clerical side I cannot forget Judy Westwood for her typing, Barbara Upton for producing the igloos with MacDraw, and Graham Scott for taking the time to help them both, and last and least, Celia Blake for helping with the proof-reading.

Abbreviations and symbols

abl	ablative
abs	absolutive
acc	accusative
adv,advan	advancement marker
AF	Actor focus
aor	aorist
APG	Arc Pair Grammar
asp	aspect
ass	assertion
aux	auxiliary
ben	beneficiary, benefactive
cau	cause
Cho	chômeur
COP	copula
cl	clitic
D	dummy
dat	dative
det	determiner
detr(ans)	detransitive (derived intransitive) marker
DO	direct object
e	empty category
emph	emphatic
erg	ergative
ev	eventive
evid	evidential
f(em)	feminine
foc	focus
fut	future
gen	genitive
ger	gerundive
GR	grammatical relation
H	head

impf	imperfect
imperf	imperfective
inf	infinitive
instr	instrument, instrumental
IO	indirect object
lk	linker
loc	locative
LSA	Linguistic Society of America
m	masculine
N	noun
neg	negative
NP	noun phrase
obl	oblique
P	predicate
part	participle
pass	passive
perf	perfect
PF	Patient focus
pl	plural
PO	primary object
POSS	possessor
PP	prepositional phrase
prep	preposition
pres	present
prt	particle
PRO	PRO-noun, unspecified nominal
purp	purposive
Q	question
R	recipient, retreat
re	reflexive
rec	recent past
recip	reciprocal
refl	reflexive
rel	relativizer
RG	Relational Grammar
s	singular
S	sentence
SC	structural change
SD	structural description
seq	sequential
sg	singular
SO	secondary object
Su	subject
subj	subjunctive

SUL	Stratal Uniqueness Law
t	trace
TG	Transformational Grammar
top	topic
tr	transitive
U	Union
UAH	Universal Alignment Hypothesis
UHS	Unspecified Human Subject
UNSPEC	unspecified nominal
V	verb
VP	verb phrase
1	subject, first person
2	direct object, second person
3	indirect object, third person
1AEX	1 Advancement Exclusiveness Law
1̂	subject chômeur
2̂	direct object chômeur
3̂	indirect object chômeur
p̂	predicate chômeur
<	derived from

Chapter 1

Outline

1.1 Basic notions

Relational Grammar (RG) was developed primarily by David Perlmutter and Paul Postal in the early 1970s. In this theory grammatical relations are taken to be undefined primitives. The set of relations recognized includes **subject**, **direct object**, **indirect object**, and an as yet undetermined number of **oblique** relations including **benefactive**, **locative**, and **instrumental**. The three relations subject, object, and indirect object are collectively called **terms**. These and the obliques form a hierarchy as in [1]:

[1]   subject   direct object   indirect object   obliques
           1   2   3

The terms are conventionally referred to by their position in the hierarchy, so a subject is referred to as 1, a direct object as 2, and an indirect object as 3. 1 and 2 are known collectively as **nuclear** relations and 2 and 3 as **object** relations.

The relational structure of a clause can be represented in a stratal diagram. The relational structure of the active sentence [2a] is displayed in [3a] and the relational structure of its passive counterpart [2b] is shown in [3b]:

[2a] The crocodile ate the woman.
[2b] The woman was eaten by the crocodile.

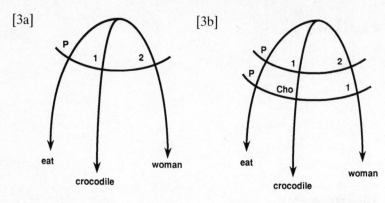

In these networks linear order has been abstracted and the substructure of the predicate and of the noun phrases has been ignored. The active clause [2a] is considered to have a predicate, designated P, a subject, designated 1, and a direct object, designated 2. There is only one **stratum** or level. In the relational structure of the passive there are two strata. The initial stratum is the same as the sole stratum of the active, but the second and final stratum reflects **revaluations**. The initial direct object has advanced to subject and the initial subject has been demoted to the **chômeur** relation (abbreviated *Cho*). The notion of chômeur is peculiar to Relational Grammar and represents one of the innovations of the theory. Informally the chômeur relation is the relation held by a nominal that has been ousted from term status, i.e. from 1, 2, or 3. A chômeur lacks at least some of the grammatical properties of the corresponding term; the subject chômeur in [3b], unlike the subject in [3a], fails to control agreement on the verb, for instance, and occupies a peripheral, optional position in the clause. The term *chômeur* comes from the French word for unemployed or idle person. The related term **chômage** is also used. Thus one could describe *the crocodile* in [2b] being 'put en chômage' or 'going into chômage'.

An agentless passive such as *Their roots had been disturbed* is allotted an initial stratum in which the initial 1 is unspecified and consequently has no realization. This generic nominal is usually represented in recent Relational Grammar literature as PRO:

[4a] Their roots had been disturbed.

[4b]

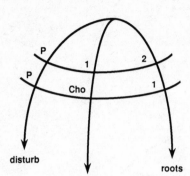

In early versions of the theory initial stratum relations were held to be linked to semantic roles in a universal way, an agent always being an initial 1, a patient an initial 2, and the recipient of a predicate like *give* an initial 3. This principle is known as the **Universal Alignment Hypothesis** (Perlmutter and Postal 1984a:97; orig. 1978). This hypothesis is untenable in its strict form (see section 2.2.), but with a two-place verb a prototypical agent and a prototypical patient, as in *The man hit the dog*, are always taken to be initial 1 and 2 respectively.

The label **indirect object** is used for the recipient in a clause like [5a] but not for the first object in the two-object construction exemplified in [5b]. A sentence like [5a] is considered to have a single stratum with initial relations being reflected directly (as shown in [6a]), but a sentence like [5b] is considered to involve two strata with the initial indirect object having advanced to direct object in the second stratum pushing the initial direct object into chômage [6b]:

[5a] Mao gave power to the people.[1]
[5b] Mao gave the people power.

[6a]

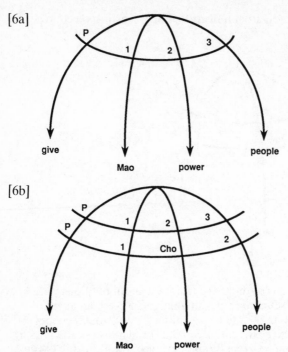

This analysis conflicts with a common traditional analysis in which the first object of the two-object construction is called the indirect object and the second the direct object. There are facts that support the Relational Grammar analysis. The most obvious one is that the notional indirect object, typically a recipient, occupies the position immediately after the verb. The other is that the first object but not the second can be the subject of the corresponding passive, as in [7a]:

[7a] The people were given power by Mao.
[7b]

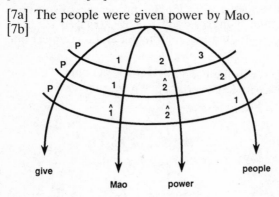

It might appear that in some varieties of English the second object can also correspond with the subject to the passive since there are sentences of the pattern *Power was given the people by Mao*. However, these are derivable from the basic pattern as in [5a] with the advancement of 2 to 1 and subsequent advancement of 3 to 2:

[8a] Power was given the people by Mao.

[8b]

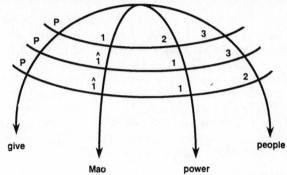

But it should be noted that this analysis is not generally agreed on. The point is taken up in section 2.7.2.

Note that in [7b] and [8b] chômeurs are indicated by the use of a circumflex (from the word chômeur!) over the sign for the term relation held in the immediate preceding stratum. This is an alternative to the abbreviation *Cho* and is useful, as here, where there is more than one chômeur. Since, however, chômeurs arise only from the demotion of terms and cannot be revalued, the distinction between a 1- a 2-, and a 3-chômeur is always apparent from the last stratum in which a term relation was held.

Where there is an indirect object construction, as in [5a], but no double object construction (see [5b]), the indirect object cannot become the subject of the passive. This is to be expected on the assumption that the passive of a transitive clause in English involves the advancing to subject of a direct object only. Thus the following have no passive with the recipient as subject:

[9a] All the workers contributed funds to the party.
[9b] Some donated money to the church.

The 3 to 2 interpretation holds for those double object constructions that have no indirect object counterpart such as the following:

[10a] No one envies you the task.
[10b] God will forgive you your sins.
[10c] They could have spared him the trouble.
[10d] Liz allowed Richard a second chance.
[10e] Waterhouse bet Golea ten grand.
[10f] They refused his wife permission to visit him.
[10g] No one begrudged the little Aussie battler his success.

It also applies to various idiomatic expressions such as *to give someone's back a rub* or *to give something or someone the once over*. It holds too in those languages such as Manam, Blackfoot, Mohawk, Tzotzil, and Huichol where there is never any indirect object alternative to the double object construction. All these constructions are interpreted as involving obligatory 3 to 2 advancement (see also section 8.2).

In English a beneficiary can be advanced to 2 where it is the potential recipient of the patient (initial 2) as in [11] but not where it is just the beneficiary of the action as in [12]:

[11a] The chef made a cake for the boss.
[11b] The chef made the boss a cake.

[12a] I washed the dishes for my aunt.
[12b] *I washed my aunt the dishes.

However, for some speakers the advancee cannot be further advanced to 1 via the passive:

[13] *The boss was made a cake by the chef.

This failure of the advancee to be able to become the subject of the passive can be related to the initial stratum. Relational Grammar allows global reference, i.e. it allows reference back to earlier strata. In this particular case it needs to be stipulated that a 2 arising from the revaluation of a beneficiary cannot advance to 1. (The mechanism for handling this problem is introduced in section 2.8.)

Consider the following pairs:

[14a] The mayor presented the sash to the winner.
[14b] The mayor presented the winner with the sash.

[15a] Bruce fed the stale bread to the pigs.
[15b] Bruce fed the pigs with the stale bread.

[16a] I supplied free milk to/for the orphans.
[16b] I supplied the orphans with free milk.

[17a] The army provided pointie-talkies for all personnel.
[17b] The army provided all personnel with pointie-talkies.

[18a] _____
[18b] My grandmother rewarded me with lots of sweets for getting top marks in Conservative Dentistry.

The [b] sentences are related to the [a] sentences in much the same way as double object constructions (as in [5b]) are to indirect object constructions (as in [5a]) or beneficiary constructions (as in [11a]). The Relational Grammar analysis would appear to be one that takes the [a] sentences to reflect initial relations directly and the direct object in the [b] sentences to be an advancee and the *with*-marked nominal to be a direct object chômeur (see, for instance, Channon 1982). Under such an analysis *reward* would be taken to reflect obligatory advancement to 2 since there is no construction in which *reward* takes the patient, or theme to be the direct object.[2]

The revaluations presented up to this point illustrate the two possible treatments of chômeurs. Either they are re-marked, as with the 1-chômeur of the passive in English, or they retain their term marking as the 2-chômeur does in English in most cases of 3–2 advancement. They also differ with respect to registration of the revaluation. In the passive the change of valency is registered by the introduction of the grammatical verb *be* and the use of the past participle form of the lexical verb. On the other hand with the advancement of indirect object to direct object there is no registration on the verb at all.

When an oblique is advanced to term status, most languages register this revaluation on the verb. In the following Indonesian example a locative is advanced to 2 and the verb is suffixed with *-i*. There is another change in the verb that indirectly reflects the new valency. The advancement of the locative creates a new 2 and hence a transitive verb. In Indonesian a transitive verb followed by a 2 is prefixed by *meng-* with the final nasal of the prefix assimilating to the initial consonant of the stem:

[19a] Ali duduk diatas banku itu.
     1   locative
     Ali sit   on   bench that
     'Ali sits on the bench.'
[19b] Ali men-duduk-i banku itu.
     1   2
     'Ali occupies the bench.'

The effect of an advancement can be essentially discourse motivated and not affect propositional or cognitive meaning. This is normally the case with the passive. However, advancements to 2 are often associated with the advancee acquiring some sense of being more affected. Example [19b] could be translated 'Ali occupies the bench' and could be used in a situation where Ali sprawls or reclines so as to take up most of the seating space. *Menduduki* in fact is also used for 'occupy' in the military sense. The problem of handling the semantic effect associated with revaluation is discussed in section 2.9.

Advancements to 2 usually feed advancements to 1 and this is the case in Indonesian with *menduduki*. Example [19c] illustrates the passive of [19b]:

[19c] Banku itu   di-duduk-i (oleh) Ali.
      bench that pass-sit-loc (by)   Ali
      'The bench is occupied by Ali.'

Indonesian also provides for the advancement of benefactives. This advancement can take place in a clause with a direct object [20a]. The advancee ousts the direct object putting it in chômage [20b]. Part of the evidence for this interpretation is the fact that the putative 2 can be further advanced to 1 [20c], but the putative 2-chômeur cannot [20d]:

[20a] Ali me-masak ikan untuk Hasan.
      Ali   cook fish for   Hasan
      'Ali cooks fish for Hasan.'
[20b] Ali me-masak-kan Hasan ikan.
      Ali   cook-ben   Hasan fish
      'Ali cooks Hasan fish.'
[20c] Hasan di-masak-kan ikan oleh Ali.
      Hasan pass-cook-ben fish by   Ali
      'Hasan is cooked fish by Ali.'
[20d] *Ikan di-masak-kan Hasan oleh Ali.[3]

The stratal diagrams for [19c] and [20c] are shown in [21a] and [21b] respectively:

8

[21a]

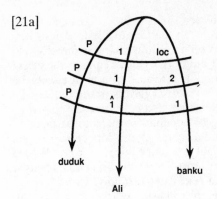

[21b]

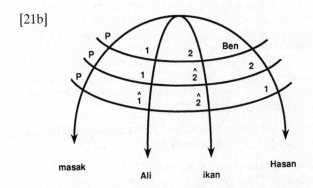

Most advancements are to the nuclear terms, 1 and 2, but there are some cases where Relational Grammarians have posited advancement to 3, as with the following German example (Wilkinson 1983):

[22a] Der Vater nahm das Spielzeug von dem Jungen weg.
      the father took the toy   from the boy: dat away
      'Father took the toy away from the boy.'
[22b] Der Vater nahm dem Jungen das Spielzeug weg.

Where there is registration of a revaluation there is an indication of markedness and thus an indication of which construction might plausibly be taken to reflect initial relations directly and which construction is likely to reflect revaluations. However, where there is no registration, as with the double object construction in English, the question arises of how a pair of paraphrases are to be related. The RG analysis seems to rest heavily on the Universal

9

Alignment Hypothesis which determines that a particular role
holds a particular initial relation. In the German pair [22a, b] the
motivation for taking [22a] to reflect initial relations directly and
[22b] to reflect a revaluation follows from a principle to the effect
that an oblique can be revalued as a term, but a term cannot be
revalued as an oblique. In [22b] *dem Jungen* is in the dative, the
case for recipients, and is therefore taken to be a 3. *Von dem
Jungen* in [22a] is taken to be an oblique, perhaps to be labelled
source, rather than a chômeur. This ascription seems to be
justified. *Von* here has its normal lexical meaning of 'from'. Where
a preposition, postposition, or an oblique case marker signals a
chômeur, this lexical meaning tends not to apply. Consider, for
instance, the preposition *by* in English. Where it marks the
demoted subject in the passive it does not carry its locative
meaning (*sit by the window*) nor its manner meaning (*travel by
rail*); similarly with the preposition *with* in those examples where
RG takes it to be the marker for a demoted object (see [14] to [18]
above). There it does not carry its comitative sense (*sit with the
patient*) nor its instrumental sense (*hit with a hammer*). For that
matter the same applies to *von* in the German passive. Example
[22c] is the bekommen passive of [22b]:

[22c] Der Junge bekam vom Vater das Spielzeug weggenommen.
'The boy had his toy taken away by the father.'

Oblique–3 advancement has been posited for a number of
languages including French (Frantz 1981:14) and Turkish
(Ozkaragöz 1986:43), but it is not nearly so common as oblique–2
advancement. The posited oblique–3 advancements are not
registered on the verb as oblique–2 advancements usually are and
it is not always clear that there are not simply alternative initial
strata. In early RG paraphrases seemed always to be related by
revaluation but more recently there have been a number of
analyses allowing separate initial strata for a single phonological
predicate.[4]

1.2 Some technicalities

The introduction of stratal diagrams in the section above overlooks
some technicalities of representation and definition that need to be
spelled out. The structure of a simple or complex sentence is
conceived of as a relational network which is a graph-theoretic
object involving three types of primitive entity (Perlmutter and
Postal 1983c:82–3):

primitive linguistic elements
primitive grammatical relations
linguistic levels.

Relations hold between elements of which there are at least four types: abstract constituent nodes, logical or semantic primitives, phonological primitives (features), and grammatical categories. Relations are represented by arcs and the levels at which the relations hold are represented by co-ordinates. The object in [23a] is an arc indicating that b (the dependent node) bears the 1 (subject) relation to a (the governing node) at levels c_1 and c_2. Example [23b] presents an equivalent notation:

[23a]

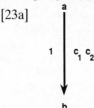

[23b] $[1(b,a) \langle c_1c_2 \rangle]$

A sentence such as [5a], above contains four relations (P, 1, 2, and 3) which could each be represented as in [23a] or [23b] with a common label to identify the common tail (the governing node). In practice the common node is represented by the intersection of arcs as in [24]:

[24]

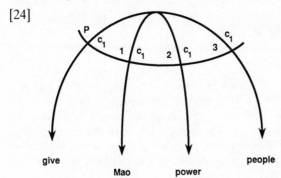

This notation is difficult to read where there are more than two strata. Compare [25] which presents the relational network of [5b] with the equivalent stratal diagram in [6b] above:

[25]

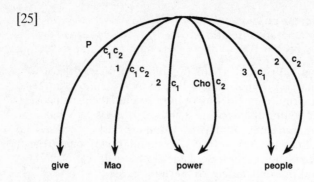

The difficulty of reading network diagrams with co-ordinates and separate arcs for every different relation held by a dependent increases greatly with the number of levels and clauses in a sentence. For this reason stratal diagrams are generally used instead where a single arc represents a dependent and strata are ruled off by 'horizontal' arcs. In some instances it is convenient to do away with a network entirely and simply write the labels for the relations borne by a dependent in columns with separate lines for each level. The relations in [7] could, for instance, be represented as in [26]:

[26] The people were given power by Mao.
     3   P   2   1
     2   P   Cho   1
     1   P   Cho   Cho

Where arcs are represented by columns, there is no graphic indication that they have the same tail. This is implicit in the columnar convention.

1.3 Relational laws

Relational Grammar seeks to formulate linguistic universals and to characterize the class of grammatical constructions to be found in human languages. Obviously not all relational networks are valid for natural language. There must be constraints that delimit the range of possible networks that characterize human language. Here are some laws or well-formedness conditions that bear on possible revaluations.

There can only be one dependent bearing a particular term relation in a particular stratum. This is known as the **Stratal Uniqueness Law** (SUL). Perlmutter and Postal (1983c:95) consider the possibility of extending the coverage of this principle to obliques, but point out that it does not apply to chômeurs (note the presence of two chômeurs in the third stratum of [26] above).[5] There is a requirement that every final stratum contain a subject. This is the **Final 1 Law**. This does not mean that there must be a surface subject. Perlmutter and Postal (1983c:100) cite the italicized clauses in the following sentences which in their analysis have a final 1 but no overt surface 1:[6]

[27a] Try and *tickle yourself*.
[27b] *Kiss one salamander* and people say you are a pervert.
[27c] Joe went home and then *called Betty*.
[27d] Which of those nurses do you think *likes Ted the most*?

Various impersonal sentences have traditionally been described as having no subject, but Perlmutter and Postal claim that all such sentences have a dummy nominal as subject which in some instances is covert (see the discussion of impersonal constructions in Chapter 3).

The **Oblique Law** requires that any dependent that bears an oblique relation bear that relation in the initial stratum (Perlmutter and Postal 1983c:90).[7] For instance, if a nominal bears the instrumental relation in any non-initial stratum, it must also do so in the initial stratum. It cannot acquire an oblique relation in a later stratum. There can be no revaluations from one oblique (e.g. instrumental) to another (e.g. locative). This, of course, does not seem a surprising claim. It is not easy to see what motivation there would be for positing a revaluation from one oblique to another. But note that the Oblique Law precludes a term relation being revalued as an oblique. On the face of it, there would appear to be such cases. The passive, for instance, typically involves the nominal that bore the subject relation in the active appearing with the case marking and/or adpositional marking of an oblique relation ('adposition' is a cover term for preposition and post-position). It would be natural to assume that a 'passive agent' that appears in the ablative has acquired the ablative relation. However, Relational Grammar denies this and asserts that the demoted subject is a chômeur.

In early versions of Relational Grammar a term could be revalued only as a chômeur, but now a nominal holding a nuclear term relation can be demoted to a lower term relation, i.e. a dependent holding a 1 relation can be demoted to 2 or 3, and a dependent holding a 2 relation can be demoted to 3. These demotions can be spontaneous; they need not arise as a result of the advancement of another nominal to a particular relation which forces the demotion under the Stratal Uniqueness Law. However, demotions to chômeur status are never spontaneous, but only arise when another nominal usurps the relation by advancement, ascension or raising (see Chapter 4) or dummy birth (see section 3.2). This is stipulated by the **Motivated Chômage Law** (Perlmutter and Postal 1983c:99). Chômeurs can never be advanced. This is prohibited in the **Chômeur Advancement Ban** (ibid.:117). Here is a list of licit revaluations:

[28] *Advancements*
2–1	3–2	Oblique–3
3–1	Oblique–2	
Oblique–1		

Demotions
1–2	2–3	3-Chômeur
1–3	2-Chômeur	
1-Chômeur		

It is natural to think of revaluations as representing stages in a process, particularly where one revaluation seems to feed another as in [7] above where 3–2 advancement seems logically to precede 2–1 advancement. However, relational networks simply represent the relations between nodes at various levels. The range of possible networks is limited by universal laws such as the Stratal Uniqueness Law, the Motivated Chômage Law and so on. The range of revaluations found in particular languages needs to be specified either by positive stipulation or by supplementing the universal laws with language-particular constraints.

At least some Relational Grammarians accept the traditional distinction between the syntax and the lexicon.[8] The **valency** (or **valence**) of a particular predicate can be stipulated in the lexicon. Informally we could consider entries for predicates with the initial stratum specified to appear as follows:

[29] P run : 1
P hit : 1 2
P give : 1 2 3

Where the valencies of particular predicates undergo a particular revaluation obligatory under specified conditions or are constrained from undergoing certain revaluations, this can be specified in the lexicon by an **extended valence** (Davies and Dubinsky 1988), i.e. a valence referring to more than one stratum. This is illustrated in section 2.8 of the next chapter.

The idea of the grammar being non-sequential is not easy to get used to and a number of linguists writing in the RG framework use process oriented terminology, sometimes with a word of apology.

Some linguists are sceptical of the distinction between a sequential derivation and a non-sequential multistratal network (e.g. Comrie 1986:784–5). The important difference between the relational networks of Relational Grammar and the sequential derivations of Transformational Grammar (see section 1.4) is that RG allows rules of one stratum to refer to other strata. For example, a rule of control, as we shall see in section 2.6, may distinguish between a final indirect object that is also an initial indirect object (i.e. one that has not been revalued) and a final indirect object that is an initial subject. Such a rule in a sequential derivation would be called a global rule (Lakoff 1970) and in most theories global rules are considered excessively powerful. However, they are used regularly in RG and numerous examples are adduced which purport to require them.

1.4 Motivation

To anyone approaching Relational Grammar from any variety of traditional grammar the basic notions should seem familiar and motivated even if some of the terminology and notation is new; in particular, the idea of describing sentence structure in terms of relations such as subject and object should seem natural enough. However, Relational Grammar began as a breakaway from the Transformational Grammar (TG) of Chomsky (1957, 1965) who sought to describe language in terms of structural notions such as dominance and precedence between categories. A Transformational Grammar consists essentially of phrase structure rules as in [30] supplemented by transformations. The phrase structure rules can be said to specify or generate a range of basic sentence patterns. Transformations are used *inter alia* to cover other patterns that are paraphrases of some in the first set such as double object structures and passives:

[30] S   →   NP VP
    VP →   V (NP) (PP)
    PP →   P NP
    NP →   N

(S = sentence, NP = noun phrase, VP = verb phrase, PP = prepositional phrase.)

    These phrase structure rules, when supplemented by lexical insertion rules specifying the nouns, verbs, and prepositions, can derive a sentence. A particular derivation will consist of a series of strings of categories that can be described in terms of a tree diagram or **phrase marker**. The two transitive phrase markers specified by [30] are as follows:

[31a]

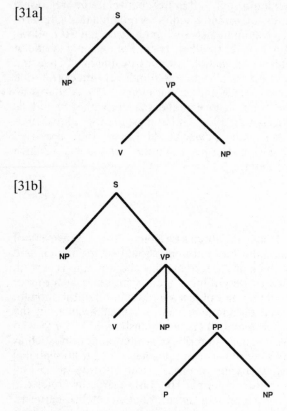

[31b]

The phrase markers [31a] and [31b] fit sentences such as the Indonesian examples [32] and [33] respectively and their English translations.

[32] Ali me-masak ikan.
      'Ali cooks fish.'

[33] Ali me-masak ikan untuk Hasan. (= [20a] above)
      'Ali cooks fish for Hasan.'

The phrase markers generated by the phrase structure rules represent the **deep structure** of a sentence.

   In order to account for sentences like [20b] above, where in Relational Grammar terms a benefactive advances to 2, a transformation of the following form would be used (SD is the structural description of the string to be transformed and SC is the structural change):

[34] *Double object forming transformation*

SD	NP	V	NP	P	NP
	1	2	3	4	5
SC	1	2	5	0	3

This will have the effect of moving the NP from within the PP to a position immediately after the verb and deleting the preposition (the PP node needs to be erased too):

[35] Ali me-masak-kan Hasan ikan. (= [20b] above)
    'Ali cooks Hasan fish.'

The operation of each transformation yields a new phrase marker. The last phrase marker in the transformational derivation is the **surface structure**.

Perhaps the most important difference to be noted between this system and the Relational Grammar one outlined above is that in Transformational Grammar the subject is defined as the function of the N(oun) P(hrase) immediately dominated by S(entence) and the object as the function of the NP immediately dominated by the V(erb) P(hrase). In such a system grammatical relations are derived or non-primitive entities. They are given a structural definition and require the positing of a VP for the definition to be maintained.

According to Perlmutter and Postal a particular deficiency of Transformational Grammar is that in such a system no universal characterization of relationships such as that between active and passive is possible, as it is in traditional grammar (1983a, orig. 1977). In English the passive clause differs from the corresponding active in terms of order, prepositional marking, and verb morphology. But none of these differences characterize the active/passive relation universally. In some languages active and passive clauses have the same order (e.g. Tzotzil), and in some the subject chômeur has postpositional marking (e.g. Turkish) or oblique case marking (e.g. Russian) rather than a preposition. Relational Grammar claims to be able to abstract what is common to these structurally diverse relationships, namely a correspondence between the 2 of the active and the 1 of the passive. In RG the passive involves a 2 in a transitive stratum advancing to 1. In particular languages there will be differences of order, agreement, case marking, and adposition, though many of these details will not be peculiar to the passive but will be part of the expression of subject, direct object, and oblique.

Technically TG can provide a universal definition of passive. TG takes the verb phrase to be universal at some deep level of structure. Under this assumption the passive can be defined universally as a transformation that moves the NP immediately dominated by VP and makes it the NP immediately dominated by S. However, the TG assumption of a VP, an assumption which is still maintained in Chomsky's Government and Binding theory (1981), the successor to TG, is very dubious. Certainly it is not a universal of surface structure. In the Celtic languages, for instance, the basic word order is Verb–Subject–Object which necessitates the extraction of V from the VP between deep and surface structure. In many languages word order is grammatically free and there is no evidence for a surface VP.

Proponents of the Government and Binding model sometimes argue for an asymmetry among the verb's dependents. Marantz (1984:23 ff.) argues that the insertion of an argument as logical object forms a predicate which in turn determines the semantic role of the logical subject. He claims that most simple verbs in English express a wide range of predicates depending on the choice of direct object, e.g. *throw a baseball*, *throw a party*, *throw a fit*, *throw a match*. On the other hand the choice of subject does not normally imply a particular role for the object, although semantic selectional restrictions sometimes narrow the choice of predicate: *the policeman threw NP*, *the boxer threw NP*, *the social director threw NP*, etc. Marantz also notes that there are countless verb–object idioms such as *kick the bucket*, while subject–verb idioms are rare. This might seem like a good argument for a universal logico-semantic VP, but Marantz posits a VP consisting of the agent NP and the verb in certain ergative languages like Dyirbal even though his point, to the extent that it is valid, is a universal of the patient–verb relationship (the reasons for establishing an agent–verb VP in Dyirbal are discussed briefly in section 7.3).[9]

However, even if no VP were posited, grammatical relations could still be distinguished by order and that is how the two objects of the double object construction are distinguished in the TG system. The important point is whether any structure other than the surface structure needs to be posited.

In Government and Binding the passive is derived from a deep structure in which the subject is empty [e]. The verb assigns a semantic role to its object, but no (abstract) case. Being passive it does not assign a semantic role to the subject. The object then moves to the subject position to fulfil the case requirement of the finite verb taking its semantic role with it but leaving behind a trace (indexed by the subscript *i* in the following examples). Here is the analysis of *Hasan is seen by Ali*:

[36a] [e] see-en Hasan (by Ali)
[36b] Hasan$_i$ is seen t$_i$ (by Ali)

The agent can be introduced in a non-nuclear phrase, the semantic role being assigned by the preposition. This analysis has the advantage that it separates the advancement and demotion aspects of the passive, or in transformational terms, the preposing and postposing movements. Van Riemsdijk and Williams (1986:44), for instance, point out that with passivization in NPs the preposing is optional: *the destruction of the city by the enemy* or *the city's destruction by the enemy*.

This analysis of the passive is still structural, but a number of grammatical models that developed in the 1970s are like RG in employing a relationally based passive. Starosta's Lexicase (1978, 1988) uses derivational rules that alter the case frame of verbs. These case frames include grammatical relations and case but need not mention order. Bresnan's Lexical Functional Grammar has the following formulation for the passive in Universal Grammar (1982:9):

[37a] (SUBJ)→ ∅(OBLIQUE)
[37b] (OBJ) → (SUBJ)

Passivization produces new intransitive lexical entries from transitive ones with the correspondences shown in [37]. The rule for the passive in English will specify (BY OBJ) for (OBLIQUE), that is, it will specify that the subject corresponds with the object of the preposition *by*.

Another argument that could be put forward in favour of a relational rather than a structural or categorial approach concerns subcategorization. Consider a verb like *put*. It is a three-place verb requiring an agent/initial 1, patient/initial 2, and a locative. The locative can be realized via a prepositional phrase or an adverb (*put him in it, put it there*). It is simpler to specify a relation rather than a disjunction of categories. In some languages the range of categories realizing a particular relation can range over noun phrase, adpositional phrase, relational noun, adverb, particle, and conjunction.

Before proceeding to a detailed discussion of the Relational model in succeeding chapters I should point out that Relational Grammar began by concentrating on the relations of arguments to predicates and that this area of grammar has proved so rich that very few other areas of grammar have received much attention. I should also add that there has been very little attempt to specify details of surface structure. As mentioned earlier, almost all the Relational Grammar literature deals in incomplete networks of the type introduced above. The level at which all revaluations are complete is the **final stratum** which is to be distinguished from the **surface structure**. The latter would include a full specification of the morphemes in linear sequence.[10] The linearization rules can be based on the **central** grammatical relations or the **overlay** relations or both. The central relations include 1, 2, 3, the obliques, and the chômeur relation. The overlay relations, as the name suggests, can be held in addition to the central relations. The overlay relations include **Topic**, **Overweight**, **Relative**, and **Question** as illustrated in the following sentences (Perlmutter and Postal 1983c:87):

[38a] *That* I would never have believed he would do.
[38b] I offered to Frederica at that time *the most beautiful pearl of the most expensive collection.*
[38c] the table *which* he is sending
[38d] *Who* do you think Ted met?

Linearization rules are illustrated in section 1.5.

The nominal dependents of the clause are treated for the most part as unanalysed wholes except for possessive phrases where the relations **possessor** and **head** are distinguished (see section 4.3.2). In theory the substructures of the clausal dependents are to be analysed, but until recently Relational Grammarians had not got around to investigating this area. In 1981 Rosen wrote the following, perhaps echoing the feeling of her fellow Relational Grammarians: 'Relations existing within sub-clausal units are needed for housekeeping purposes, since they must figure in language-specific linearisation rules, but it is not yet clear whether any interesting discoveries about them are to be expected' (1981:10). Ironically Rosen has now emerged as a co-proposer, along with Davies, of an interesting new analysis of the verbal group (see sections 5.3.1 and 5.3.2) and she has begun to explore relations within the noun phrase with promising results (see section 5.3.3). However, it must be said that an enormous amount remains to be done about details of the structure of phrases and words.

1.5 Linearization

Relational networks are unordered representations. Surface structure word order is introduced by linearization rules which for the most part can be based on final stratum grammatical relations. Basic word order in English can be specified as in [39] (Perlmutter's afterword to Perlmutter and Postal 1983b):

[39] 1–P–2–3–Non-term

Its application can be seen in [40]:

[40a] The students gave silver   trays to Bazza and the boss.
           1   P   2   3

[40b] The students gave Bazza and the boss silver trays.
           1   P   2   Cho

[40c] The government was overthrown by Rabuka.
           1   P   Cho

Marked word order typically involves an overlay relation such as **Question** or **Topic**. Overlay relations are held in addition to central relations. In English question words are normally fronted except in echo questions. The position of *what* in [41] will be accounted for by assigning it the overlay relation of **Question** and a language particular linearization rule for placing question words first in the clause:

[41] What sayest thou?

This is an example of early modern English conveniently chosen to avoid the complication of *do*. The RG treatment of overlay relations is programmatic only. One question that arises is whether an extraposed nominal with a topic function always bears a central relation. Does *ice-cream* in [42], for instance, bear the direct object relation?[11]

[42] Ice-cream, I love it.

1.6 Arc Pair Grammar

In the late 1970s Postal, in conjunction with David Johnson, developed a variant of Relational Grammar known as Arc Pair Grammar. The major reference is Johnson and Postal's *Arc Pair Grammar* (1980). It is extremely heavy going largely because of its difficult-to-read relational networks and bizarre terminology. Pedagogically useful material can be found in Postal 1982, Postal 1986, and Aissen 1987.

Arc Pair Grammar employs the relational network rather than the simpler stratal diagram (compare [25] and [6b] above). Two relations that hold between arcs are represented, namely the **sponsor** and **erase** relations. Here is an Arc Pair Grammar relational network for the passive given previously as [2b] *The woman was eaten by the crocodile*:

[43]

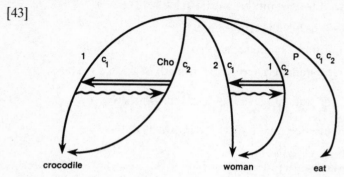

The initial 1 arc is said to sponsor the Cho arc. The sponsor relation is shown by the wiggly arrow. The Cho arc erases the initial 1 arc, i.e. in simple terms the chômeur arc occurs instead of the initial 1 arc in a later stratum not as well as the initial 1 arc. The erase relation is shown by the double arrow. As [43] shows the initial 2 sponsors the final 1 and the final 1 erases the initial 2. Initial relation arcs are self-sponsoring and some arcs self-erase, i.e. they simply do not appear in surface structure. The initial 1 arc is also referred to as the **predecessor** of the Cho arc; conversely the Cho arc is the **successor** of the initial 1 arc. These two terms are useful in describing the career of a nominal over successive strata and are sometimes used in RG.

Chapter 2

Some clause-internal revaluations

2.1 Introduction

This chapter confines itself to advancements and demotions within a simple sentence. The notions of advancement and demotion presuppose a hierarchy against which the directions of revaluation are gauged and revaluation implies a set of initial relations distinct from final relations. The two sections immediately below discuss the establishment of initial relations (2.2) and the hierarchy (2.3). Subsequent sections introduce some revaluations and discuss problems of analysis that arise in connection with the establishment of initial relations and the hierarchy.

2.2 Establishing initial relations

Suppose we demarcate sets of grammatical relations in particular languages on the basis of morphological and syntactic behaviour. If we identify these relations across languages according to the roles they encode in unmarked constructions, we generally find that each relation so identified tends to exhibit similar grammatical characteristics. Thus the relation identified across languages as subject on the basis of encoding, *inter alia*, agents will usually exhibit features such as controlling person agreement on the verb or being obligatorily suppressed with non-finite verb forms. Given this correlation between semantic role and grammatical relation it is not surprising that Relational Grammarians proposed that roles were related to grammatical relations in a universal way, i.e. that initial grammatical relations could be assigned on the basis of semantic roles. This was known as the Universal Alignment Hypothesis (UAH) (Perlmutter and Postal 1984a:97; orig. 1978). It means taking an agent, experiencer, or cognizer to be an initial 1, a patient to be an initial 2, and a recipient to be an initial 3.[1] Instruments, locations, and the like can be expected to be encoded

Relational Grammar

as obliques though there has been practically no discussion of
how many obliques there might be or how each is to be
demarcated.
The Universal Alignment Hypothesis in its strict form is
untenable. Consider for a start the following sentences and their
English translational equivalents:

[1] *Latin*
    Utor   cratere.
    use:I   mixing:bowl:abl
    'I use a mixing bowl.'

[2] *Russian* (Wierzbicka 1980:24)
    Ivan požal   plečami.
    Ivan shrugged shoulders:instr
    'Ivan shrugged his shoulders.'

[3a] *Yidiny* (based on Dixon 1977:305)
    Bunya   nyanggaadyin   yidiinydya.
    woman   speak   Yidiny:loc
    'The woman speaks in Yidiny.'
[3b] Bunya   yidiny   nyanggaadyin.
    woman   Yidiny speak
    'The woman speaks Yidiny.'
[3c] Bunyaang   yidiny   nyanggaadyinga.
    woman:erg Yidiny speak:loc/advan
    'The woman speaks Yidiny.'

The Latin and Russian sentences, when put alongside their
English translational equivalents, are good illustrations of the fact
that the objective world can be conceived of in different ways. It is
not surprising that Latin chooses to encode the 'used' complement
of *uti* in the ablative, since the ablative is the case that encodes
instruments and the entity used is somewhat like an instrument in
that it is used in connection with affecting something. However, it
is itself affected by the using activity and English chooses to
encode the used entity as a direct object, i.e. in the relation used
prototypically to encode affected patients as in *The man hit the
dog*. Much the same thing is true of the Russian example and its
English equivalent. When we shrug our shoulders we are not
trying to affect our shoulders; the moving of the shoulders is for
the purpose of signalling an attitude. Russian chooses to encode
the instrumental aspect of the gesture, whereas English does not
pick this out at all. Now if objectively determined roles are
encoded in terms of initial grammatical relations in a universal
way, then the non-actor argument of shrugging predicates will

24

have to be allotted the 2 relation and obligatorily demoted in a language like Russian, or allotted the oblique relation of instrument and obligatorily advanced in a language like English. The former possibility would run into a technical difficulty inasmuch as demotion to instrumental would have to be demotion to chômage (remember obliques cannot be created by revaluation) and this is only possible in Relational theory where another nominal usurps the initial relation (the Motivated Chômage Law). There is no evidence for a non-initial 2, no indication that the Russian instrumental is not marking an oblique, and no morphological evidence for a revaluation in either direction. All this applies, *mutatis mutandis*, to the Latin example.

The Yidiny examples [3a] and [3c] demonstrate that in this language the complement of a predicate meaning 'speak (in) language x' can appear in the locative or be advanced to direct object. The presence of the suffix *-nga* in [3c] *vis-à-vis* its absence in [3a] indicates that [3c] is likely to reflect a revaluation, rather than [3a]. Since chômeurs cannot be advanced, this forces the interpretation that the locative is the initial grammatical relation. However, a comparison of languages reveals that different languages encode the analogous complement in a variety of cases. Among other Australian languages we find the instrumental in Malak-Malak, the ablative in Ngalakan, the perlative ('through', 'along') in Djapu, the dative or special locative ('against', 'opposite') in Kalkatungu, and the accusative in Diyari. Another common possibility is to use the unmarked case in a detransitivized construction as in the Yidiny example [3b] (Dixon 1977:305, 364).[2] Since there can be no advancements or demotions between obliques, the choice of any one oblique as the initial grammatical relation will fail to be generalizable to other languages where the case marking indicates a different oblique.

The basic problem with the UAH is that it operates on objective, referential roles and ignores the fact that the world can be conceived of in different ways. Postal (1982:411), writing about the **Principle of Initial Determination**, which is the equivalent of the UAH in Arc Pair Grammar,[3] admits that converse predicates like *buy* and *sell* are a problem:

[4a] Mark bought a car from Fred.
[4b] Fred sold a car to Mark.

If one considers that *Fred* is objectively a source in both sentences, and *Mark* a destination, then there is an insuperable problem. However, if one allows that *Mark* is conceived of as the initiator of the transaction in [4a] and as the recipient in [4b] while *Fred* is conceived of as a source in [4a] but an initiator in [4b], no problem arises.

The only argument against the UAH to appear in the RG literature comes from Rosen. This is discussed in section 2.4 below. However, it seems that Relational Grammarians have abandoned the strict version of the UAH, since there are now quite a few references in the literature to alternative ways of encoding roles in initial grammatical relations (Perlmutter and Rosen 1984:xvii; Aissen 1983:294 (illustrated in [33], [34] in Chapter 4); Postal 1986:31; and Legendre 1986:149). If the UAH were valid, then it is difficult to see why one would need initial grammatical relations.

What can be salvaged from the UAH is that certain prototypical roles are consistently aligned with certain initial relations. A prototypical agent and a prototypical patient as in *John killed Fred* are probably always initial 1 and initial 2 respectively. Such an assumption is implicit not only in RG analyses but in most analyses.

2.3 Hierarchy

As noted in section 1.1 the term relations are ranked hierarchically with respect to one another and to the obliques:

[5] subject   direct object   indirect object   obliques
    1   2   3

Little if any attempt has been made in the RG literature to justify this hierarchy. It is taken very much for granted. Perhaps it is felt that the evidence for it is obvious. Nevertheless it seems to be worth pointing out some of the ways the hierarchy manifests itself as a prelude to discussing advancements and demotions in later sections.

The hierarchy represents the unmarked word order in various languages including English and French (with non-pronominal dependents). It also frequently shows up in case marking: there are languages where only the subject is unmarked by an affix or adposition (Quechua) and some where only the nuclear terms are unmarked (Malay, Halkomelem). It also appears in the distribution of person–number agreement (typically cross-referencing and typically on the verb).[4] Indo-European languages normally exhibit agreement with the subject only; some languages such as Swahili have agreement with subject and object, and others such as Georgian have a third set of agreement markers for indirect object as well. A few languages exhibit cross-referencing with some obliques.[5]

While the presence versus absence of case marking and adpositions tends to be associated with the oblique end of the hierarchy, agreement, whether cross-referencing or not, normally runs from the 'top' of the hierarchy. The arrowheads in [6] indicate the direction of the distribution of these features and common cut-off points along the hierarchy:

[6]   1   2   3   obliques
  case   ←——←——←———
  agreement ›———→

The notion that the subject end of the hierarchy is the 'top' is justified in terms of grammatical privileges. Keenan and Comrie (1977), for instance, have demonstrated that this hierarchy, or an elaboration of it, can also be found in accessibility to relativization, with the relations at the subject end having greater accessibility to relativization across languages. However, the hierarchy in RG applies not just to surface structure but to all strata. This makes sense if one considers that the hierarchy is one of grammatical privilege. A single stratum clause is one where there is an unmarked relationship between role and relation. Revaluations represent marked associations of role and relation. The passive, for instance, represents the choice of a patient as opposed to an agent for the most privileged relation.

RG recognizes two defined term relations, **ergative** and **absolutive**. Ergative is the subject in a transitive stratum and absolutive embraces the subject in an intransitive stratum and the direct object in a transitive stratum.[6] These relations manifest themselves most obviously in case marking or in cross-referencing agreement, but as we shall see in Chapter 6 they can have more covert instantiations.[7] Note that ergative and absolutive may be held simultaneously with subject and object. These relations represent a cross-cutting classification of the nuclear relations, not separate relations holding their own positions on the hierarchy.

In a few Caucasian languages the ergative-absolutive dichotomy shows up in both case marking and agreement. Such a language is Avar (Bechert 1977:57):

[7a] Aḥmad v-ač-ana.
     Ahmad msg-come-past
     'Ahmad came.'
[7b] Paṭimat y-ač-ana.
     Fatima fsg-come-past
     'Fatima came.'

[8a] Aḥmadi-cca Paṭimat y-ecc-ana.
Ahmad-erg Fatima fsg-praise-past
'Ahmad praised Fatima.'
[8b] Paṭimati-cca Aḥmad v-ecc-ana.
Fatima-erg Ahmad msg-praise-past
'Fatima praised Ahmad.'

As can be seen, the actor in the transitive clause is marked by a suffix glossed as ergative, whereas the intransitive subject and the patient of the transitive verb are unmarked. However, it is the unmarked actant that is cross-referenced on the verb. *V* represents masculine singular and *y* represents feminine singular.

In terms of the criteria referred to above for establishing the relational hierarchy absolutive outranks ergative.

One might question the establishing of indirect object as the lowest ranking term relation rather than as one of the obliques. After all indirect objects are typically marked like obliques. However, in many languages there are criteria that group the indirect object with the terms, the most common being the availability of clitic representation. In French, for instance, there are indirect object clitics distinct from the direct object series (at least in the third person) and the subject series. In [9b] *il* (subject), *les* (direct object) and *lui* (indirect object) are all unstressable proclitic forms:

[9a] Jean donne les escargots à Paul.
'John gives the snails to Paul.'
[9b] Il les lui donne.
'He gives them to him.'

But one might object that in French there is also a clitic for directional phrases but these are not taken to be terms. In [10] *y* replaces *Dijon*:

[10a] Michel est allé à Dijon.
'Michael has gone to Dijon.'
[10b] Michel y est allé.
'Michael has gone there.'

In fact properties characteristic of nuclear terms often extend to a number of non-nuclear relations. In some Australian languages a variety of animate obliques can be represented by clitic forms just as subject and object can. A survey across languages certainly shows that the relation encoding the recipient of 'give' is most likely to show up at the top of the non-nuclear hierarchy. Besides being the most likely relation to be cross-referenced the putative indirect object is the relation most likely to be advanced to direct object (without registration of the advancement) and is often nuclear-like in that it can be represented by zero when third person. However, in many languages there seems to be no internal evidence to show that the indirect object is term-like rather than oblique. RG allows an analysis to be underdetermined. This is not a characteristic exclusive to RG, but it is striking in the case of indirect objects. There does not appear to be any theoretical reason to assume that the indirect object occurs in every language, but I know of no RG analysis of a language which does not identify one. Some further discussion of indirect objects comes up in section 2.5, in all the subsections of 2.7 and in section 6.3

2.4 The Unaccusative Hypothesis

Perlmutter and Postal (1984a, orig. 1978) pointed out that in English some intransitive verbs allow pseudo-passives (as in [11]) while others do not [12]:

[11a] The bed was slept in by the shah.
[11b] The bridge was skied under by the contestants.
[11c] The bed was jumped on by the children.
[11d] The package was stepped on by a camel.

[12a] *The bridge was existed under by trolls.
[12b] *The oven was melted in by the ice cube.
[12c] *The sink was oozed into by the toothpaste.
[12d] *The woods were vanished in by Little Red Riding Hood.
[12e] *The bed was happened in by something disgusting.
[12f] *The test tube was united in by the ingredients.

They attribute the difference to a difference in initial stratum relations. The predicates in [11] are said to have an initial 1 as we would expect. The predicates in [12], however, are analysed as having an initial 2. The former class are called **unergative** (a stratum with a 1 but no 2 is unergative) and the latter class **unaccusative** (a stratum with a 2 but no 1 is unaccusative), hence the **Unaccusative Hypothesis**. Clauses with unaccusative predicates will normally involve at least two strata, an initial one with a nominal holding the direct object relation, and a second one in which the object has advanced to subject (fulfilling the Final 1 Law). The contrast between an initially unergative predicate and an initially unaccusative one is illustrated in the following (Perlmutter and Postal 1984a:95):

[13a] Martians dream.   [13b] Martians exist.
[13c]   [13d]

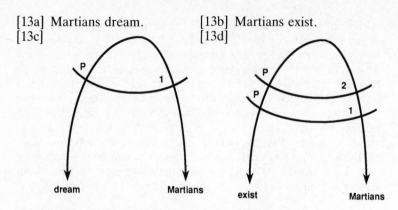

The failure of unaccusative predicates to permit pseudo-passives is attributed to the **1 Advancement Exclusiveness Law** (1AEX) which limits advancements to subject to one per clause.[8] Since a sentence such as *Trolls existed under the bridge* involves the advancement of *trolls* from 2 to 1, it cannot have another stratum in which *the bridge* advances from its oblique locative relation to subject.[9] The stratal diagram for **The bridge was existed under by trolls* would be as in [14]:[10]

[14]

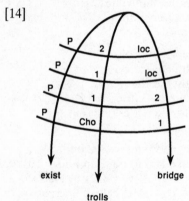

It is not immediately obvious that the difference between the passives in [11] and [12] is syntactic. After all, [11] can be rendered infelicitous by substituting a comparatively small agent such as a flea, a fly or a tick. This suggests that the difference between the two sets of passives is pragmatic. For a passive (plain or pseudo) to be acceptable it must involve saying something significant about the patient or location or whatever role is advanced. Passives of unergatives such as *The bed was jumped on*

30

by the tick are hard to find a context for that would make them
felicitous, and one could suggest that passives of unaccusatives are
always unacceptable because it is difficult to conceive of the
putative initial 2, which in terms of its semantic role is generally
inert, having a significant effect on the other argument of the verb.

In order to establish the Unaccusative Hypothesis one needs
evidence from another domain of grammar. If we take the subject
of verbs that are unergative on the basis of the pseudo-passive test
we find that they tend to be treated like ergative subjects with
respect to nominalization, i.e. they tend to be encoded by the
genitive determiner: *John's jumping, John's reading of the will.*
Conversely the subjects of unaccusative verbs tend to be treated
like direct objects, i.e. they are usually encoded in an *of*-phrase:
the melting of the ice, the destruction of the city. However, this is
only a tendency not an absolute and is related to a broader
tendency for animates to be encoded by a determiner phrase and
inanimates by an *of*-phrase.

Certain derivational affixes in English tend to pick out
unaccusative verbs as opposed to unergative ones. L. Horn (1980)
shows that *re-, un-, -able*, and *-ee* can be used with unaccusative
verbs or transitive verbs, but not unergative ones. When used with
transitive verbs they indicate properties of the object not the
subject:

[15] *transitive*	*unaccusative*	*unergative*
repaint	reappear	*resneeze
rewash	re-enter	*rego
unfold	unfold	*unswim
washable	perishable	*sneezable
draftee	absentee	*dancee

However, as one might expect with lexical derivation, there are
various exceptions. *Escapee* is synchronically a derivative of
escape, an unergative verb under the pseudo-passive test (*This
prison has never been escaped from*); *biographee* has no verbal
counterpart, which highlights the fact that derivational relationships
are not part of regular syntax, and *laughable* shows a correspondence
between its subject and the object of the preposition *at* of the
phrasal verb *laugh at*. There is nothing in the behaviour of these
affixes that cannot be attributed to semantics or dismissed as
idiosyncratic (e.g. *escapee* which incidentally is now in competition
with a new formation *escaper*).

At this point one might be inclined to reject the notion of a
previously undiscovered syntactic distinction between intransitives
with subjects that are initial 1s and intransitives with subjects that

are initial 2s, dismissing the evidence as a reflection of semantic or pragmatic factors. However, in some languages the evidence cannot be easily dismissed. In Italian and French, for instance, it can be demonstrated that a split in intransitives shows up in more than one area of grammar, with the evidence from different areas showing close alignment.

Rosen, developing points made in unpublished work of Perlmutter, demonstrates that in Italian an unergative/unaccusative distinction shows up in three separate domains of the grammar (Rosen 1981, 1984; see also Perlmutter 1983b):

(a) auxiliary selection
(b) scope of the partitive clitic
(c) absolute construction.

With transitive verbs compound 'tenses' are formed with *avere* 'to have', but with intransitive verbs we find that some take *avere* and others take *essere* 'to be' (with agreement of the past participle with the subject):

[16] E arrivata Maria (essere).
      is arrived Maria
      'Maria (has) arrived.'

[17] Maria ha dormito (avere).
      Maria has slept
      'Maria (has) slept.'

Essere-taking verbs include *cadere* 'to fall', *partire* 'to leave, to depart', *tornare* 'to return', *morire* 'to die', *nascere* 'to be born', *andare* 'to go', *venire* 'to come', *entrare* 'to enter', and *bastare* 'to be enough'. *Avere*-taking verbs including *dormire* 'to sleep', *nuotare* 'to swim', *telefonare* 'to telephone', *viaggiare* 'to travel', *scherzare* 'to joke', and *tacere* 'to be silent'. The subjects of *essere*-taking verbs are predominantly referential patients and the subjects of *avere*-taking verbs are predominantly agents.

The proclitic *ne* 'of it, of them' can only be used with a direct object or with the apparent subject of the patient-like group, i.e. with *essere*-taking intransitives (the hedge implied by 'apparent' is made clear in section 3.2). *Ne* is used with headless quantified nominals. Example [18] illustrates its use with a direct object, [18a] showing a quantified nominal and [18b] showing how *ne* serves as a pro-form for the missing head:

[18a] Ho   visto tre   dischi volanti.
       I have seen three discs flying
       'I saw three flying saucers.

[18b] Ne   ho   visti tre.
of: them I: have seen three
'I saw three (of them).'

With transitive verbs in compound tenses formed with *avere* the
participle agrees with a preceding direct object including *ne*.
The next pair exemplify *ne* used with an *essere*-taking intransitive:

[19a] Sono venuti tre   ragazzi.
are   come three boys
'Three boys came.'
[19b] Ne   sono venuti tre.
of:them are   come three
'Three (of them) came.'

Ne cannot be used with the subject of an *avere*-taking verb
whether that verb be intransitive or transitive. Thus one cannot
substitute *dormire* 'to sleep' in [19b].

Where a phrase based on a past participle is used absolutely the
nominal accompanying it must be a patient-type intransitive
'apparent' subject or a direct object. In [20] *assolvere* is transitive
and in [21] *partire* is intransitive:

[20] Assolto   l'imputato,   scoppiarano gli applausi.
acquitted the:defendant exploded   the applause
'The defendant having been acquitted, applause broke out.'

[21] Partiti   i   Frabiani, scoppiarano gli   applausi.
departed the   Frabrians exploded   the   applause
'The Frabians having departed, applause broke out.'

The first phrase in [20] must be interpreted as referring to the
initial stratum direct object of *assolvere*; it cannot be construed
with the initial subject. The first phrase in [21] would become
ungrammatical if an intransitive verb of the *avere*-taking group
were substituted, for example *viaggiare* 'to travel': *I Frabiani
viaggiati, . . .*

It might be thought that the unergative–unaccusative distinction
could be captured semantically. In fact Perlmutter and Postal
originally proposed the Universal Alignment Hypothesis (discussed
in section 2.2. above) to account for the semantic basis of the
unergative–unaccusative distinction (Perlmutter and Postal 1984a:
97ff., orig. 1978). They suggested that predicates describing willed
or volitional acts (e.g. *work*, *play*, *speak*) and certain involuntary
(sic) bodily processes (e.g. *cough*, *defaecate*, *sleep*, *cry*) were
initially unergative, while the following types of predicate were
initially unaccusative: predicates expressed by adjectives in

English,[11] including those describing sizes, shapes, weights, colours, smells, and states of mind; predicates whose nuclear term is a patient (e.g. *fall, trickle, darken*); predicates of existing or happening; those referring to involuntary emission of stimuli that impinge on the senses (e.g. *shine, crackle, stink*); aspectuals (e.g. *begin, continue*), and duratives (e.g. *last, remain*). This hypothesis is subject to the objections raised in section 2.2 above. Rosen demonstrates that there is no strict semantic basis for the unergative-unaccusative distinction though obviously the distinction operates on an approximately semantic basis. She posits a **Little Alignment Hypothesis** according to which there is a fixed mapping between roles and initial relations for a particular predicate. She shows that this does not work, therefore *a fortiori* the Universal Alignment Hypothesis does not work. Consider the following examples (Rosen 1984:53):

[22a] Il pubblico ha fischiato il tenore.
'The audience booed the tenor.'
[22b] Il pubblico ha fischiato.
'The audience booed.'

[23a] Bertini ha calato il sipario.
'Bertini lowered the curtain.'
[23b] Il sipario è calato.
'The curtain fell.'

[24a] Aldo ha fuggito ogni tentazione.
'Aldo fled all temptation.'
[24b] Aldo è fuggito.
'Aldo fled.'

[25a] Bertini ha deviato il colpo.
'Bertini deflected the blow.'
[25b] Il colpo ha deviato.
'The blow went awry.'

Examples [22] and [23] illustrate the regular case where the intransitive verb has an auxiliary consistent with the role we expect on the basis of the relationship between the intransitive verb and its transitive counterpart. If this pattern were maintained in [24] and [25] the auxiliaries would be reversed. In [24b] *Aldo* could be expected to be agent-like and treated as an initial 1 on the basis of the parallelism with [24a], but the auxiliary is *essere*. Likewise in [25b] we would expect *il colpo* to be patient-like and treated as an initial 2 yet the auxiliary is *avere*. In these cases the tests for the unergative/unaccusative distinction all match. The examples cannot be dismissed on the basis of just the auxiliary choice being aberrant. They demonstrate that a strict version of the Universal Alignment Hypothesis does not work.

There are plenty of examples of apparently synonymous intransitive predicates being treated differently in different languages. As Rosen points out (1984:61), 'die', for instance, is treated as unergative in Choctaw and unaccusative in Italian. The evidence in Italian is the choice of the auxiliary *essere* as opposed to *avere*. In Choctaw the evidence is more direct. Choctaw is one of a minority of languages that mark some intransitive subjects like transitive subjects and others like direct objects. The first person, for instance, can be represented by -*li*- or -*sa*-, the former being used for the ergative relation and for a group of intransitive subjects that are predominantly agent-like, and the latter for direct objects and intransitive subjects that are predominantly patient-like. RG not unnaturally interprets these various manifestations of a split in intransitives along agent–patient lines as evidence of an unergative–unaccusative split. The first bound pronoun in [26a] is interpreted as unergative as opposed to the form -*sa*- in [27b] below, which is interpreted as unaccusative:

[26a] *Choctaw*
    Illi-li-tok   kiyo.
    die-1st-past not
    'I did not die.'
[26b] *Italian*
    Non sono morto.
    not I: am dead
    'I did not die.'[12]

Rosen notes that it might be argued that 'die' is conceived of differently in different cultures, that the Choctaw people may see dying as a step one takes rather than as something that happens to one. However, she notes that a more banal concept such as 'sweat' can be treated in different ways in different languages. In Italian *sudare* takes *avere* as its auxiliary indicating that it is unergative, whereas the translational equivalent in Choctaw takes the objective first person bound form -*sa*- (compare -*li*- in [26a] above) indicating that it is unaccusative:

[27a] *Italian*
    Ho   sudato.
    I have sweated
    'I sweated.'

[27b] *Choctaw*
    Sa-laksha.
    1st:acc-sweat
    'I sweated.'

Rosen concludes that there is some arbitrariness in the assigning of initial grammatical relations.

There certainly is apparent arbitrariness from the point of view of referential or objective properties of predicates. The Universal Alignment Hypothesis operates in effect on the basis of abstract predicates extracted from sets of translational equivalents. However, as pointed out in section 2.2, languages encode conceptualizations and there is scope for alternative conceptions of what is the same from an objective point of view. It seems that some languages make an overt distinction between two classes of one-place predicate, and a larger group, including English, make the same distinction covertly. The distinction is essentially an agent–patient one and prototypical agents and prototypical patients will normally align across languages. However, some predicates will receive different treatments in different languages or alternative treatments in a particular language (see [28] below) reflecting differences in perception. Given that the number of categories is only two, it is natural that some assignments will be apparently arbitrary from an objective point of view.

Where a single phonological predicate is treated in alternative ways, it can be treated as two homophonous predicates, one unergative, the other unaccusative. Rosen quotes the following pair of Choctaw sentences from Davies (1981a) to illustrate two different treatments according to whether an activity is perceived to be under protagonist control or not (note the -*sa-/-li-* contrast again):

[28a] Sa-ttola-tok.
    1st:acc-fall-past
    'I fell.'
[28b] Ittola-li-tok.
    fall-1st-past
    'I fell (on purpose).'

However, she adds that this distinction of protagonist control does not apply with all intransitive verbs in Choctaw. In fact it seems that a number of factors such as agentive or volitional control or accomplishment can be relevant to the treatment of intransitive verbs in various languages. In Italian some verbs of motion are unergative when referring to carrying out a motion activity, but unaccusative when referring to the reaching of a goal. Thus one says *Ha corso per venti minuti* 'He ran for twenty minutes', but *È corso a casa* 'He ran home.'[13]

In sum it seems that at least in some languages there is good evidence for accepting a syntactic distinction underlying the class of intransitive surface subjects. In an attempt to avoid any non-surface level of syntax one could try to capture the unergative–unaccusative distinction in terms of semantic roles with a list of predicates that involve a marked or 'exceptional' relationship between role and grammatical relation. Perhaps this would be plausible in some instances, but on the basis of Rosen's data it would not be a reasonable way of describing Italian. The listing of exceptional predicates would be relevant to at least three areas of grammar and such a listing would undermine the whole point of establishing grammatical relations.

As noted above, some languages make an overt distinction between two classes of intransitive predicate. They include some Caucasian languages such as Bats, for instance, and some American Indian languages such as Dakota, Arikara, and Seneca. These languages mark the sole argument of some one-place predicates like the subject of a two-place predicate and the sole argument of the other one-place predicates like the object of two-place transitive predicates (see Choctaw examples above). Thus they make a distinction between an agent-like class and a patient-like class that shows up irrespective of transitivity. They can be said to make overt a distinction that the Relational Grammarians have found covert in languages like Italian and English.

As more and more languages are studied in the framework of Relational Grammar more and more evidence for the unergative-unaccusative distinction is being unearthed. It remains to be seen how widespread the distinction is. It is probably not universal. Gibson, for instance, comments that there does not seem to be any evidence for it in Chamorro (1980:27).

As indicated at the beginning of this section Perlmutter and Postal sought to explain the apparent impossibility of pseudo-passives with the class of verbs they designated 'unaccusative' by invoking the 1 Advancement Exclusiveness Law. It is possible to maintain 1AEX without maintaining the Unaccusative Hypothesis and vice versa. Gerdts (1980b) argues that intransitive predicates from Halkomelem exhibit an unergative-unaccusative distinction and that some unaccusative predicates allow advancement of obliques to 2 and then to 1 via the passive, thus violating 1AEX. In this language a certain class of obliques which occur with intransitive verbs expressing a psychological state or event can be advanced to 2. Gerdts calls this class 'causal' though they appear to be the translational equivalents of what are usually encoded as indirect objects or direct objects of non-activity verbs, e.g. the non-subject complements of verbs meaning 'tired of', 'astonished at', 'ashamed of', etc. Example [29a] illustrates the oblique and [29b] the advancement of the oblique to 2. The illustrative sentences do not have the same nominal as initial oblique since the advancement is used with an animate causal and eschewed with an inanimate one. The advancement marker is *-me?*:

[29a] ni cen q'el   ?e kʷθe smeθ'enqinems.
     asp I   believe obl det lies:his
     'I believed his lies.'
[29b] ni cen q'el?-me?-t kʷθe leplit.
     asp I   believe-adv-tr det priest
     'I believed the priest.'

The advancee can be further advanced to 1 in the passive. The problem is that there is evidence to suggest that 'psychological' predicates are unaccusative. If they are, the passive would violate 1AEX since there would be unaccusative advancement and passive advancement to 1 in the same clause. The evidence for unaccusativity is as follows. Predicates meaning 'fall', 'spill' (as in *the milk spilled*), etc., which are likely to be unaccusative on semantic grounds, cannot be causativized, whereas predicates that mean 'eat' (intransitive), 'walk', and 'sit down', which are likely to be unergative, can. The psychological predicates behave like the unaccusative group in that they cannot be causativized, i.e. there are no causative formations of the type *I made John happy* or *I made John be astonished*. Example [30a] is another example of *-me?* advancement and [30b] is the passive equivalent:

[30a] ni lciws-me-t-es   kʷθe swiw?les kʷθe sqʷemey?
     asp tired-adv-tr-erg det boy   det dog
     'The boy is tired of the dog.'
[30b] ni lciws-me-t-em   kʷθe sqʷemey ?e kʷθe swiw?les.
     asp tired-adv-tr-intr det dog   obl det boy
     'The dog was gotten tired of by the boy.'

The strata that would need to be posited for the passive if the 'psych' verbs are unaccusative are as follows:

[31]   experiencer neutral
   P   2   obl
   P   1   obl
   P   1   2
   P   Cho   1

As can be seen both arguments are advanced to 1 in such an analysis. It is not certain how this conflict can be resolved. Both 1AEX and the Unaccusative Hypothesis are well motivated. It seems to me that these 'psych' predicates may have an initial 1. The causative test Gerdts refers to operates on a one-place predicate. It may be that when there is a second argument present, the experiencer is interpreted as an initial 1 (Bickford (1987:276) makes much the same point).

There is another analysis that resolves the conflict and that is to eliminate the advancement of the initial 2 to 1 (assuming for the moment that the experiencer is an initial 2). The oblique can advance to 2, which will put the initial 2 in chômage, and then advance to 1. Such a solution does not violate 1AEX, but it means analysing the relevant sentences as something other than passive. This would mean finding a new basis for the distribution of passive marking. The point will come up again in section 3.3.2 with reference to apparent instances of impersonal passive with unaccusatives which appear to violate 1AEX.

The unergative-unaccusative distinction has been adopted in the Government and Binding (GB) framework. Burzio (1986:20ff.) analyses the Italian sentences [32a] as unaccusative by deriving it from a transitive structure with the apparent surface subject in object position and an empty [e] subject position as in [32b].[14] This is the natural structural analogue of the RG analysis. The variant with the subject before the verb [32c] is derived via a movement rule that leaves a trace (t). The moved NP and the trace are indexed by a subscript i [32d]:

[32a] Affondarono due navi.
     'Two ships sank.'
[32b] [e] affondare due navi.
[32c] Due navi affondarono.
[32d] [due navi$_i$] affondare t$_i$.

The verb *affondare*, like its translational equivalent in English, can also be used transitively:

[33] L'artiglieria affondò due navi.
    'The artillery sank two ships.'

The transitive and unaccusative patterns can both be derived from a single lexical subcategorization frame [_NP]. A verb like *affondare* is considered to assign semantic case to the subject position optionally. Where it does, the subject position must be filled by an argument as in [33]; where it does not, we have the subject position empty and the unaccusative pattern as in [32b].

With an ergative verb such as *dormire* the subject position is assigned semantic case, but there is no post-verbal complement. Marantz (1984:35ff.) developing a theory akin to Government and Binding distinguishes the classes as follows:

[34] *unergative*
     swim [∅] [+logical subject]
     unaccusative
     arrive (patient) [−logical subject]

These are lexical entries characteristic of the two classes. To see how this system works it is necessary to compare the entry for a typical transitive verb:

[35] *transitive*
     hit (patient) [+logical subject]

As in Government and Binding only the verb phrase is considered relevant to the subcategorization of the verb. The role of the NP of VP, i.e. the object, is given in round brackets as **patient** (Marantz uses **theme**) for the unaccusatives like *arrive* and transitives like *hit*. However, while *hit* is marked [+logical subject], *arrive* is marked [−logical subject]. A general rule for accusative languages assigns the **agent** role to the logical subject (or whatever other role is appropriate).[15] Since *arrive* does not have a logical subject, the patient assumes the surface subject relation. *Swim* on the other hand is allotted no argument within VP (note (∅) in the lexical entry). It has only the agent role assigned by the logical subject.

Both these theories accept the Unaccusative Hypothesis and translate it into structural terms. Essentially for Burzio and Marantz an unaccusative has a deep object (NP of VP) but no deep subject (NP of S), while an unergative has an NP of S but no NP of VP.

There is a further complication. In RG apparent post-verbal subjects in Italian are not analysed as subjects at all but as chômeurs. Example [32c] would be analysed as a subject verb sequence, while [32a] would be taken to be a sequence of verb plus 2-chômeur with a silent dummy as final 1. This analysis of post-verbal 'subjects', which is in dramatic contrast to the traditional one, is described in the next chapter in the section on impersonal constructions, 3.2.

2.5 Antipassive and 2–3 retreat

Many languages have pairs of constructions with the same subject which express the same propositional content but differ in transitivity. Such a pair is illustrated in [36] from Yup'ik Eskimo (based on Reed *et al.* 1977):

[36a] Qimugte-m neraa   neqa.
      dog-erg   eat:3s:3s fish
      'The dog ate the fish.'
[36b] Qimugta ner'uq neq-mek.
      dog   eat:3s fish-abl
      'The dog ate fish.'

The members of such pairs usually differ in semantic transitivity (Hopper and Thompson 1980). In this instance the intransitive member of the pair is being used to indicate a non-specific patient; it can also be used in the negative. In some Eskimo dialects the intransitive construction is used to indicate a partitive sense. The intransitivity of [36b] is apparent from the absolute marking of the subject (compare the ergative marking in [36a]), from the oblique marking on *neq-*, and from the monovalent cross-referencing on the verb. Where the intransitive member of such a pair is morphologically derived, it suggests that a demotion of the direct object is involved. There is no transparent indication that the intransitive verb in [36b] is marked with respect to the transitive one in [36a], but the intransitive construction is marked from the point of view of its syntactic and semantic domain. In RG [36a] would be taken as reflecting initial stratum relations directly with *qimugtem* as 1 and *neqa* as 2 (see [37a] below). A natural interpretation of [36b] would be that it reflects the demotion of 2 to a 2-chômeur. However, RG does not countenance spontaneous demotion to chômage. A term dependent can only be revalued as a chômeur if its relation is usurped by another dependent. Postal (1977) has suggested that this requirement can be met by demoting the initial 1 to 2 which would push the initial 2 into chômage (the initial 2 would have to be revalued to preserve Stratal Uniqueness). In the absence of any other advancement to 1 the second stratum 2 would revert to 1 in accordance with the Final 1 Law. This interpretation is presented in the stratal diagram [37b]:[16]

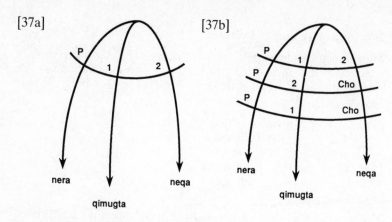

[37a]   [37b]

Postal (1977) called this demotion **antipassive**, but this label is confusing since the label antipassive was introduced into the typological literature in Silverstein (1976 orig. 1973) to cover a range of detransitivized constructions in ergative languages, some of which are probably to be interpreted in RG terms as involving 2–3 retreat (Postal 1977:309, fn. 43):

Typological   RG

antipassive   ⎡ antipassive (2-Cho)
              ⎣ 2–3 retreat

As noted in sections 1.3 and 2.3, RG originally allowed demotion only to chômage, but on the basis of data from Kinyarwanda, discussed in section 2.7.1 below, spontaneous demotion from 2 to 3 was admitted. Demotion from 1 to 3 is employed in the interpretation of Inversion constructions, see section 2.6, but demotion from 1 to 2 seems hardly to be needed except in the antipassive where it has no motivation other than to save the Motivated Chômage Law.

In the antipassive construction in Choctaw the subject is cross-referenced on the verb by accusative forms. Davies (1984:356) takes the presence of this accusative marking as evidence that supports Postal's analysis of antipassive as involving 1–2 retreat, a conclusion endorsed by Perlmutter (1982:306). The accusative marking is interpreted as being based on the intermediate stratum in which the initial 1 has retreated to 2 before advancing back to 1:

[38] Shokha anopa chi-yimmi   ho?
     story   2acc-believe Q
     'Do you believe the story?'

2–3 retreat is often obligatory for a relatively small subset of initially transitive predicates. Ozkaragöz (1986:45) argues that this is so in Turkish. An example is *hohlamak* 'to blow on':

[39] Sema ayna-ya   hohla-dï.
Sema mirror-dat blow:on-past
'Sema blew on the mirror.'

Part of the evidence for taking it to be initially transitive is that there is a corresponding passive. Only transitive verbs can be passivized and there is no 3–2 advancement in Turkish.

Example [40b] illustrates 2–3 retreat in the Australian language Kalkatungu. Example [40a] is a transitive clause with the subject in the ergative and the direct object in the unmarked case, the absolutive. Example [40b] is intransitive as can be seen from the absolutive marking for the subject. The initial 2 appears in the dative and the verb is marked with a suffix -*li* which registers the detransitivization. In this language 2–3 retreat is productive and is used, as detransitivized constructions usually are, to signal reduced semantic intransitivity (Hopper and Thompson 1980) such as generic patient and/or continuing or habitual activity:

[40a] Ngarrkun-tu ari kanyirr.
wallaroo-erg eat grass
'The wallaroo eats the grass.'
[40b] Ngarrkun ari-li   kanyirr-ku.
wallaroo eat-detrans grass-dative
'The wallaroo eats grass.'

Example [41] illustrates a two-place intransitive. As can be seen [40b] and [41] are examples of the same construction:

[41] Thuku nanti ngarrkun-ku.
dog   bark wallaroo-dative
'The dog barks at the wallaroo.'

As pointed out above the typological literature does not distinguish between 2-Cho and 2–3 revaluations, and constructions like the one illustrated in [40b] are referred to as 'antipassive'. However, since RG does distinguish two types of detransitivization, the question arises of what criteria are relevant to the distinction. Klokeid (1978:588) labels the analogues of [40b] in a number of other Australian languages as exhibiting 2–3 retreat on the grounds that the demotee appears in the case used for recipients of verbs meaning *give* (namely the dative case) and recipients are likely to be initial 3s. In Kalkatungu, however, the recipient of *anyi* 'to give' appears not in the case I have labelled dative, but in another case generally used for expressing 'to', the allative (illustrated in [77a] later in this chapter). However, within RG theory the retreatant in a construction like [40b] must be interpreted as a 3 rather than a chômeur since it can be advanced. A chômeur cannot be advanced (the Chômeur Advancement Ban) but a 3 can. A demonstration follows.

The suffix *-nytyama* registers the advancement of a 'dative' to 2. In [42b] the second person singular pronoun has been advanced to 2 as indicated by the fact that it can be represented by an enclitic on the verb:

[42a] Nga-thu intyi-mi nyun-ku utyan.
      I-erg   chop-fut you-dat wood
      'I will chop the wood for you.'
[42b] Nga-thu intyi-tyama-mi-kin   nyini utyan.
      I-erg   chop-dat:adv-fut-you you   wood
      'I will chop you some wood.'

Reflexive-reciprocal formations are derived intransitives marked by the suffix *-ti*. Example [43] illustrates the reflexive-reciprocal of *lha-* 'to hit':

[43] Ngarrkun maltha lha-ti.
      wallaroo mob   hit-refl/recip
      'The wallaroos are fighting.'

In order for a two-place intransitive to undergo this detransitivizing derivation it must be first transitivized with *-nytyama*, which presumably registers the advancement of the dative to 2. Example [44] should be compared with both [41] and [43]:

[44] Thuku nanti-tyama-ti.
      dog   bark-dat:adv-refl/recip
      'The dogs are barking at one another' (or 'The dog is barking at itself').

The crucial point relating to the status of dative marked nominals is that with a few verbs such as *ngkuma* 'to seek' and *thu-* 'to cook' which are frequently detransitivized (*ngkuma* is always detransitivized in independent clauses) the *-nytyama* suffix is used to feed reflexive-reciprocal formation. In other words these verbs are retransitivized before undergoing reflexive-reciprocal formation:

[45a] Ngata ngkuma-yi-mi   maa-tyi.
      we   seek-detrans-fut food-dat
      'We will look for food.'

[45b] Ngata ngkuma-tyama-ti-mi.
we   seek-dat:adv-refl-fut
'We will look for one another.'

Since chômeurs cannot be re-advanced, the dative marked arguments must be 3s.[17] The argument hinges on a handful of verbs that alternate between having a transitive construction and an intransitive one, but it is possible that two-place intransitives like *nanti* 'to bark' should be analysed as exhibiting 2–3 retreat also.

A side effect of this analysis is that the recipient of *anyi* 'to give' is probably to be analysed as an oblique (labelled **directional**) since it is marked by the allative rather than the dative (see [77a] below). See also Rosen's analysis of clauses with recipients illustrated in the latter part of section 6.3.

2.6 Inversion

In a number of languages there is a marked construction in which the nominal that normally would be the subject appears with the marking of an indirect object. This construction is referred to in the RG literature as Inversion, the name by which it is known among Georgian linguists (Harris 1984b:259). The following examples are from Georgian. Example [46a] illustrates the ergative construction, [46b] the nominative construction, and [46c] the Inversion construction.[18] The alternation between the first two is determined by tense and verb class. The Inversion construction occurs with many verbs in the evidential mode; [46c] is the evidential counterpart of the other two (Harris 1984b):

[46a] Rezo-m gačuka   samajuri (šen).
Rezo-erg you:gave:3s:it bracelet (you-dat)
'Rezo gave you a bracelet'
[46b] Rezo gačukebs   samajur-s   (šen).
Rezo you:give:3s:it bracelet:dat (you:dat)
'Rezo gives you a bracelet.'
[46c] Turme   Rezo-s   učukebia   samajuri šen-tvis.
apparently Rezo-dat gave:3s:it:evid bracelet you-ben
'Apparently Rezo gave a bracelet to you.'

Examples [46a] and [46b] can be considered to reflect initial 1, 2, and 3 directly with no revaluations, the difference in the case marking patterns being attributed to tense and verb class. Harris analyses [46c] as reflecting the demotion of the initial 1 to 3 and the advancement of the initial 2 to 1. The demotion of the initial 1 to 3 puts the initial 3 in chômage:

[47] Rezo   micema   samajuri   šen
      Rezo   'give'   'bracelet'   'you'

1	P	2	3
3	P	2	Cho
3	P	1	Cho

The verb in Georgian displays cross-referencing for final subject, direct object, and indirect object. In the Inversion construction the nominative nominal (*samajuri* in [46c]) controls subject agreement and the dative nominal indirect object agreement. Note that in [46c] *šen-tvis* is marked by a benefactive suffix and does not get cross-referenced on the verb. This suggests it is not a term which is to be expected under the Inversion analysis (see [47]) (the cross-referencing form for second person is *g-*).

Third person subjects trigger number agreement on the verb, but in the Inversion construction the dative nominal controls the number agreement. In [48] *-t* is the plural number marker (Harris 1984b:268):

[48] Turme   studentebs   gamougzavniat   gela.
      apparently students:dat sent:him:evid:3pl Gela
      'Apparently the students sent Gela.'

[49] Turme   gelas   gamougzavnia studentebi.
      apparently Gela-dat sent:him:evid students
      'Apparently Gela sent the students.'

Harris suggests that this can be accounted for if number marking is based on initial terms.

The Inversion construction is an alternant of the ergative subject construction [46a] and the nominative subject construction [46b] and it is the marked alternant in that it occurs in a restricted range of mode, namely when the intention is to indicate that speakers lack direct evidence of the truth of their statement. Since it expresses the same propositional content as the other constructions, Harris follows RG practice in assuming it to be based on the same initial stratum, namely one that manifests the common alignment of agent-initial 1, patient-initial 2, and recipient-initial 3.

Harris notes that with certain 'affective' predicates there is only a construction with the experiencer in the dative and the neutral entity in the nominative (1984b:269):

[50] Gelas   uqvars   Nino.
      Gela-dat love:he:her Nino
      'Gela loves Nino.'

Some clause-internal revaluations

She argues that these constructions are also examples of Inversion, reflecting the same revaluations as the inverted alternants in the evidential mode. In Latin, Inversion is used with the gerundive form of the verb which expresses roughly obligation:

[51a] Vos defenditis hanc   provinciam.
You defend:2pl this:acc province:acc
'You are defending this province.'

[51b] Haec vobis   provincia est defendenda.
this you:dat province is defend:ger
'You have to defend this province.'

In the passive the initial 1/final chômeur is expressed in the ablative with the preposition *a(b)*. However, the ablative is also used with gerundive when there is an initial 3 in the clause:

[52] Haec a nobis senatui   sunt nuntiandae.
These by us:abl senate:dat are announce:ger:pl
'These things should be announced to the senate by us.

Although RG allows spontaneous demotion of 1 to 3, demotion to chômage must be motivated by an advancement. Example [52] must be interpreted as passive with *haec* the initial 2 advancing to 1 and pushing *nos* 'we' into chômage:

[53] Nos   nuntiare   haec   senatus.
    1   P   2   3
    Cho   P   1   3

Examples analogous to [50] above are common in European languages, i.e. examples where the only active construction available for certain verbs is one with the experiencer encoded as indirect object and the neutral entity as a subject. These are prima facie candidates for an Inversion analysis in so far as the correlation between semantic role and grammatical relation is the inverse of what can probably be considered normal on a cross-linguistic statistical basis. They occur, for instance, with the following predicates all of which mean 'like, please'. German *gefallen*, Italian *piacere a*, Spanish *gustar a*, French *plaîre à*, and English *appeal to* (as in *It appeals to me*). The following examples are from Italian. Example [54] is taken to reflect initial stratum relations directly, but [55a] and [55b] are interpreted as examples of Inversion. Example [56] is included to illustrate a third way of encoding 'to like' or 'to love'. It is probably to be interpreted as an example of 2–3 retreat:

47

[54] Giorgio ama Roma.
'George loves Rome.'

[55a] A te piace lo spettacolo?
'Do YOU like the show?'
[55b] Ti piace lo spettacolo?
'Do you like the show?'

[56] Enrico vuol bene a Maria.
Enrico wish well to Maria
'Enrico likes Maria.'

In [55a] the indirect object is marked by the prepositional phrase *a te* which is used for emphasis; the form *ti* in [55b] is an unstressable proclitic for indirect object. In the first and second person the same form is used for direct and indirect object, but the two relations are represented differently in the third person.

Since the Universal Alignment Hypothesis is not tenable in its strict form the ascription of Inversion to predicates like Italian *piacere a* and English *appeal to* needs some syntactic evidence to support it. Here are two pieces of evidence for the analysis, one from Italian and the other from English.

In Italian the Inversion nominal behaves like an indirect object in terms of its marking. It is marked by the preposition *a* (as in [55a]) or it can be represented by an indirect object proclitic (as in [55b]). However, it behaves like a subject in that it controls the missing subject of various non-finite constructions including *da*+ infinitive (the following examples are adapted from Perlmutter (1982)):

[57] Giorgio mi ha rimproverato tante   volte da farmi   paura.
George me has reproved   so:many times to make:me fear
'George rebuked me so many times that he scared me.'

[58] A Giorgio è talmente piaciuta una compagna d'ufficio da lasciarci.
To George is so   pleased a companion-of-office to leave:us
[lit.] 'To George was so pleasing an office co-worker that he left us.'
'George was so taken with a girl at the office that he left us.'

In [57] *Giorgio*, the main clause subject, is understood as the subject of the infinitive *fare* (*far paura* = 'to make fear'). In [58] it is the Inversion nominal that is understood as the missing subject of *lasciar(e)*. This is interesting in that the Inversion nominal is marked like an indirect object yet ordinary (initial stratum) indirect objects cannot control the missing subject of non-finite clauses. In [59] the initial/final 3, *Giorgio*, cannot control the subject of the infinitive. To express the sentiment of [59] one would need to use a finite subordinate clause *che si è arrabiato* 'that he got (himself) angry':

[59] *Ho telefonato a Giorgio tante volte da arrabiarsi.
I:have telephoned to George so:many times to get:angry
'I telephoned (to) George so many times that he got angry.'

The same point applies to the antecedents of reflexives. An Inversion nominal can antecede a reflexive (as in [60]) just like a subject can, but an initial/final 3 cannot (Rosen 1981:27):

[60] A Mario piace solo sé stesso.
to Mario please only self emph
'Mario likes only himself.'

RG attributes this subject property of the Inversion nominal to the fact that it is an initial stratum 1 though a final 3 (see also section 6.6).
    The second piece of evidence comes from English. Perlmutter and Postal consider the following sentences to be instances of Inversion (Perlmutter and Postal 1984a, orig. 1978):

[61a] That girl matters to me.
[61b] That belongs to me.
[61c] That occurred to me.
[61d] That happened to me.
[61e] That dawned on me.

The 1 Advancement Exclusiveness Law (only one advancement to 1 per clause permitted) predicts that these clauses will not have pseudo-passives since this would involve two advancements to 1: the advancement of the initial 2 and the advancement of the Inversion nominal (see [63a] below and compare [47] above). This prediction is borne out. There are no pseudo-passives such as *I was mattered to by that girl* for the sentences in [61]. Thus the analysis that attributes Inversion to the sentences in [61] and assumes there can only be one advancement to 1 per clause is supported.
    Perlmutter and Postal also attribute an Inversion analysis to the predicates illustrated in the following pair, neither of which can be passivized:

[62a] The reason for that escapes me.
[62b] His motivations elude me.

Here they assume the Inversion nominal advances to 2 in the final stratum. Example [63a] is the stratal diagram for [61a] and [63b] the stra tal diagram for [62a]:

[63a]   [63b]

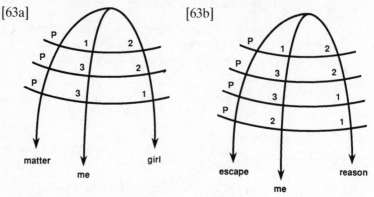

The unmarked alignment across languages is for an experiencer to be encoded as an initial/final 1 and for the neutral entity opposed to it to be an initial 2/final 2 or an initial 2/final 3. Where the reverse alignment occurs, the dative-marked experiencer tends to acquire subject properties. In the history of English, Inversion nominals came to be treated as subjects in co-ordination before they had lost their dative marking and acquired nominative marking and control of verb agreement, that is, before they had become initial 1s. Lightfoot (1979:235) quotes from Malory *the kynge lyked and . . . . loved this lady wel* where the *kynge* is dative reflecting its Inversion status. Note, however, *lyke* which took the Inversion construction, is conjoined with *love* which had an experiencer as initial 1/final 1 as it does in contemporary English. This suggests that *kynge* is being treated as a subject, at least as far as co-ordination is concerned.

2.7 Problems with objects

The following three subsections deal with problems concerning the status of apparent objects. Section 2.7.1 deals with what appear to be double object constructions in Kinyarwanda. The challenge to RG theory provided by this data led to the abandoning of the Chômeur Law which had required that all demotions must be to chômeur. In section 2.7.2 are discussed passives of the type *Mercy will be denied you* which appear to involve the advancement to 1 of the chômeur in the double object construction. Section 2.7.3 introduces a radically different analysis of double object and related constructions.

Some clause-internal revaluations

2.7.1 Kinyarwanda

Gary and Keenan 1977 argued that Kinyarwanda has two objects (strictly two final stratum objects) and hence was an exception to the Stratal Uniqueness Law. The claim is based on sentences such as [64a] and [64b] (Gary and Kennan 1977:91):

[64a] Yohani y-oher-er-eje   Maria ibaruwa.
      John   he-send-R-asp Mary letter
      'John sent Mary a letter.'
[64b] Yohani y-oher-er-eje   ibaruwa Maria.
      John   he-sent-R-asp letter   Mary
      'John sent Mary a letter.'

Kinyarwanda appears to have only one construction for recipients, a variety of the double object construction. This involves putting the unmarked patient and unmarked recipient after the verb in the order recipient patient as in [64a], the preferred order, or in the order patient recipient as in [64b]. The suffix glossed as *R* marks the presence of a recipient. The subject is obligatorily represented or cross-referenced on the verb and the patient and recipient may both be represented or cross-referenced. The same set of forms is used for patient and recipient; where both are present they appear in the order patient recipient:

[65] Yohani y-a-yi-mw-oher-er-eje.
     John   he-past-it-her-send-R-aspect
     'John sent it to her.'

Both the object-like noun phrases in sentences such as [64a,b] exhibit the properties of the direct object of a single object verb, properties such as being able to be advanced to the subject of the passive or being able to be relativised. Gary and Keenan argued therefore that there were two objects. Perlmutter and Postal (1983c, orig. 1978), however, suggest that the string in [64a] is structurally ambiguous, that is, that it corresponds to a sentence in which 3 has advanced to 2 and to a sentence without any advancement. The same applies of course to the string in [64b] since there appears to be no relational difference between them. They suggest that Kinyarwanda differs from most other languages in that it does not flag indirect objects with an affix or adposition. This means that one cannot distinguish a final stratum in which a recipient is encoded as 3 from one where the recipient has advanced to 2. Under this interpretation the apparent phenomenon of two nominals exhibiting object properties is accounted for. Either we have a stratum as in [66a] serving as the basis for passive (or relativization) or we have a second stratum as in [66b] serving as a basis:

[66a]	Yohani	oher	ibaruwa	Maria	
	1	P	2	3	
	Cho	P	1	3	(passive)
[66b]	Yohani	oher	ibaruwa	Maria	
	1	P	2	3	
	1	P	Cho	2	(3–2)
	Cho	P	Cho	1	(passive)

However, this treatment does not account for the fact that there are clauses in which the patient is relativized and the recipient advanced to subject. Consider the following relative clause:

[67] ibaruwa [Maria y-ø-oher-er-ej-w-e].
    letter   [Mary she-past-send-R-asp-pass-asp]
    'the letter that Mary was sent'

As Perlmutter and Postal point out, this suggests that a 3 has advanced directly to 1. If the passive subject, *Mary*, had advanced to 2 in a second stratum, it would have forced the initial 2 into chômage. That this is not the case is evidenced by the fact that the initial 2 can be relativized. Chômeurs in Kinyarwanda cannot be relativized.

In this language the advancement of a locative to 2 pushes the initial 2 into chômage as expected. The putative chômeur cannot be relativized. However, the expected 2-chômeur arising from instrumental advancement can be relativized and this cannot be handled by positing direct advancement from 3 to 1.[19] Perlmutter and Postal give the following examples from Kimenyi (1976). Example [68a] illustrates the instrumental phrase marked with the preposition *n(a)*. Example [68b] illustrates the advancement of the instrument to direct object. Note that the instrumental nominal loses its prepositional marking and the advancement is registered on the verb by the suffix *-iish*. Example [69] illustrates the relativization of the patient nominal in a clause in which the instrument has advanced to 2:

[68a] Umugabo a-ra-andik-a   ibaruwa n'   ikaramu.
      man   he-pres-write-asp letter   with pen
      'The man is writing a letter with a pen.'
[68b] Umugabo a-ra-andik-iish-a   ibaruwa ikaramu.
      man   he-pres-write-instr-asp letter   pen
      'The man is writing a letter with a pen.'

[69] Ng'iiyi ibaruwa umugabo y-aandik-iish-a   ikaramu.
      this   letter   man   he-rel:write-instr-asp pen
      'Here is the letter that the man is writing with a pen.'

Relativization in clauses like [69] poses a challenge to the RG
system in that relativization in this language is restricted to final
terms, but the initial 2 in a clause exhibiting advancement to 2
should be a 2-chômeur. Perlmutter and Postal resolve this conflict
by allowing a 2 to retreat to 3. They posit that instrumental
advancement to 2 forces the initial 2 to retreat to 3. This fits in
neatly with their analysis of strings like that in [64], that is, with
their assumption that indirect objects in Kinyarwanda are
indistinguishable from direct objects. This analysis is laid out in
[70]:

[70] Umugabo   andik   ibaruwa   ikaramu.
     man   write   letter   pen
     1   P   2   instr
     1   P   3   2

Perlmutter and Postal discuss a suggestion to the effect that
instrumental advancement could force the initial 2 into chômage
and that the chômeur subsequently advances to 3. They rightly
dismiss this possibility since it would rob the notion of chômage of
its significance.

They also discuss a suggestion that the instrument advances
directly to 3 rather than to 2. This would be compatible with the
Kinyarwanda data and would allow retention of the principle that
all demotions are to chômage. However, they decline to adopt this
analysis since it conflicts with an emerging generalization to the
effect that instrumentals always advance to 2.[20]

In sum Perlmutter and Postal demonstrate that the double
object construction in Kinyarwanda can be accommodated in the
RG framework if it assumed that 3s are not marked differently
from 2s and if a 2 is allowed to demote to a 3.[21] Prior to being
confronted with the Kinyarwanda data RG had incorporated as
one of its principles the Chômeur Law which required all
demotions to be to the chômeur relation. A consideration of the
Kinyarwanda material led Perlmutter and Postal to abandon this
law and allow demotion from 2 to 3. As we have seen in previous
sections of this chapter RG recognizes 2–3 retreat in a number of
languages. It also posits 1–3 retreat in Inversion constructions and
1–2 in antipassive. These demotions need not be forced under the
Stratal Uniqueness Law by the advancement of a nominal or the
introduction of a dummy. They can be spontaneous. However,

although the Chômeur Law (all demotions go to chômeur) has been abandoned, the Motivated Chômage Law remains in force (all demotions to chômeur are forced under the SUL; no spontaneous chômage).

2.7.2 Tertiary passives and the Nuclear Novice Law

In some varieties of English, including the literary one, there is a passive in which the subject appears to correspond to the second object of the double object construction:

[71a] A book was given him.
[71b] Your sins will be forgiven you.
[71c] Beg for love and it will be denied you. (Wilde, *Lady Windemere's Fan*, Act III)

The construction hardly occurs with a non-pronoun recipient and the agent (the subject chômeur) is typically omitted.[22] Such passives appear to be based on the advancement of the patient object from a stratum that results from the earlier advancement of the initial 3 to 2. But since 3–2 advancement puts the patient object or initial 2 into chômage, this is not a licit revaluation; a chômeur cannot advance. However, there is an alternative. If the initial 2 advances to 1 and in a subsequent stratum the initial 3 advances to 2, we will have a network that accounts for sentences like those in [71]. The stratal diagrams [73a] and [73b] display the networks for [72a] and [72b] respectively:

[72a] Someone gave a book to him.
[72b] A book was given him by someone.

[73a]

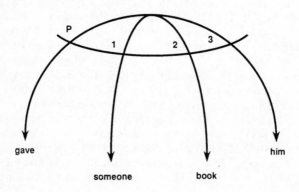

[73b]

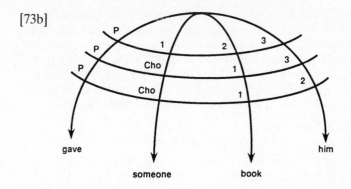

Relational networks in which an advancement to 2 follows a passive revaluation are accepted by Postal (1986:81) who calls them **tertiary passives**. (He uses **primary passive** for *The bananas were given to Mary by John* and **secondary passive** for *Mary was given the bananas by John*.) However, Bickford (1987) surveys a number of languages that have advancements to 2 and passive and finds that none of them allow an advancement to 2 to follow the passive. The languages surveyed include Indonesian (see [20d] in Chapter 1), Chamorro, Seri, and several Bantu languages. On this basis he seeks to exclude the possibility by establishing the **Nuclear Novice Law** which states that a nuclear novice arc begins before all nuclear experienced arcs with the same tail. A nuclear experienced arc has a nuclear predecessor, a nuclear novice one does not. This Law means that advancement to 2 (yielding a nuclear novice) must occur in an earlier stratum than passive (which yields a nuclear experienced arc). Bickford examines, in the light of the proposed Nuclear Novice Law, a number of languages that appear to allow advancement to 2 in a later stratum than passive and shows that the evidence for the putative 2 is ambivalent in every instance. In the case of English he argues that the putative 3–2 advancee could be in fact a 3 that is not flagged or marked as such. In other words an idiosyncracy of marking is responsible for making a 3 look like a 2. Certainly he succeeds in showing that there is no clear, convincing evidence that a nominal like *him* in [72b] is a genuine 2. Recently, however, the Nuclear Novice Law has been challenged in another context (see note 6 in Chapter 3).

2.7.3 Primary and secondary objects

Dryer (1986a) has suggested that some languages operate in terms of the grammatical relations **primary object** (PO) and **secondary**

object (SO). These relations are held simultaneously with direct and indirect object in the same way that ergative and absolutive are held at the same time as subject and direct object. In a 'giving' sentence the recipient will be the initial IO and the patient the initial DO by the Universal Alignment Hypothesis or a modified version thereof. However, the double object construction will be analysed as follows in terms of IO, DO, PO, and SO:

[74] Jae sent the minister a letter
     Su   IO(PO)   DO(SO)

Note that *the minister* is analysed as holding the IO relation at the initial and final stratum. There is no revaluation. The double object construction is taken to be monostratal. Dryer defends this interpretation on the grounds that this construction is the preferred alternative across languages and therefore should be analysed as having only a single stratum. Note too that *a letter* is analysed as being a DO. This allows for the fact that in English the second object can be relativized and questioned. It will also take care of the double object constructions in Kinyarwanda where the patient object can be relativized (see the discussion above, especially [67]).

Dryer takes the alternative to the double object construction, i.e. where the recipient appears as an oblique, to be a marked construction cross-linguistically and he analyses it as involving a demotion of the IO to chômeur, a demotion he calls **antidative** (compare antipassive in section 2.5):

[75] Jae sent a letter to the minister.

    Su   DO(SO)   IO(PO)
    Su   DO(PO)   Cho

    Jae   letter   minister

Dryer's proposal is essentially a return to the traditional analysis, at least as far as his interpretation of the double object construction is concerned, and it captures the fact that the recipient normally takes precedence over the patient and the fact that the patient retains grammatical privileges even when the recipient takes precedence. However, Dryer's proposal plays havoc with a number of definitions and principles of revaluation. The same effect could be achieved by simply recognizing two object relations, PO and SO, and modifying the alignment principle to ensure a recipient is encoded as PO where PO is opposed to SO. This would allow [74] and [75] to be analysed as in [76a] and [76b]:

[76a] Jae sent the minister a letter.
     1   PO   SO
[76b] Jae sent a letter to the minister.
     1   2/PO   3?Cho?

Dryer's analysis of the *to*-phrase and its analogues in other languages is likely to be controversial. One could consider that the demotion is to 3 or one could consider that clauses with the *to* alternative and its analogues are also monostratal with the recipient being encoded as an initial 3 as in standard RG. This would mean recognizing that a particular role can be encoded as more than one initial relation, but such a principle is needed anyway (see section 2.2).

Under Dryer's analysis the oblique-marked recipient in languages like German, which do not have the double object construction, is an initial and final 3, but the apparently analogous entity in a language with the double object construction is a chômeur. It remains to be seen if such a distinction finds syntactic support.

Dryer's analysis is interesting with respect to languages that can detransitivize double object constructions. In several Australian languages this combination occurs and both the recipient object and the patient object get demoted. The following example is from Kalkatungu:

[77a] Nyin-ti anyi-mpa-n   maa nga-tyinha?
      you-erg give-perf-you food me-allative
      'Have you given food to me?'
[77b] Nyin-ti anya-ngi (ngai) maa?
      you-erg gave-me (me)   food
      'Did you give me some food?'
[77c] Nyini anyi-minha-n   nga-tyi maa-tyi?
      you   give-imperf-you me-dat food-dat
      'Are you giving me any food?'

Example [77] illustrates the counterpart of English *You gave the food to me*, although, as pointed out in section 2.5, the recipient is not encoded as an indirect object. Example [77b] shows the double object construction where the recipient is the privileged object as shown by the fact that it can be represented on the verb as an enclitic. Example [77c] illustrates the effect of detransitivizing the double object construction. This is the construction illustrated in 2.5 and interpreted as 2–3 retreat. Note that both 'objects' demote. This does not make much sense under the standard RG analysis, since the patient object should in theory be a chômeur. There is no precedent for re-marking a chômeur in the RG

literature. Dryer could interpret [77c] as involving both objects
going into chômage, but since the dative in Kalkatungu marks 3s,
it could be that there is demotion to 3. One possibility under
Dryer's proposal would be that an existing IO (PO) would become
simply (IO) and the DO (SO) would become a chômeur:

[78] Nyini   anyi ngai   maa
     Su(erg) P   IO(PO)   DO(SO)
     Su   P   IO   Cho

Another possibility would be to recognize primary and secondary
indirect objects, but I know of no criteria to establish such an
analysis.

2.8 Revaluations and valency

Here is a check-list of the clause internal revaluations allowed in
Relational Grammar. All occurring types have been illustrated in
Chapter 1 or in earlier sections of this chapter.

2–1 advancement

2–1 advancement from a transitive stratum is **passive** (see [2] and
[7] in Chapter 1) and is extremely common. 2–1 advancement
from an intransitive stratum is **unaccusative advancement** and
occurs in response to the Final 1 Law (see section 2.4). It too
would appear to be common. Unaccusative advancement is not
directly apparent from a comparison of alternative surface
structures since it is obligatory under the Final 1 Law, but see
section 5.2 on Causative Clause Union.

3–1 advancement

3–1 advancement has been posited for a few languages including
Kinyarwanda (see discussion of [67] in this chapter), Japanese,
and Quechua.

Oblique–1 advancement

Oblique–1 advancement occurs in English (see the pseudo-passive
examples in [11] of this chapter). It seems to be common in Bantu
languages (Siewierska 1984:64ff.). Under one RG analysis numerous
Philippine-type languages would have oblique–1 advancement,
but in at least some of them I would argue the relevant
advancements should be interpreted as oblique–2 (this is discussed
in section 7.4).

3–2 advancement

3–2 advancement is common. It is an option in numerous languages such as English, Indonesian, and Arabic. It is obligatory in Tzotzil (Aissen 1987) but prohibited in Turkish (Ozkaragöz 1986).

Oblique–2 advancement

Advancements of obliques such as benefactive, locative, and instrumental to 2 are common. See [11], [19], and [20] in Chapter 1 and [29], [42], [68], and [77] in this chapter.

Oblique–3 advancement

Examples analysable as reflecting oblique–3 advancement like [22b] in Chapter 1 from German have been claimed for some languages including French (Frantz 1981:14) and Turkish (Ozkaragöz 1986:42–4).

1–3 Inversion

Inversion structures have been posited for numerous languages including English, French, Italian, and Georgian. See section 2.6.

2–3 retreat

Examples of 2–3 retreat have been reported from various languages including German, Turkish, Japanese, and Kalkatungu (see section 2.5).

1–2 antipassive

Antipassive has been reported from numerous languages including various dialects of Eskimo, Indonesian and numerous other Austronesian languages, Dyirbal (which also has 2–3 retreat) and a number of other Australian languages, Archi, and Hebrew.

All demotions to chômage occur as side effects of other revaluations such as 2–1 and 1–2.

It is not entirely clear how information about revaluation is related to particular predicates in RG. Some Relational Grammarians such as Davies, Dubinsky, and Rosen accept the conventional notion of the lexicon in which predicates appear with a valence. Here are examples adapted from Davies (1987) and Davies and Dubinsky (1988) with some simplification of the notation:

[79a] $P(run,b)c_1$ → $1(a,b)c_1$
[79b] $P(hit,b)c_1$ → $1(a,b)c_1$
                              $2(d,b)c_1$

[79c]   P($write$,b)c_1 →   1(a,b)c_1
                            (2(d,b)c_1)
                            (3(e,b)c_1)

Example [79a] is an implicational statement which reads 'If clause *b* has a P arc with head *run* with co-ordinate c_1, then included in the set of arcs with tail *b* must be a 1-arc with co-ordinate c_1 headed by some element *a*.' Example [79b] indicates that *hit* has a 2-arc in the initial stratum as well as a 1-arc, and [79c] indicates that *write* must have an initial 1 and may have an initial 2 and/or initial 3 (*Mary wrote a letter to John, Mary wrote to John, Mary wrote a letter, Mary wrote*) (Davies and Dubinsky 1988:3–4).

In this system obligatory revaluations peculiar to certain predicates can be listed in the lexicon using an **extended valence**, i.e. a valence referring to more than one stratum. Davies provides the following illustration for the Choctaw predicate *īshahli* 'to prefer', which is one of a restricted set of predicates requiring obligatory Inversion, i.e. 1–3 demotion (Davies 1987:3):

[80]   P(*īshahli*,b)c_1 →   1(a,b)c_1
       'to prefer'   2(d,b)c_1
                              3(a,b)c_j & j > 1

The first two lines of this entry are the same as that given for *hit* in [79b] above, but the third line indicates that the nominal that heads a 1-arc in the initial stratum must head a 3-arc in a subsequent stratum c_j (where j > 1).

Davies also provides an example involving the predicate *kan* 'meet, find' in Mam. It is a transitive predicate that can occur only in passive and antipassive structures. Davies suggests that this can be captured by means of the following extended valence statement in its lexical entry:

[81]   P(*kan*, b)c_1 →   1(a,b)c_1
                            2(d,b)c_1
                            ¬2(d,b)c_f

This indicates that *kan* takes an initial 1 and an initial 2, but that the 2 may not be a 2 in the final stratum, c_f. (¬ = NOT).

Universal laws such as the Oblique Law, the Stratal Uniqueness Law and the Chômeur Advancement Ban restrict the range of possible revaluations and hence of possible networks. In Postal's view (1982, 1986), which perhaps holds only for Arc Pair Grammar, these universal laws are supplemented by language particular rules which ban a particular revaluation across the board or with a certain set of predicates. The extended valence notation can be used to stipulate such rules. Suppose we use x to stand for any predicate then a rule like [82] will prohibit passive (2–1 advancement from a transitive stratum):

[82] $P(x,b)c_j$ → $1(a,b)c_j$
$2(d,b)c_j$
$\neg 1(d,b)c_k$ & $k > j$

This indicates that for a predicate x at some stratum with a 1 and a 2, the nominal heading a 2-arc cannot head a 1-arc at a later stratum.

However, this notion of allowing all revaluations that are not banned by universal law or language particular rule would be unwieldy in the common situation where a revaluation such as Inversion or antipassive occurs with a minority of predicates and must be constrained from occurring with a majority. Davies and Dubinsky seem to adopt the more common approach of positive specification for what actually can occur. If Inversion occurs with a minority of predicates, then this will be indicated via positive specification in the valence of a predicate (as in [80]) and in the absence of such specification it is to be assumed that Inversion cannot occur.

Rules like [80] are presented by Davies and Dubinsky with respect to particular predicates, but they can be presented with respect to a list of predicates by substituting the list {x,y,z} in place of the particular predicate. This is essentially what Postal envisages in Arc Pair Grammar. He suggests rules of the following type (informally stated): if a 3-arc is the local successor of a 1-arc, then the predicate is x, y, or z. He denies that there is a lexicon distinct from the well-formedness conditions on relational networks. For him there are only well-formedness conditions which can be universal laws, general rules, or rules specific to a handful of predicates or even to just a single predicate (Postal 1982:343ff.). This raises the question of how initial strata are specified. Is there, for instance, a rule to the effect that if a predicate occurs with an initial 1 and an initial 2 it is one of a certain set? Davies and Dubinsky seem to accept that an initial valence will be specified for each predicate in the lexicon. However, there are unanswered questions about initial strata. How do non-subcategorizing complements and adjuncts get specified? There has been no attempt so far as I know in RG to establish a universal set of obliques. If such a set were established, the next question would be whether the set was instantiated in every language. But leaving this aside and considering for a moment only local dependents, which we can safely assume are universal, we need to distinguish an outer type and an inner type as in the following:

[83] In Africa Kief saw lions in the country around Nairobi.

The outer and inner types need to be distinguished at least for the purposes of linearization (the outer type cannot come between the predicate and the inner type), but often with respect to advancement. Locative advancement is usually if not always limited to the inner type which usually specifies the location of the patient (*in the country around Nairobi* gives the location of *lions* in [83]). However, since neither type of locative subcategorizes the predicate, it is not clear that they should be specified in particular lexical entries. Perhaps their presence could be predicted by a universal law specifying the universal set of obliques. If there are language particular obliques, these could be specified by general rule. Their availability to the initial stratum would follow without further stipulation and the fact that they could only be introduced in the initial stratum of a particular predicate would follow from the Oblique Law.

The distinction between outer dependents and inner ones (clearest with locative phrases) would probably have to be made by labelling, there being no VP or other structural device available to capture the distinction.

2.9 Some semantic considerations

Early RG seems to have assumed that propositional content remains constant under revaluation. This is reminiscent of the Katz–Postal Hypothesis (1964) according to which meaning could be captured in the deep structure of a Transformational Grammar, meaning being unaffected by transformations.

In general, semantic roles do hold constant under revaluation (symmetric predicates like *buy* and *sell* are not related by revaluation), but this does not mean that no difference in meaning is involved. A pair like the following would be related via revaluation, but as Fillmore (1968:48) and others have pointed out there is a difference of some 'cognitive content':

[84a] The constable loaded the hay onto the wain.
[84b] The constable loaded the wain with hay.

Example [84a] has as its unmarked interpretation that all the hay was loaded, while [84b] suggests the whole wain was filled with hay. The holistic reading also applies to the subject of the corresponding passives. This is natural enough. If one makes a predication about an entity, then, in the absence of any indication to the contrary, it is natural that the predication be taken to refer to the whole. However, this does not necessarily apply to entities that are represented peripherally as obliques or chômeurs.

Although the term relations can express a variety of roles, they each express a prototypical role and revaluations to these term relations can result in an increment of meaning. The ergative relation (a 1 in a transitive stratum) primarily expresses an agent, the direct object an affected patient, and the indirect object a sentient entity indirectly affected by the action or state designated by the predicate. These are the characteristic roles that are assigned to them in the initial stratum. In the following Kalkatungu examples the advancement to 2 results in the 'holistic effect' referred to above:

[85a] kalpin nuu-mi irratyi-thi.
       man   lie-fut girl-loc
       'The man will lie with the girl.'
[85b] kalpin-tu nuu-nti-mi   irratyi.
       man-erg   lie-loc:advan-fut girl
       'The man will lay the girl.'

The notion of sleeping with someone involves contiguity and effect. In [85a] the *irratyi* is conceptualized as a location, as in the English euphemism, but in [83b] *irratyi* has been advanced to direct object which emphasizes the notion of effect. What appears to be involved is this. The prototypical direct object is a patient, thus the typical reference of direct object and hence the meaning associated with this relation is patient. This should not be a problem for RG. It simply means recognizing that there is a meaning associated with the final 2 relation which can be relevant to the interpretation of a particular example. Davies and Dubinsky (1988) allow for an increment of meaning in certain constructions that they analyse as containing a union of predicates within a single clause. More than one predicate can assign roles and certain affixes are analysed as predicates. This is taken up in section 5.4 in the context of Clause Union.

The idea that roles remain constant across strata applies to chômeurs. A chômeur arises from the forced revaluation of a term. The chômeur may take no new marking or it may be marked like an oblique. Any oblique marking a demotee acquires is not interpreted at face value; in fact the marking is taken to be arbitrary.

The idea that the oblique marking that a demotee acquires is to be taken at face value is worth considering. If the putative chômeurs are really interpreted as the oblique that the marking indicates, then the possibility arises of reducing the class of grammatical relations. This would strengthen the theory and at the same time provide motivation for the marking. Of course putative chômeurs that do not get re-marked would have to be re-analysed too before the chômeur relation could be eliminated.

Consider the marking in the following groups of sentences from Latin and English. The [a] sentence in each group contains a putative chômeur and the other sentences in the group contain an oblique with the same marking:

[86a] Caesar interfectus est a   Bruto   Cassio-que.
      Caesar killed   is by Brutus:abl Cassius:abl-and
      'Caesar was killed by Brutus and Cassius.'
[86b] Ab   Athenis proficisci in animo habui.
      from Athens set:out   in mind had:I
      'I had in mind to set out from Athens.'

[87a] He was forced to study GB by a strict mistress.
[87b] He stood by the window.
[87c] They read 'Aspects' by candlelight.

One could consider the view that the prepositions and cases in the [a] sentences used to encode the chômeur signal a change of conceptualization; that the agent in [86a] has been recategorized as a source as in [86b], the action being seen as proceeding from the conspirators. However, this view proves unworkable. Consider the English sentences in [87]. If *by* in [87a] is to be taken at face value, then the question arises of whether it indicates locative as in [87b] or manner as in [87c]. If it indicates location, then it should be able to be used to answer *where*? It clearly does not. If it indicates manner, then it should be able to be used to answer *how*? Once again it does not. It seems clear that the *by*-phrase of the passive is in fact marking that same group of roles that appear as initial 1 in the corresponding active. It is marking subjects that have been demoted from a central relation to a peripheral one. The marking is iconic with relation to the peripheral status of the demotee but not with respect to its semantic role. This argument applies to the Latin example and presumably more widely. It seems in fact that the failure of an oblique marker to signify its characteristic role or roles can be diagnostic of chômeur status.

The notion of final 3 is interesting with respect to semantics. Typically it is marked like an oblique (e.g. dative) and it is a target of revaluations. However, in the RG interpretation a distinction is made between demotion to 3 and demotion to chômage though the two demotions often look alike since they involve acquiring similar or in some instances the same marking. The distinction seems to correlate in a number of instances with a semantic difference. It was shown above that when a subject is demoted in a passive construction and marked like an oblique it does not become an oblique; it is not reinterpreted as an oblique. However, demotion to 3 seems not only to involve acquiring the relation indicated by the marking but also the meaning associated with this relation. Consider the following examples:

[88] *Kalkatungu*
[88a] Nga-thu mani-mi maa ntia-(ng)ku.
      I-erg   get-fut food money-instr
      'I'll get food with the money.'
[88b] Nga-thu mani-nti-mi ntia   maa-tyi, urtimayi-mpa-θ.
      I-erg   get-adv-fut money food-dat use:up-seq-I
      'I used the money for food, I used it all.'

[89] *French*
[89a] Je ferai voir la lettre à Paul.
      I make see the letter to Paul
      'Ill get Paul to have a look at the letter.'
[89b] Je montrerai la lettre à Paul.
      'I'll show the letter to Paul.'

The indirect object encodes entities that are involved in the activity or change of state only indirectly. The action may be directed towards them. In [88a] the money, *ntia*, is expressed as an instrument, a means of getting food. In [88b] the sense is something like 'I used the money for food'. The holistic sense is evident here with the advancee, note the way the passage continues, '. . . I used it up'. But note too that the dative here seems to be interpretable as a normal lexical dative indicating purpose: *maatyi* 'for food'.

In the French example it is clear that the 'derived' indirect object used with the causative (see Chapter 5) has the same meaning as the 'lexical' indirect object that occurs with a single-morpheme verb like *montrer*.

It is not certain whether the semantic difference between demotion to 3 and demotion to chômage always shows up so clearly, but there is some evidence to suggest a reflection of the syntactic analysis in the semantics.

Chapter 3

Reflexives and impersonals

In the examples presented up to this point each nominal has had a continuous career from the initial to the final stratum. This chapter introduces arcs that have no final co-ordinate and arcs that have no initial coordinate. The former type is posited for one type of reflexive and the latter type for impersonal constructions.

3.1 Reflexives

3.1.1 True reflexives

In a reflexive clause an argument bears more than one semantic role. For instance, in the following sentence:

[1] Bob criticized himself.

we understand *Bob* to be the patient of the verb as well as the agent. Since an agent is encoded as an initial 1 and a patient as an initial 2, the natural way of treating a sentence like [1] is to allow a nominal to be both 1 and 2 in the initial stratum. One early Relational Grammar analysis of [1] is shown in [2]. The nominal *Bob* heads a 1-arc and a 2-arc in the initial stratum and these arcs share the same head node and the same tail node. This is **multiattachment**. In the second stratum *Bob* loses its 2-hood which is taken up by the reflexive pronoun *himself* (Perlmutter and Postal 1984b:135):

[2]

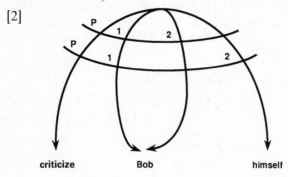

criticize   Bob   himself

In some languages there is no reflexive pronoun, but the verb is intransitivized and the reflexivization is marked on the verb. This is the situation in many Australian languages. The following example is from Yalarnnga. Note that the subject is marked by the ergative in the transitive clause [3] but not in the intransitivized reflexive [4]:

[3] irri-nhthu nanyi-mu ngarrkunu.
    man-erg   see-past   wallaroo
    'The man saw the wallaroo.'

[4] irri   nanyi-nyama-mu kunhu-ngka.
    man see-refl-past   water-loc
    'The man saw himself in the water.'

The Relational Grammar interpretation of [4] is shown in [5]. Note that *irri* is both an initial 1 and 2 in the initial stratum, which fits the semantics, but only a 1 in the final stratum, which fits the surface structure. The suffix *-nyama* would be described as registering the resolution of the multiattachment or the cancellation of the lower relation of the multiattachment, not as a reflexive pronoun. It is invariant for person and number:

[5]

    nanyi   **irri**   **kunhu**

Rosen has argued that clauses like [1] with a reflexive pronoun should be allotted an initial and only stratum with the agent as 1 and the reflexive pronoun as 2:

67

[6]

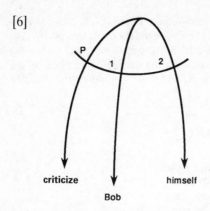

criticize   Bob   himself

On the other hand reflexive clauses where there is no reflexive pronoun should be analysed as in [5]. She notes that *si* in Italian is 'not referential and not a nominal, but a marker signalling the resolution of a multiattachment' (Rosen 1982:531). This means that she treats *si* like *-nyama* in [4] above, even though it varies for person and number (*si* is the third person form and is used here to stand for the series *mi*, *ti*, etc.; see [7] below). Clauses like the following would be analysed as in [5] above.[1]

[7a] Ugo si è difeso.
     'Ugo defended himself.'
[7b] Mi vedo.
     'I see myself.'
[7c] Come ti senti?
     'How do you feel?'

Rosen's suggested analysis of English reflexives as having a reflexive pronoun in the initial stratum is in line with more recent transformational analyses. In early Transformational Grammar anaphoric forms including reflexives replaced lexically filled noun phrases in the deep structure. In more recent treatments pronouns, including reflexives, appear in deep structure and interpretive rules specify when co-reference between nominals is possible or impossible (see Jackendoff (1972:108ff.) for arguments). Rosen's analysis of reflexive pronouns (as in [6]) seems to be the accepted one in RG. There are a number of arguments that could be adduced in favour of it from different languages. Many of them involve the simple fact that reflexive pronouns more often than not behave like non-reflexive nominals undergoing 2–3 retreat, etc. Sentences like *John thought a lot about himself* present a problem for the multiattachment analysis (compare [2] above) since the

68

reflexive pronoun would have to be 'born' as an oblique. This would break the Oblique Law which requires that all obliques be initial obliques.[2]

3.1.2 False reflexives

Rosen (1984:51–2) also discusses Italian clauses like those in [8] below where there is a reflexive marker but no semantic reflexivity, 'false reflexives' as they are sometimes called. (I assume semantic reflexivity in [7c] above: 'How do you feel yourself (to be)?', but compare [10] and [11] below):

[8a] La funa si è rotta.
     'The rope broke.'
[8b] Il motore si è fermato.
     'The motor stopped.'
[8c] Il bottone si è staccato.
     'The button came off.'
[8d] Arturo si è svegliato.
     'Arturo woke up.'
[8e] Arturo si è arrabiato.
     'Arturo got angry.'

Rosen considers these to be initially unaccusative on semantic grounds (cf. *Luigi ha rotta la fune* 'Luigi broke the rope'), but when the initial 2 advances to 1 it still heads a 2-arc in the second stratum. This is called **retroherent** advancement. It allows a generalization about the distribution of reflexive markers, i.e. they mark the presence of multiattachments:[3]

[9]

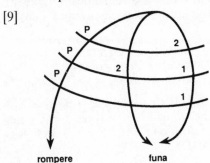

rompere   funa

The unaccusative verbs with retroherent advancement cannot be distinguished systematically from unaccusatives with plain 2–1 advancement (see section 2.4) and the presence of retroherence must be specified for particular verbs. Presumably this would be done using the notion of 'extended valence' as described in section 2.8.

Steele (1986:18) argues that in sentences like the following German examples there is an unergative initial stratum followed by multiattachment in the second stratum:

[10] Udo benimmt sich gut.
'Udo behaves well.'

[11] Er drückt sich gut aus.
'He expresses himself well.'

The stratal chart for [11] is shown in [12]:

[12] 1   Manner P
      1,2 Manner P
      1   Manner P
      ──────────────────────
      er   gut   ausdrücken

The form *sich* can be a stressable pronoun or, as here, a reflexive marker.[4]

3.1.3 Reflexive passives

Italian is one of a number of languages that has a reflexive passive, or perhaps better a personal reflexive passive, since there are also impersonal reflexive passives (see section 3.4). A personal reflexive passive is personal as opposed to impersonal in that it takes a referential subject, and it is reflexive in that it exhibits marking associated with clauses that are semantically reflexive. Consider the following Italian example (Lepschy and Lepschy 1977:213):

[13] Questo giornale si legge da moltissima gente.
     this   paper re reads by very many people
     'This paper is read by very many people.'

This would be analysed as in [14] essentially as a passive with retroherent advancement, the retroherent advancement being posited to maintain the generalization that reflexive morphology signals the presence of multiattachment:

[14]

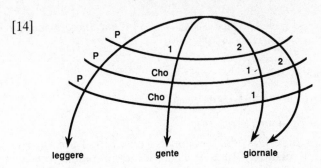

leggere   gente   giornale

In [13] there is an overt agent so it is clear that the clause is passive. But examples like [13] are unusual. Normally there is no agent expressed and the question arises of whether a particular clause is a reflexive passive or an unaccusative with retroherent advancement as in [8].

The following is an example of a reflexive passive with no expressed agent (Rosen 1981:99):

[15a] Gli avanzi   si buttano via.
        the leftovers re throw   away
        'The leftovers are thrown away.'

[15b] gives an analysis in tabular form with PRO, the unspecified nominal, as initial 1/final 1-chômeur:

[15b]

1	2	P
Cho	1,2	P
Cho	1	P

| PRO | avanzi | buttano via |

Under the multiattachment analysis the auxiliary *essere* can be said to be used wherever a nominal heads a 1-arc and an object arc. *Essere* is used in the passive, with unaccusatives (see section 2.4) and reflexives. With reflexives a nominal heads a subject arc and an object arc in the same stratum. *Essere* is not used with the emphatic reflexive *sé stesso*. For instance, corresponding to [7a] above, *Ugo si è difeso*, where *si* is a reflexive marker, there is *Ugo ha difeso sé stesso* 'Ugo defended HIMSELF'. This fits in with the analysis of emphatic pronouns as separate nominals. *Ugo ha difeso sé stesso* would have the analysis shown in [6] and there would be no multiattachment (Rosen 1981:140).

3.1.4 Summary

In sum RG treats reflexives in the following way:

(a) reflexive pronouns

These are treated like other nominals and allotted appropriate initial stratum relations. Rules of semantic interpretation would be needed to handle antecedence. These would presumably have to be based on surface structure since word order is sometimes relevant.[5]

(b) reflexive markers

These are taken to reflect multiattachment. True (semantic) reflexives exhibit multiattachment in the initial stratum while false reflexives are assigned multiattachment in a non-initial stratum.

3.2 Dummies and impersonal constructions

Consider the italicized elements in the following sentences:

[16] *There*'s some soup on my fly.

[17] *It* rained cats and dogs.

[18] *It* seems that you don't really want it.

[19] I like *it* when she sings.

None of these is referential and it is appropriate therefore that they do not appear in the initial stratum. They are all **dummies**. With meteorological predicates like *rain* it is appropriate to assume no initial stratum relations other than the predicate itself, with the dummy being introduced in the second stratum. The **birth** of the dummy *it* in *It rained* is illustrated in [20b] (Rosen 1981:17):

[20a] It rained

[20b]

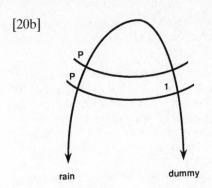

rain   dummy

In the other cases the dummy replaces a nominal, as in [16], or a clause, as in [18] and [19]. The stratal diagram for [16] is as follows,

[21]

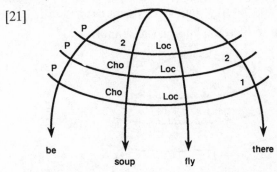

be   soup   fly   there

In clauses like [16] the dummy seems to be the subject since it occupies the subject position and appears in tags in subject auxiliary inversion (*There's soup on my fly, isn't there?*) but the verb agrees with the displaced nominal, the chômeur. In Relational Grammar the nominal displaced by the dummy is called the **brother-in-law** of the dummy and a principle of **brother-in-law agreement** is established (the strict definition of brother-in-law appears in [25] below):

[22] Where the nominal referenced by an agreement rule is a dummy, agreement is determined by the dummy's brother-in-law instead.

The distribution of dummies is constrained by the **Nuclear Dummy Law** which states that dummies can only be 1s or 2s. Example [19] has a dummy as a 2, assuming *it* is not referential (*I like the look on the kiddies' faces when she sings*, nor an appositional 'copy' of the subordinate clause analogous to *him* in *I knew him, Horatio, a fellow of infinite merit and jest* which is a copy of *a fellow of infinite merit and jest*.

The brother-in-law relation can be used to state agreement even where agreement on a matrix verb is determined by a nominal in a lower clause (Perlmutter and Zaenen 1984). In [23a] the verb *seem* agrees with *bugs* which is in a clause analysed as holding the initial 2/final chômeur relation to *seem*. The analysis is shown in [23b] (see section 4.3.1 for more examples of clausal ascension):

[23a] There seem to be some bugs in the soup.
[23b]

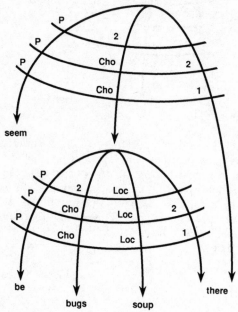

Although *bugs* is not in the same clause as *seems*, it is the brother-in-law of a nominal that is. Perlmutter and Zaenen (1984:186)

point out that without the brother-in-law relation one would have to write a complicated verb agreement for English as follows:

[24] A finite verb agrees with the final 1 of its clause, unless the final 1 is the dummy *there*, in which case the verb agrees with the nominal *there* puts en chômage in the lowest clause and earliest stratum in which *there* heads an arc.

Against this it could be said that the relation of brother-in-law cloaks just such a complicated rule since the strict definition of brother-in-law reads as follows:

[25] *The Brother-in-Law Relation*
The brother-in-law relation holds between a dummy and a nominal if the dummy puts the nominal *en chômage* in the lowest clause and earliest stratum in which the dummy heads an arc.

However, Perlmutter and Zaenen point out that in a cross-language perspective [22] is preferable to a complicated language-particular rule like [24] because the brother-in-law relation is needed in a number of languages. The brother-in-law relation captures a cross-language regularity and its motivation derives from the basic goals of linguistic theory, that is, to make explicit the ways languages differ and the ways they are alike.

Rosen (1981:91ff.) following Perlmutter posits a silent dummy in Italian clauses such as *È piovuto* 'It rained' (cf. [20] above). The presence of a dummy which appears in a non-initial stratum and advances to 1 fits in with the generalization that *essere* is the auxiliary wherever a nominal heads a 1-arc and an object arc:

[26] P
    P   2
    P   1
    —————————
    piovere D

Rosen and Perlmutter take Italian clauses with apparent post-verbal subjects to be impersonal constructions with a silent dummy as final 1 and the apparent subject to be in fact a chômeur. Example [27a] is an unergative clause and [27b] gives the inverted alternants. Example [28a] is an unaccusative clause and [28b] gives the inverted forms:

[27a] Molti stranieri hanno lavorato in quella fabrica.
'Many foreigners (have) worked in that factory.'
[27b] i. Hanno lavorato molti stranieri in quella fabrica.
ii. In quella fabrica hanno lavorato molti stranieri.

[28a] Dei profughi ungheresi sono rimasti nel paese.
       'Some Hungarian refugees (are) remained in the country.'
[28b] i. Sono rimasti dei profughi ungheresi nel paese.
       ii. Sono rimasti nel paese dei profughi ungheresi.

The analysis of [27a] is straightforward. *Molti stranieri* is the initial and final 1 and [28a] is also straightforward with *dei profughi ungheresi* being an initial 2 that advances to final 1. The stratal networks posited for [27b] and [28b] are shown in [29] and [30] respectively (Perlmutter 1983b:141ff.):

[29]	lavorare	stranieri	fabrica	D
	P	1	Loc	
	P	Cho	Loc	1
[30]	rimanere	profughi	paese	D
	P	2	Loc	
	P	Cho	Loc	2
	P	Cho	Loc	1

Part of the evidence for this analysis derives from the fact that the post-verbal NP in [27b] and [28b] does not exhibit certain control properties characteristic of subjects. As noted in section 2.6 and 6.6 a final 1 and an Inversion nominal (initial 1/final 3) can control the missing subject of the *da*+infinitive construction. In [31] the final 1 controls the subject of the non-finite clause, but this is not possible if the apparent final 1 is placed after the verb:

[31] Dei profughi ungheresi sono rimasti a Roma tanto tempo
      dopo la guerra da sentirsi romani.
      'Some Hungarian refugees remained in Rome so long after
      the war as to feel themselves to be Romans.'

For sentences like [28a] with an unaccusative initial stratum there is evidence of another kind. As pointed out in section 2.4 *ne* can be associated only with a 2, to be more precise, with a nominal that is a 2 in some stratum but not a 1 in any stratum (Perlmutter 1983b:152ff.). Now this provides a litmus for the pre-verbal NP and post-verbal NP variants of initially unaccusative clauses. If the conditions for the emergence of *ne* are as stated, it should be able to appear with the post-verbal NP (initial 2 and 2-chômeur (see [30] above)), but not with the pre-verbal NP which is an initial 2 and final 1. This is in fact what happens.

[32a] Sono rimaste due persone.
       'Two people remained.'
[32b] Ne sono rimaste due.
       'Two (of them) remained.'

[33a] Due persone sono rimaste
[33b] *Due ne sono rimaste.

These examples might suggest that *ne* can emerge only from a
post-verbal NP, i.e. that word order *per se* is relevant. However,
ne can be associated with a 2/non-1 that is fronted either because it
is contrastively stressed [34] or because it bears the overlay
relation of **Question** [35], [36] (Perlmutter 1983b:151ff.):

[34] Molte ne sono rimaste, non poche.
      'Many (of them) remained, not few.'

[35] Quante ne hai comprate.
      'How many (of them) did you buy?'

[36] Quante ne sono rimaste.
      'How many (of them) remained?'

The analysis of 'inverted subjects' as chômeurs leaves the question
of accounting for their control of agreement and their case. The
agreement will be in accordance with the brother-in-law agreement
principle [22]. The case needs to be accounted for by an analogous
principle to the effect that the dummy's brother-in-law agrees with
the dummy in case. The dummy in [27b] and [31b] is the final 1 and
is in the nominative case.

   This interpretation will probably seem strange to anyone used to
the traditional analysis, but consider the following French example
(Rosen 1981:96):

[37] Il est arrivé des   journalistes.
      It is arrived some journalists
      'Some journalists arrived.'

It is clear in [37] that *des journalistes* is not the subject since it does
not control verb agreement and that *il* is the subject by virtue of its
form (*il*), its position, and the fact that it and the verb are singular
in form. If one bears in mind that French must fill the subject
position by a noun phrase or a subject clitic, and that Italian, being
a cross-referencing language, does not need to, then one can see a
parallel between the two languages. The Italian equivalent of a
construction like that in [37] would simply look like a sentence
with the subject placed after the verb since there would be no need
for an overt dummy. However, in Italian the verb agrees with the
post-verbal subject-like nominal (the brother-in-law of the dummy)
so there is no superficial evidence to suggest the nominal in
question is anything other than a subject. In French on the other
hand the verb agrees with the dummy.

Rosen also posits a dummy for all clauses in Italian that have impersonal *si*, **Unspecified Human Subject** (UHS) clauses as she calls them. Example [38] is the impersonal of an unergative, [39] the impersonal of an unaccusative, and [40] the impersonal of a transitive (Rosen 1981:106ff.) (PRO stands for the UHS):

[38a] Non si scherza.
        'One isn't kidding.'
[38b]

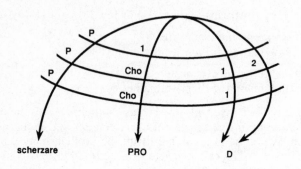

[39a] Si arriva.
        'One arrives.'
[39b]

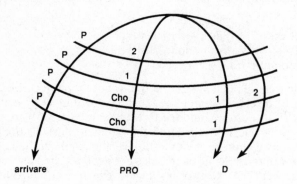

[40a] Si pronunciava/pronunciavano le acca.
        'One pronounced the aitches.'

[40b]

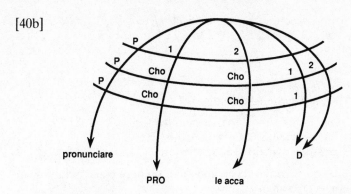

Here there is double dummy birth in a non-initial stratum. In the case of unaccusatives like *arrivare* the dummy cannot be born in a non-final stratum and advance to 1 since this would be in violation of 1AEX. The allotting of multiattachment to the dummy is to preserve the generalization mentioned earlier that *si* is associated with multiattachments. Note that in the transitive case [40] the birth of the multiattached dummy creates two chômeurs alias brothers-in-law. Verb agreement is determined by the brother-in-law of the dummy. Here where the analysis posits two brothers-in-law, there could be two controllers of agreement and that is in fact what we find. The verb can agree with PRO which always determines singular agreement, or with the other brother-in-law which in this case is *le acca* which determines plural agreement.

There is no space here to present all the well-developed argumentation that Perlmutter and Rosen bring to bear in support of the analyses described in this section and section 3.1, but it should be noted that the notions of multiattachment and dummies between them can contribute a great number of relational networks. They represent a powerful combination. However, the onus is on those who favour less abstract theories to produce an analysis of comparable generality and elegance.

3.3 Plain impersonal passives

3.3.1 Impersonal passive

Quite a number of languages have constructions with passive marking but no referential subject (as with the impersonal *si* construction described in section 3.2). Usually there is no subject at all (but see discussion below) as in the following Latin examples:

[41] Sic i-t-ur   ad astra.
thus go-3-pass to stars
'Thus it is gone to the stars.'

[42] Nobis ab amicis   persuasum est.
us:dat by friends:abl persuaded is
'It was persuaded to us by friends.'

In Dutch and German there may be a dummy place holder as in the following German example:

[43] Es wurde dem   Lehrer geholfen.
it was   the:dat teacher helped
'The teacher was helped.'

The verb form used is usually the unmarked option (except for the passive morphology) and in a language with person and number marking for subject this means third person singular as in the examples above. The presence or absence of any non-referential pronoun is incidental to the construction, the choice being determined by morpho-syntactic requirements extraneous to the construction in question. In German, for instance, *es* seems to be used to preserve the verb-second requirement in main clauses where there is no motivation to front another constituent. If a constituent is fronted, as in the following, no *es* is required:

[44] Dem Lehrer wurde geholfen.
'The teacher was helped.'

These constructions are generally known as impersonal passives. They tend to be used with one-place intransitive verbs like Latin *ire* 'to go' as in [41] or two-place intransitive verbs like Latin *parcere* 'to spare' and German *helfen* [44], both of which take dative complements as does Latin *persuadere* [42], though this verb can also take an optional clausal complement. However, in some languages they can occur with transitive verbs. An example from Welsh appears as [55] below.

The RG analysis of impersonal passives involves positing a dummy. The dummy is introduced as a 2 in a non-initial stratum (usually the second); it then advances to 1 in a subsequent stratum putting the initial 1 into chômage. The fact that the dummy 2 advances to 1 from a transitive stratum justifies the interpretation passive. Here is a Dutch example with an intransitive verb and a non-referential *er*, which is in form a locative deictic like English *there* as in *There is someone at the door* (Perlmutter and Postal 1984b:126):

[45a] Er wordt door de kinderen op het ijs geschaatst.
    it is   by   the children on the ice skated.
    'It is skated by the children on the ice.'

[45b]

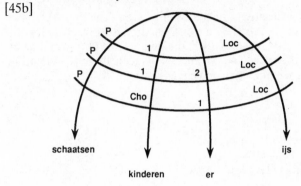

The dummy has no denotation, hence it is appropriate that it never occurs in an initial stratum. It is to be distinguished from an unspecified argument which does appear in an initial stratum (see examples of PRO in section 3.2). In [45] *er* is interpreted as representing the dummy; however, essentially the same analysis is posited for sentences like [44] above where there appears to be no subject at all. In such cases RG posits a silent or invisible dummy.

3.3.2 Impersonal passive and unaccusatives

The dummy advancee analysis in conjunction with 1AEX (the 1 Advancement Exclusiveness Law) predicts that there can be no impersonal passive of an unaccusative predicate. This would necessitate two advancements to 1: the advancement of the initial 2 and the subsequent advancement of the dummy 2. The argument is parallel with the one presented in section 2.4 about the impossibility of pseudo-passives with unaccusatives.

    This prediction is borne out by a wide range of data in numerous languages. However, apparent examples of impersonal passives with unaccusatives have been reported from some languages including Lithuanian, Sanskrit, Turkish, and German (Perlmutter and Postal 1984a:111; Postal 1986:140ff.; Shannon 1987:252). The following examples are from Turkish (Ozkaragöz 1986:230; see also 1980):

[46] Burada düş-ül-ür.
here fall-pass-aor
'Here it is fallen.'

[47] Bu yetimhane-de çabuk büyü-n-ür.
this orphanage-loc quick grow-pass-aor
'In this orphanage it is grown quickly.'

Assuming unaccusative advancement and assuming that the dummy enters as a 2 to yield a transitive departure stratum for the advancement of the dummy to 1, the analysis for [46] would be as in [48]. Since there are two advancements to 1, there is a violation of the 1 Advancement Exclusiveness Law:

[48]	P	2		Loc
	P	1		Loc
	P	1	2	Loc
	P	Cho	1	Loc
	düş	PRO	D	burada

Faced with examples like these a Relational Grammarian can try to explain them away by claiming the verbs are not ones that determine unaccusative initial strata or by claiming they do not involve two advancements to 1. The first strategy will not work in Turkish since there is independent language-internal evidence that the verbs involved are indeed unaccusative. The other strategy provides a loophole. The idea that the clauses in question are passive is based on the morphology, but just as not all clauses with reflexive morphology are reflexive not all clauses with passive morphology are passive. In Latin deponent verbs have passive morphology but are syntactically active. Consider the following relational networks which can be applied to sentences like [46] and [47]:

[49a]   [49b]

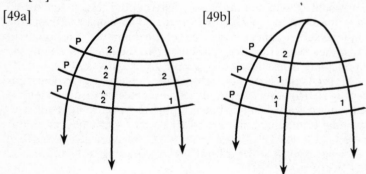

[49a] is a network in which the dummy appears as a 2 in the second stratum and pushes the initial 2 into chômage before it itself advances to 1. [49b] is a network in which the initial 2 advances to 1 and is displaced by a dummy. Since the dummy is born as a 1 and does not advance to 1 there is no violation of 1AEX (Perlmutter 19864b:158ff.) and Postal (1986:143–4).

If these solutions are adopted, they leave two problems. The first is how to frame a generalization to account for the distribution of passive marking. If [49b] is accepted, then a generalization along the lines that the passive indicates the demotion of a 1 might be a suitable basis. The second problem is more serious. If some constructions that look like impersonal passives are analysed as in [49a] or [49b] are all such constructions to be so analysed? Are there any genuine impersonal passives and how are the true ones to be distinguished from the false? If the claims based on the Universal Alignment Hypothesis and 1AEX about the impossibility of impersonal passives with unaccusatives are to have any substance, then evidence has to be found to distinguish the two types. In principle this is possible, in practice it is going to be difficult (see the discussion in Postal 1986:174ff.).

Turkish is notable for also having an impersonal passive of a personal passive. In all instances the initial 1 and 2 are both PRO, a generic, unspecified NP, and the tense is aorist (Ozkaragöz 1986:242). Note the two instances of the passive suffix:

[50] Bu şato-da   boğ-ul-un-ur.
      this chateau-loc strangle-pass-pass-aor
      'One is strangled (by one) in this chateau.'
      'It is strangled in this chateau.'

Ozkaragöz's analysis is as in [51]:

[51]			
P	1	2	
P	Cho	1	
P	Cho	1	2
P	Cho	Cho	1
	PRO	PRO	D

This assumes personal passive (second stratum), which accounts for the first passive marker, followed by the birth of a dummy as a 2 to yield a transitive stratum (third stratum). The advancement of the dummy 2 from the transitive stratum to become a final 1 justifies the impersonal label and the appearance of a second passive marker. [51] contains two instances of advancement to 1. Ozkaragöz accepts [51] and also [48] as the analysis of impersonal passives of unaccusatives. She suggests that the preferred way of resolving the conflict of RG principles that arises with these problematic examples is to abandon 1AEX as a law and reduce it to the status of a language particular rule (1986:238). She states that 1AEX 'does not work' in Turkish (ibid.:236) and that attempts at alternative analyses to [48] and [51] all require extra stipulation beyond what would be needed if violations to 1AEX are accepted.[6]

The dummy advancement analysis in conjunction with 1AEX also predicts that there can be no impersonal passive of Inversion clauses (see section 2.6), since, once again, this would imply two advancements to 1 (Perlmutter and Postal 1984b:113–15). However, there can be impersonal Inversion constructions. Perlmutter (1983b:174) suggests that in Italian alongside personal Inversion clauses like [52a] there are impersonal Inversion clauses like [52b]:

[52a] Molte sinfonie di Mozart gli piacciono.
'He likes many of Mozart's symphonies.'
[52b] Gli piacciono molte sinfonie di Mozart.

Example [52b] is given an analysis similar to that of [28b] above (see [30]):

[53]

P	1	2	
P	3	2	
P	3	Cho	2
P	3	Cho	1

| piacere | gli | sinfonie | D |

The reasons for taking [52b] to be impersonal are analogous to those given earlier in connection with the other Italian examples of 'inverted subject'.[7]

3.3.3 Impersonal passive and transitives

The application of the dummy advancement analysis of the impersonal passive to transitive verbs results in two chômeurs. The introduction of the dummy as a 2 in the second stratum forces the initial 2 into chômage. The dummy then advances to 1 forcing the initial 1 into chômage. The following example is from Welsh. Example [54] is a transitive clause and [55] the impersonal passive:

[54] Lladdodd draig   ddyn.
    killed   dragon man:acc
    'A dragon killed a man.'

[55] Lladdwyd dyn (gan ddraig).
was:killed man by draggon
'A man was killed (by a dragon).'

The analysis posited for [55] is displayed in [56]:

[56]
P	1	2	
P	1	Cho	2
P	Cho	Cho	1

| lladu | draig | dyn | D |

The analysis has strong theory-internal motivation. The positing
of a dummy as a 2 in a transitive stratum which advances to 1
justifies the passive morphology; the dummy advancement fulfils
the requirements of the Motivated Chômage Law (no spontaneous
demotion to chômeur), and the dummy satisfies the Final 1 Law
(every clause must have a final 1). However, this analysis is
controversial and has not been universally accepted (Keenan 1975;
Comrie 1977, 1986; Siewierska 1984). The best known dissenting
view is that of Comrie who argues that there is no subject at all in
sentences like [55] and that the initial subject goes into chômage
spontaneously. Perlmutter and Postal point out that there is no
principle that 'all dummy nominals must be present superficially as
well as in more abstract terms' (1984b:128). This would seem to be
true since in a broader range of cases we need to distinguish
invisible presence from non-presence.

The spontaneous demotion analysis (as in Comrie 1977) and the
dummy advancement analysis make different predictions about
the status of the initial direct object. Under the assumption of
spontaneous demotion of the initial subject the initial direct object
should remain a 2. However, in the RG analysis the initial 2 should
be pushed into chômage by the dummy. Thus the final status of the
initial 2 can provide support for the hypothesized dummy.

The initial 2 retains one object property in the impersonal
passive. A pronominal direct object in an active clause (initial and
final 2) can be represented by proclitic *i* on the verb, when the
assertion marker *fe* is present:

[57] Fe'i lladdodd (ef) draig.
ass:him killed (him) dragon
'A dragon killed him.'

This proclitic, otherwise exclusive to direct objects, can represent
the initial 2 in the impersonal passive:

[58] Fe'i   lladdwyd (ef) gan ddraig.
ass:him was:killed (him) by dragon
'He was killed by a dragon.'

This provides some evidence in favour of the spontaneous demotion analysis in that the initial 2 is behaving like a final 2, but it is not fatal to the RG analysis, since that theory makes no predictions about which term properties are lost when a nominal becomes a chômeur.

What the RG dummy advancement analysis needs is some positive indication that the initial 2 is not a final 2. There is one piece of prima facie evidence noted by Perlmutter and Postal (1984b:142). If we compare [55] with [54] we see that *dyn* in [55] does not undergo soft mutation to *ddyn* which it would do if it were a direct object (*dd* represents the soft mutation (fricative) of *d*). However, this is not positive evidence since there is no mutation with the direct object of non-finite verbs and the impersonal verb form appears to be non-finite in that it does not allow a referential subject nor does it bear any person marking. This property of the object of a non-finite can be seen in [59b] as opposed to [59a] (Zwicky 1984:387):

[59a] Gwelodd y   dyn gi (<ci).
saw:3sg the man dog
'The man saw a dog.'
[59b] Yr oedd   y dyn yn gweld ci.
prt was:3sg the man in see:inf dog
'The man saw a dog.'

Perlmutter and Postal admit that a rule of the following form could describe direct object mutation:

[60] The initial consonant of the final 2 of a clause with a finite verb mutates.

But they claim that this is not so simple as their rule:

[61] The initial consonant of a final 2 mutates.

But although their analysis is compatible with the data, it is underdetermined by the data. There is no positive evidence for the dummy advancement analysis. There are many cases where an RG analysis that is well motivated in some languages can apply in others though there is no internal evidence, but in this instance there is not a lot of evidence to establish the analysis of impersonal passives of transitives in the first place.

The claim that [61] is superior to [60] because it is simpler is a specious argument. Simplicity can only reasonably be applied to a whole analysis, not to a part of one.

Marlett (1984) presents some evidence that the initial 2 in Seri is not a final 2 in the impersonal passive construction. There is a rule of epenthesis that inserts *-k(o)-* in a certain environment. This environment needs to be specified phonologically and morphologically. The position involved is in the pre-stem part of the verb and the morphological specification is that the preceding morpheme can be a subject prefix or an object prefix but not an oblique one. This is illustrated in [62]. Example [62a] contains a subject prefix, [62b] an object prefix, and [62c] an oblique prefix. Examples [62a] and [62b] show the epenthetic segment(s) (highlighted in capitals), but [62c] does not:

[62a] im-tKm-ataX.
    thou-mood-go
    'You can go.'
[62b] ma-sKOm-kasni   ?a?a.
    thee-mood:neg-bite aux
    'It won't bite you.'
[62c] me-t-m-afp?
    to:thee mood-neg-arrive
    'Didn't he come to you?'

Significantly the epenthetic segment(s) can not be inserted after a prefix representing the patient in the impersonal passive. Thus there is no epenthesis in [63] despite the fact that the phonological requirements are met:

[63] masi-s-m-a:?-kasxa   ?a?a
    you-mood:neg-pass-bite aux
    'You (plural) will not be bitten.'

This indicates that the initial 2 is not behaving like a final term and its failure to trigger epenthesis is consistent with the dummy advancement analysis under which the initial 2 is pushed into chômage by the dummy.

Siewierska (1984) argues against the RG analysis by pointing out that in a number of languages the initial 2 shows a range of final 2 characteristics. Unfortunately hardly any exhaustive treatments of particular languages are available, so it is possible that further research would unearth evidence like the failure of *-k(o)-*epenthesis in Seri which would indicate that the initial 2 was not a final 2 and therefore a candidate for analysis as a 2-chômeur. This in turn would support the dummy advancement analysis. At present the strongest evidence for silent dummies comes from intransitive clauses, particularly the arguments from Italian in Rosen (1981) and Perlmutter (1983b).

3.4 Reflexive impersonal passives

Reflexive impersonal passives occur in a number of languages including the Slavic and Romance languages as well as in German:

[64] Hier   tanzt   sich's gut.
There dances self:it well
'There's good dancing here.'

This would be given the following analysis. This is NOT the analysis given in Perlmutter and Postal (1984b: 137) which assumes pronoun birth for *sich* as in [2]. I am assuming that *sich* marks the cancellation of the lower relation of a multiattachment resulting from retrohorent advancement as in [5]:

[65]	P	1		Manner
	P	1	2	Manner
	P	Cho	1,2	Manner
	P	Cho	1	Manner

tanzen   PRO   er   gut

Perlmutter and Postal claim that their analysis of impersonal passives makes possible a 'non-ad hoc account of the existence of reflexive impersonal passive clauses and provides a formal mechanism linking these to reflexive personal passive clauses, as well as to reflexive clauses in general' (1984b:138–9).[8] The following summary illustrates the four possible passives and the RG analysis for each. As can be seen the reflexive impersonal passive is related to the plain impersonal passive in the same way as the reflexive personal passive is related to the plain personal passive. Adverbial modifiers have been omitted from the stratal charts:

[66]   *plain personal passive*: German
[66a] Solche Sachen werden nicht oft gesagt.
'Such things are not often said.'

[66b]	P	1	2
	P	Cho	1

sagen   PRO   solche Sachen

[67]   *reflexive personal passive*: Italian (Rosen 1981:99)
[67a] Gli avanzi si buttano via.
       'Leftovers are thrown away.'

[67b]	P	1	2
	P	Cho	1,2
	P	Cho	1

buttare via	PRO	avanzi	

[68]   *plain impersonal passive*: German
[68a] Es wird hier getanzt.
       [lit.] 'It is danced here.'

[68b]	P	1	
	P	1	2
	P	Cho	1

tanzen	PRO	D

[69]   *reflexive impersonal passive* (=[64] above)
[69a] Hier tanzt sich's gut.
       'There's good dancing here.'

[69b](=[65])	P	1	
	P	1	2
	P	Cho	1,2
	P	Cho	1

tanzen	PRO	D

As can be seen from a comparison of the charts, impersonal passives have a dummy advancing from 2 to 1 and reflexive passives have retroherent advancement from 2 to 1 resulting in multiattachment which is resolved by the cancellation of the lower relation in the multiattachment. This cancellation is registered by a reflexive marker.

Chapter 4

Multinode networks

Up to this point discussion has been confined to simple sentences and the internal structure of phrases has been ignored. This chapter introduces complex sentences and deals with relations within one type of phrase, the possessive phrase. The following sections cover in turn the Relational Grammar treatment of Equi NP Deletion, Extraposition, and Raising. The last section on **Raising** or **Ascension**, as it is also known as in RG, covers clausal ascension and possessor ascension.

4.1 Cross-clausal multiattachment

In the following sentences there is a non-finite complement clause:

[1] Graham wanted to go to Land's End.

[2] I told Graham to go to Land's End.

In each case the missing subject is determinable. In [1] it is understood as being co-referential with the subject of the main clause and in [2] it is understood as being co-referential with the direct object of the main clause. In Transformational Grammar the missing subject was introduced as an NP in deep structure and deleted before surface structure under identity with the NP that controlled it in the governing clause.[1] The relevant transformation was known as Equi NP Deletion. In Relational Grammar Equi is handled by cross-clausal multiattachment. The following example is from K'ekchi (Berinstein 1985:137–8):

[3a] Lix Rosa ta:ø-xic   chi lok'oc re li tib.
       Rosa fut-3abs-go prep buy:inf dat the meat
  'It's Rosa who will go to buy the meat.'

[3b]

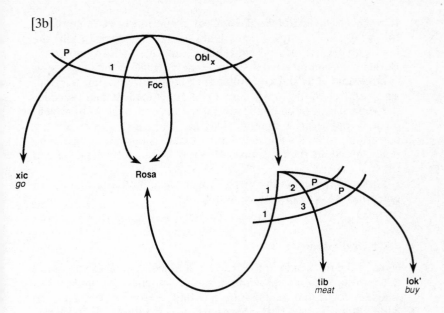

Note that *Rosa* heads a 1-arc in the main clause and in the complement clause. This is cross-clausal multiattachment. *Rosa* is also multiattached within the main clause since it heads an overlay arc (Focus) as well as the central relation of subject. This particular construction provides a nice example of how the notion of cross-clausal multiattachment can be exploited. To demonstrate this it is necessary to describe 2–3 retreat and how the subject of such a clause must hold an overlay arc. The following pair illustrate an ordinary transitive clause [4a] and its counterpart with 2–3 retreat [4b]. The basic word order is verb–object–subject (ibid. 149–50):

[4a] X-ø-x-lop   li   cui:nk li   c'anti'.
     rec-3abs-3erg-bite the man   the snake
     'The snake bit the man.'
[4b] Li c'anti' x-ø-lop-o-c   re li   cui:nk.
     the snake rec-3abs-bite-R-asp dat the man
     'It was the snake that bit the man.'

The retreat in [4b] can be seen from the absence of any ergative cross-referencing form on the verb, the presence of a marker registering retreat, and the dative preposition with the patient. In

K'ekchi the final subject of a retreat clause must head one of the following overlay arcs: Focus, Question, or Relative. In [4b] the final subject is focused and hence appears before the verb. Berinstein demonstrates that where 2–3 retreat occurs in an Equi-complement it is the controller that bears the overlay relation. This can be seen in [3a] where *Lix Rosa* is focused and precedes the verb. This can be neatly accounted for under the **Multiattachment Hypothesis**. A nominal like *Lix Rosa* in [3a] satisfies the constraint on final subjects of retreat clauses because it heads the final 1-arc in the retreat clause (see [3b]) as well as the final 1-arc in the main clause.

Further arguments involving cross-clausal multiattachment are given towards the end of section 4.3.1.

4.2 Extraposition

Most of the discussion in the RG literature concerning extraposition deals with extraposition within a simple sentence. Perlmutter and Zaenen, for instance, illustrate indefinite extraposition in Dutch with sentences like [5b] where *er* is a non-referential form like English *there* in *There are many reasons for this behaviour* (1984:173–4):

[5a] Twee kinderen spelen in de tuin.
     two   children play   in the garden
     'Two children are playing in the garden.'
[5b] Er   spelen twee kinderen in de tuin.
     there play   two   children in the garden
     'There are two children playing in the garden.'

The analysis of [5b] is shown in [6] where the dummy, instantiated by *er*, is introduced as a non-initial 1 which puts the initial subject in chômage.

[6]	P	1		Loc
	P	Cho	1	Loc
	spelen	twee kinderen	er	de tuin

This type of analysis is applicable to examples like [7a] where the initial 1/final chômeur is a clause:

[7a] It strikes me that the government has a case to answer.

Here is an analysis of [7a] in tabular form:

[7b]		1		P	2
	1	Cho		P	2

D(it)	[the government	strikes	me
	. . . to answer]		

4.3 Ascension

4.3.1 Clausal ascension

In the following sentence *John* is the grammatical subject of *seem*, but semantically it is an argument of the verb of the complement clause:

[8] John seems to work too hard.

This can be seen from the fact that there are no selection restrictions between *seem* and its subject, whereas there are between the subject of *seem* and the verb of the complement. In various models of Transformational Grammar *John* in [8] would be treated as an underlying subject of *work* which is raised to become the subject of *seem*. In Government and Binding, for instance, a raising predicate like *seem* or *appear* has an empty subject position [e] to which the complement subject is moved leaving a co-indexed trace (t) (Chomsky 1981:62ff.):[2]

[9] [e]   seem [John work too hard]
$\quad$ John$_i$ seem [t$_i$ work too hard]
$\quad$ John seems to work too hard.

A raising analysis is also posited for examples like [10] and [11]:

[10] Long shifts are tough to work.

[11] I expect the glass to fall.[3]

In [10] there are selection restrictions between the subject of *are tough* and the object of *work* (cf. *It is tough to work long shifts*). In [11] there are selection restrictions between *glass* and *fall*, though *glass* is grammatically the direct object of *expect*. The raisings illustrated in [8], [10], and [11] have been classified in the transformational literature as follows:

[12] *subject-to-subject raising*
$\quad$ John seems to work too hard.
$\quad$ [seem [John work too hard]]

[13] *object-to-subject raising*
Long shifts are tough to work.
[be tough [PRO work long shifts]]

[14] *subject-to-object raising*
I expect the glass to fall.
[I expect [glass fall]]

The posited underlying structures have been shown below each example and it is easy to see how the labels are justified. However, even in traditional terms the notion of 'raising to subject' is misleading, since there are no examples of raising to the subject in a transitive stratum. As we shall see below, RG extracts a more accurate generalization about the target of raising.

In their 1974 Linguistic Institute lectures Perlmutter and Postal (see also Perlmutter's afterword to Perlmutter and Postal 1983b:53) proposed the following universal laws about raising or **ascension**, as it is generally known in RG:

[15] *Relational Succession Law*
An NP promoted by an ascension rule assumes the grammatical relation borne by the host out of which it ascends.

[16] *Host Limitation Law*
Only a term grammatical relation can be host of an ascension.

Predicates such as *seem, appear, be likely*, and various modals in their epistemic sense (e.g. *may* in *Kylie may become a star*) are taken to be unaccusative. The stratal diagram for [8] (=[12]) is displayed in [17]. Note that in the initial stratum [*John work too hard*] is a 2. Under the Relational Succession Law *John* must ascend to hold the 2 relation in the higher clause. This puts the initial 2, or what is left of it, in chômage:

[17]

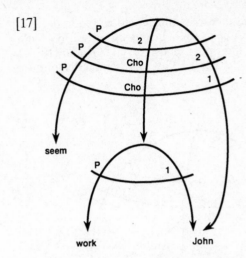

Predicates like *tough*, *easy*, and *difficult* are also taken to be unaccusative. The stratal diagram for [13] is shown in [18]. Once again the ascendee, this time the final 2 of the lower clause, becomes a 2 in the upper clause putting the remnants of the initial 2 in chômage:

[18]

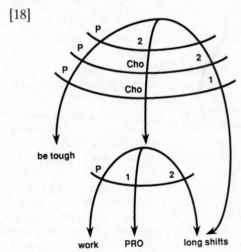

95

In [14] the complement clause is interpreted as the initial 2 of *expect*, so *the glass* must ascend to 2. In this instance it does not have to advance to 1 in the upper clause, as in [17] and [18], to fulfil the requirements to the Final 1 Law. The stratal diagram for [14] is shown in [19]:

[19]

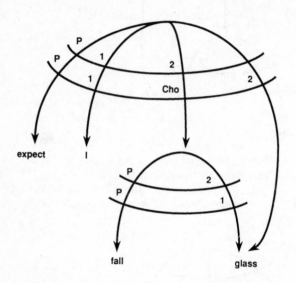

The generalization that emerges from this treatment regarding the target of raising is that the target is always a 2.

The analysis of verbs like *appear* and *seem* as taking a clausal 2 in the initial stratum fits in with the Inversion analysis of clauses in which an experiencer is expressed as a 3. This analysis involves taking the experiencer to be an initial 1 as outlined in section 2.6. Verbs like *appear* and *seem* can take an experiencer dependent that is a candidate for Inversion and a clausal dependent from which ascension takes place. The experiencer is an initial 1 and the clause an initial 2. One analysis is shown in [20b]. Under an alternative analysis the complement clause can advance to 1 and the ascendee ascend directly to 1 [20c] (Perlmutter and Postal 1983b:70; Perlmutter 1984b:328):

[20a] Marcia seemed to me to be joking.

[20b]

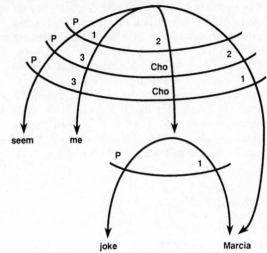

[20c]

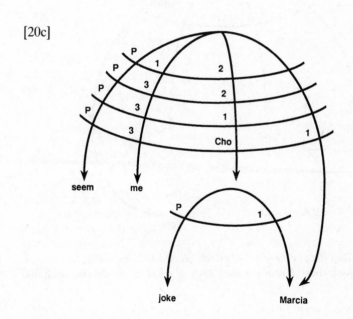

The following argument for the advantages of cross-clausal multiattachment is derived from Legendre (1987). It has been held over from section 4.1 since it involves raising (ascension).

Legendre argues that the only nominals that can take part in object raising in French are those that 'head only 2-arcs'. Advancees to 2, demotees to 2, advancees from 2, demotees from 2: none of these qualify for raising. Interestingly a 2 that is an Equi-controller cannot raise. Under the Multiattachment Hypothesis this follows since the controller heads a 1-arc in the complement clause and therefore does not head only a 2-arc. Consider the following sentence where *Pierre* is the initial/final 2 of the main clause and controls the initial/final 1 of the complement (Legendre 1987:44ff.):

[21] On a forcé Pierre à courir.
    'One has forced Peter to run.'

The multiattachment is shown in [22]:

[22]

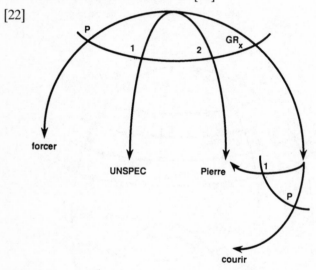

A nominal like *Pierre* in [21] which holds a non-2 relation via multiattachment cannot raise with a raising predicate such as *difficile* [23b]:

[23a] Pierre sera difficile à trouver.
    'Peter will be difficult to find.'
[23b] *Pierra sera difficile à forcer à courir.
    'Peter will be difficult to force to run.'

Legendre also points out that where a 2 controls a reflexive pronoun it can still take part in object-to-subject raising (ibid. 49–50):

[24] Pierre sera impossible à protéger   de lui-même.
'Peter will be impossible to protect from himself'

This is not surprising since in RG *Pierre* will be simply an initial 2 and *lui-même* will be an independent co-referent nominal. However, the distinction between [23b] and [24] would be a problem for Government and Binding where the missing subject of an infinitival complement is filled by an abstract element PRO which can be co-indexed to its controller. This is essentially the same mechanism that is used to describe the relationship of a reflexive pronoun to its controller or antecedent. Legendre claims that a distinction between multiattachment [21] and a pair of co-referent nominals [24] proves useful and that a theory that uses the same mechanism to cover both relationships would have difficulty accounting for the different behaviour of an object that is an Equi-controller [21] and an object that is a reflexive controller [24].

4.3.2 Possessor ascension

Consider the following pairs of sentences. The first pair is from Lardil (Klokeid 1976:265ff.) and the second from Stoney (Frantz 1981:30):

[25a] Ngithun relka kalka kun.
     me:gen head ache ev
     'My head aches.'
[25b] Ngata kalka kun relka.
     I   ache ev head
     'My head aches.'
     'I've got a headache.'

[26a] Ma-thiha n-uzazach.
     my-foot 2s-wash
     'You washed my foot.'
[26b] Thiha ma-n-uzazach.
     foot 1s-2s-wash
     'You washed my foot.'

In [25a] the first person is expressed as a genitive marked dependent on *relka* 'head', the phrase *ngithun relka* being the subject of *kalka* 'ache'. In [25b] the first person is expressed as the subject of *kalka*. In RG this and similar pairs have been related by assuming that the construction in [25a] reflects initial stratum relations directly whereas [25b] reflects the ascension of the possessor from the possessive phrase to the clause proper. The analysis proposed for [25b] is displayed in [27]. The relations posited in the phrase are POSS(essor) and H(head). I have assumed *kalka* is unaccusative:

[27]

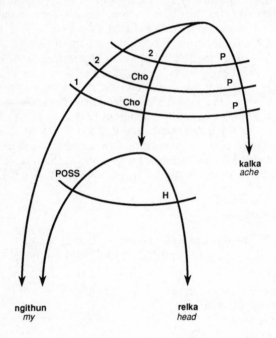

In [26a] the first person is expressed as a possessor via a pronominal prefix to the noun *thiha* which is the direct object of the verb. In [26b] the first person is expressed as a direct object via a pronominal prefix on the verb. An analysis analogous to the one given in [27] can be provided for [26b] (see Frantz 1981:31) in which the possessor ascends into the clause proper:[4]

[28]

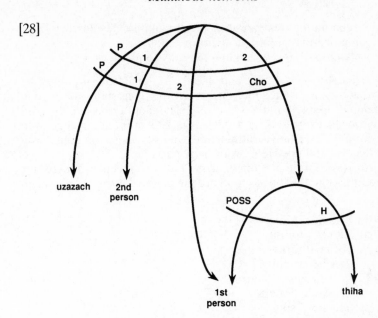

Possessor ascension works neatly here. In ascending the possessor assumes the relation borne by the host in conformity with the Relational Succession Law and pushes the host into chômage according to the Stratal Uniqueness Law. There are various pieces of evidence to support the analysis of the initial 2 as a chômeur in constructions like this. In [26b], for instance, the object pronominal form represents the initial possessor/final 2 and there is no provision for representing the initial 2 on the verb (it would appear from [26a] that the form would have been zero anyway).

Examples like [25b] and [26b] also conform to the Host Limitation Law which limits the hosts of ascensions to terms (see section 4.3.1 above). However, in some languages examples are to be found where the host is an oblique. In the following example from Kalkatungu the host is in the locative:

[29] Ithi ngai-ngu thapantu-thi thuna malhtha.
    ant me-loc   foot-loc   run   mob
    'A mob of ants is running over my foot.'

If examples like [25b] and [26b] are analysed as reflecting possessor ascension, then it would be consistent to analyse examples like [29] in the same way. The first person in [29] could have been expressed by a dative-marked pronoun analogous to *ngithun* in [25a] above, although it is unusual in Kalkatungu to use dative-marked possessors with body parts.[5]

A possessor ascension analysis has also been proposed for examples like the following where the putative possessor shows up as a 3:

[30]   *French* (Frantz 1981:31)
[30a] Sa tête tourne.
      his head turns
      'His head spins.'
[30b] La tête lui   tourne.
      the head 3s:IO turn
      'His head spins.'

[31/32] *Spanish* (Tuggy 1980:98; Bickford 1982:127)
[31]   Le   cortaron la   mano.
      3:IO cut:they the hand
      'They cut his hand off.'

[32]   Le   robaron el auto a Guillermo.
      3:IO stole:they the car to William
      'They stole William's car.'
      'They stole the car on Bill.'

However, such an analysis does not conform to the Relational Succession Law. If one tries to salvage the Succession Law by assuming that the ascendee first assumes the relation of the host and then revalues, one finds that this will not work. The putative host retains its term status and is clearly not a chômeur. In [30b] *tête* is obviously a final 1 and in [31] *la mano* and in [32] *el auto* can be shown to be final 2s. If the ascendee had assumed the relation of the host, these hosts would have become chômeurs and chômeurs cannot revalue to term status.

The possessor ascension analysis is based on the assumption that clauses with an 'unascended possessor' are synonymous with those that are analysed as reflecting an ascension. This is at best a dubious assumption and in some instances it is scarcely plausible. With examples like [26] from Stoney one would expect that in the version with *ma-thiha* 'my foot' as a final 2, *ma-thiha* is presented as an affected patient, whereas in the version with *ma-* 'me' as final 2 then the first person is the affected patient. In examples where the putative ascendee is a 3, it seems that a beneficiary or maleficiary sense is typically indicated. Consider the Spanish example [32]. Does the indirect object indicate a possessor or does it indicate a maleficiary? I believe it is the latter and I have tried to capture that in the second translation with the English preposition *on* which in many varieties of colloquial English has this adversative sense as in *He cheated on his wife, He did the dirty on me.*[6]

Sentences that Relational Grammarians have tried to relate via possessor ascension probably reflect different conceptualizations of a situation. In early RG a number of analyses were floated which were based on an adherence to the Universal Alignment Hypothesis and a loose idea of synonymy.[7] There seemed to be no allowance for alternative conceptualizations each with its own initial relations. Recently, however, a number of analyses have appeared which allow for alternative initialization. Aissen (1983: 294–5) allows for 'a notional benefactive' to be encoded initially as a possessor or as a 3 in Tzotzil. In [33] the possessor is expressed as the possessor of the obligatorily possessed noun stem *-u?un*:

[33] ?Iskomcan hun kampana y-u?un   hc'ultottik San-torenso.
    3s:3s:left   bell   his-u?un Our-Holy-Father
                                                San Lorenzo
    'They left a bell for Our Holy Father St Lawrence.'

In [34] the possessor is expressed as a direct object, but the verb is suffixed with *-be* which indicates the advancement of 3 to 2. This advancement is obligatory:

[34] ?Ismil-be-ik   cih.
    3s:3s:kill-adv-3pl sheep
    'They killed sheep for him.'

Aissen writes (1983:294): 'I assume here that notional benefactives may occur in two distinct underlying syntactic relations. Those that surface as possessors of *-u?un* I assume to be underlying possessors of oblique nominal phrases . . . Those that function as final direct objects to verbs suffixed with *-be* I assume to be underlying indirect objects which advance to direct object by the rule of Indirect Object Advancement.'

Recently Rosen has suggested that possessor ascension in Tzotzil can be handled by 'nominal union', the union of a, noun phrase with a clause. This is described briefly at the end of Chapter 5 in which Unions are described.

Chapter 5

Clause Union

5.1 Clause Union

Relational Grammarians recognize a class of constructions that they analyse as complex at the initial stratum, but as simple in the final stratum. Consider the following pair of Spanish sentences (Aissen and Perlmutter 1983:365, orig. 1976):

[1a] Quiero mostrártelos.
    I:want show:thee:them
    'I want to show them to you.'
[1b] Te   los   quiero mostrar.
    Thee them I:want show
    'I want to show them to you.'

Example [1a] is a complex sentence which in early Transformational Grammar would have been analysed as involving deletion of the subject of the dependent verb under identity with the subject of the main verb (Equi NP deletion) and which in RG is handled via cross-clausal multiattachment with cancellation in the lower clause (see section 4.1). The dependent verb is in the infinitive form and the conjunctive pronouns (*te* and *los*), representing arguments of the infinitive (*mostrar*), are enclitic to it. In Spanish bound pronouns are enclitic to non-finite verb forms and proclitic to finite ones. In [1b] the bound pronouns appear as proclitic to the finite governing verb even though they belong semantically with *mostrar*. This suggests that there is some kind of amalgamation of what are separate clauses in [1a]. The RG analysis involves an initial stratum with two clauses (as in [1a]). These two clauses collapse into one at a subsequent stratum with the lower or downstairs verb assuming the grammatical relation **Union** (U) and the dependents of the downstairs clause becoming dependents of the upstairs clause. This is illustrated in [2] where the downstairs clause is taken to be a 2 of *querer* at the initial stratum:

[2]

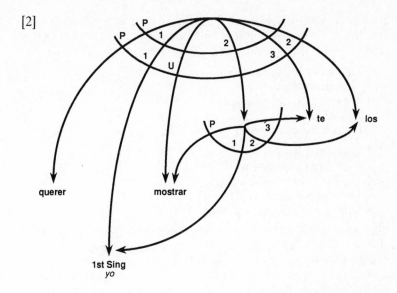

Yo, *los*, and *te* are initial 1, 2, and 3 in the downstairs clause. In the
second stratum, the Union stratum, *los* and *te* ascend into the
higher clause. *Yo* is already in the higher clause. *Mostrar* ascends
to become a Union predicate which can be considered to be a
predicate chômeur. Indeed as shown in section 5.3 below, the
notion of predicate chômeur has now superseded Union predicate,
at least in the Davies and Rosen analysis. The stratal diagram
shows the final relations. To complete the surface structure would
require transferring the person and number specification of the
subject to the verb, the linearization of the dependents including
the placement of *te* and *los* with respect to *querar* (not *mostrar*)
and provision for the optional omission of *yo* (pro-drop).

It might be thought that the appearance of the clitics *te* and *los*
with what appears to be the main verb of a complex sentence in
[1b] can be explained in terms of some kind of Raising or Clitic
Climbing. However, as Aissen and Perlmutter point out, either all
clitics climb or none does. One cannot put *te* or *los* in front of
quiero without putting the other there too. This confirms the
analysis in terms of Clause Union. In various types of Raising a
single constituent is raised and the others remain behind. With
Union all dependents of the downstairs clause become dependents
of the upstairs clause.

Here are two examples from Italian illustrating epistemic and
root modals. The [a] sentences are bi-clausal and the [b] sentences

are uniclausal Union equivalents. These examples are from Davies and Rosen (1988:59), but it should be noted that their considered analysis is not the one given in [5a,b] but the one given in [34a, b]:

[3a] Ugo deve invidiar-te-lo.
Ugo must envy-thee-it.
[3b] Ugo te   lo deve invidiare.
Ugo thee it must envy
'Ugo must envy you it.'

[4a] Ugo deve spiegar-te-lo.
Ugo must explain-thee-it
[4b] Ugo te   lo deve spiegare.
Ugo thee it must explain
'Ugo must explain it to you.'

The sentences in [3] have a natural reading 'It must be that Ugo envies you it' and can be used to illustrate the epistemic sense where *Ugo* bears no semantic role in relation to *dovere*. The sentences in [4] have a natural reading 'Ugo is obliged to explain it to you' and can be used to illustrate the root sense where *Ugo* bears the 1 relation to *dovere*. Example [3a] would be interpreted in terms of raising or ascension (see section 4.3.1) and [4a] in terms of multiattachment (see section 4.1). The Union analyses of [3b] and [4b] are shown below:

[5a] epistemic

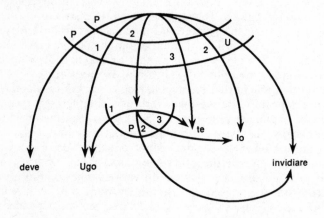

[5b] root

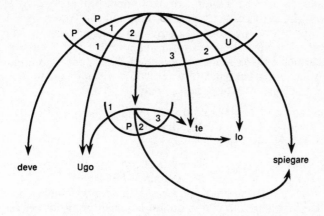

The amalgamation of clauses has been described in a transformational framework by a number of linguists including Radford
(1977), Rizzi (1978), and Burzio (1986), though Radford ultimately
argues for the superiority of RG. All three describe Italian, which
is similar to Spanish in affording evidence for Clause Union in the
form of clitic placement. Aissen and Perlmutter (1983) discuss
Rizzi's account of restructuring in Italian. Rizzi (1978:117–18)
gives the following example [6a] and shows how the intermediate
structure [6b] which follows Equi can be restructured so that a
single node is created to dominate the matrix verb and the
embedded verb yielding [6c]:

[6a] Gianni la deve presentare a Francesco.
     'John should introduce her to Francis.'
[6b] Gianni deve [presentare la a Francesco]
[6c] Gianni [deve presentare] la a Francesco.

The clitic *la* can then be placed with respect to the verb *deve
presentare* and will be placed in front of it since it is finite and clitics
precede finite forms of the verb in Italian as in Spanish. Aissen and
Perlmutter (1983:395) claim that the transformational description
predicts that restructuring will be found only in languages where a
single node can be posited dominating the verbs of the complement
and the matrix clause, whereas the RG analysis can apply even
where the two verbs are not adjacent, since it operates over

relationally defined structures to which linearization applies subsequent to Clause Union. In fact there do appear to be languages where there is a Union of non-adjacent verbs. Aissen and Perlmutter cite the following Ancash Quechua example from Cole. In this language there is a form which Cole calls a 'validator'. This can attach only to elements of a main clause, but in examples like the following it attaches to what would be an element of the subordinate clause in a two-clause analysis:

[7] Noqa muna-a Lima-chaw-mi yacha-y-tz.
    I   want-I Lima-in-val   live-infin-acc
    'I want to live in Lima.'

This suggests a Union with *yacha-y-tz* becoming a Union predicate and *Lima-chaw* becoming a dependent of *muna-*.

Jacaltec is another language that has structures which have been analysed as involving the Union of non-adjacent predicates (Craig 1977:362). Note the position of the first person plural marker in [8]:

[8] Cho-oñ y-a'   naj munlahoj.
    asp-us 3s-make he work
    'He makes us work.'

This is an example of Causative Clause Union, a subtype of Union which exhibits a number of interesting regularities across languages. Causative Union is treated in the next two sections.

Aissen and Perlmutter's claim that the transformational approach cannot handle the union of non-adjacent predicates is not correct for the simple reason that in Transformational Grammar a node can be created to dominate predicates at one level of structure and then subsequently be dismembered by movement rules. Consider the following example from German where the order of the pronouns is part of the evidence for Causative Clause Union:

[9] Ich liess es ihn machen.
    I   let it him do
    'I let him do it.'

This can be derived in the following steps: VP movement and then rightwards verb movement:

[10a] Ich liess [ihn es machen]
[10b] Ich liess [es machen] ihn (VP movement)
[10c] Ich liess es ihn machen (verb movement)

It is hard to find something that early Transformational Grammar cannot do. That was one of its shortcomings and it led to the introduction of various revisions aimed at reducing its power. However, here as elsewhere the positing of a deep structure incorporating dominance and precedence raises needless problems. Even in the simple example shown there are alternative underlying word orders, even more if other constituents are added. However, Marantz, working in a comparatively constrained framework similar to Government and Binding, still appeals to 'merger and splitting' as a means of capturing discontinuities in surface structure, including causative verbs and separated dependent verbs in what RG analyses as Union constructions (Marantz 1984:285–6).

5.2 Causative Clause Union

Besides the Unions described in section 5.1 there is a type of construction analysed in RG as **Causative Clause Union** or simply **Causative Union**. These constructions are taken to consist of two clauses in the initial stratum which collapse into one clause at a subsequent stratum. The·following examples are from Italian:

[11a] Maria parla.
      'Maria speaks.'
[11b] Anna fa   parlare Maria.
      Anna makes speak   Maria
      'Anna makes Maria speak.'
[11c] Anna la   fa   parlare.
      Anna her makes speak
      'Anna makes her speak.'

[12a] Maria scrive una lettera.
      'Maria writes a letter.'
[12b] Anna fa   scrivere una lettera a Maria.
      Anna makes write   a letter to Maria
      'Anna makes Maria write a letter.'
[12c] Anna gliela   fa   scrivere.
      Anna 3dat:3sgfem makes write
      'Anna make her write it.'

Example [11a] is an intransitive clause and [11b] its causative counterpart. The direct object of [11b] corresponds to the subject of the intransitive verb in [11a]. The status of *Maria* as a direct object in [11b] is shown by the fact that a direct object proclitic can be substituted as in [11c]. The form *la* is a feminine singular object proclitic. The order *fa parlare* and the position of the clitic are suggestive of Union. Example [12a] is a transitive clause and [12b]

is its causative counterpart. The indirect object of [12b] corresponds
with the initial 1/final 1 of [12a]. That *a Maria* is indeed an indirect
object and neither an oblique nor a chômeur is demonstrated in
[12c]. In Italian an indirect object can be represented by the clitic
gli but obliques and chômeurs cannot. The position of both the
indirect object clitic *gli* and the direct object clitic *la* in front of *fa*
rather than attached to *scrivere* confirms that there is a Union
construction, since both these clitics represent arguments of
scrivere.

There is general agreement that sentences such as [11b], [11c],
[12b], and [12c] are uniclausal, but many would deny that they are
biclausal at some non-surface or non-final level. There is some
evidence for taking causatives to be biclausal in the initial stratum.
Consider the following argument provided by Rosen (1987b:461):

[13a] Zoe ha confessato di essere mancina/*mancino.
      Zoe has confessed of be   left-handed
      'Zoe has confessed to being left-handed.'
[13b] Max ha fatto confessare a Zoe di essere mancina/*mancino.
      Max has made confess   to Zoe of be   left-handed
      'Max has made Zoe confess to being left-handed.'

In [13a] the predicative adjective agrees with the deleted subject of
essere which is controlled by *Zoe* and therefore must be feminine
singular, i.e. *mancina*. This control relationship would be captured
via multiattachment (see section 4.1). Example [13b] is the
causative counterpart. Note that the predicative adjective must
still be *mancina* to agree with *Zoe* even though *Zoe* is now an
indirect object. It would be 'costly', Rosen argues, to explain why
Zoe controls the subject of the infinitive *essere* and ultimately
mancina if it is only a 3. If it is analysed as the downstairs subject,
then the agreement of *mancina* conforms to normal agreement
principles.

The following much quoted examples are from Turkish where
the causative is morphological (by suffix) and productive. The
examples cover in turn a one-place intransitive, a two-place
transitive, and a three-place transitive with an indirect object
(Comrie 1981:168–9):

[14a] Hasan öl-dü.
      Hasan die-past
      'Hasan died.'
[14b] Ali Hasan-ı   öl-dür-dü.
      Ali Hasan-acc die-caus-past
      'Ali killed Hasan.'

[15a] Müdür mektub-u imzala-dı.
director letter-acc sign-past
'The director signed the letter.'
[15b] Ali mektub-u müdür-e   imzala-t-tı.
Ali letter-acc director-dat sign-caus-past
'Ali got the director to sign the letter.'   *

[16a] Müdür Hasan-a   mektub-u göster-dı.
director Hasan-dat letter-acc show-past
'The director showed the letter to Hasan.'
[16b] Ali Hasan-a   mektub-u müdur   tarafından göster-t-ti.
Ali Hasan-dat letter-acc director by   show-caus-past
'Ali got the director to show the letter to Hasan.'

The intransitive subject of [14a] shows up as a 2 in the
corresponding causative [14b], and the transitive subject (ergative)
of [15a] shows up as a 3 in the corresponding causative [15b]. This
pattern of correspondence obviously parallels what is found in
Italian. Example [16b] illustrates the causative of a verb that has a
1, 2, and 3; the nominal corresponding with the 1 of [16a] shows up
marked by the same postposition as is used for the 1-chômeur of
the passive. This correspondence can also be matched in Italian:

[17a] Maria scrive una lettera a Mirna.
'Maria writes a   letter to Mirna.'
[17b] Anna fa   scrivere una lettera a Mirna da Maria.
Anna makes write   a   letter to Mirna by Maria
'Anna gets Maria to write a letter to Mirna.'

A number of languages exhibit the correspondences between
causative and non-causative valencies illustrated in [11] and [12]
from Italian and [14] and [15] from Turkish. These include French,
Czech, Hindi, Punjabi, Persian, Jacaltec, and Georgian. In their
1974 Linguistic Institute lectures Perlmutter and Postal proposed a
Union Law to account for the correspondences:

[18] *Union Law*
     Downstairs absolutive → upstairs 2
     Downstairs ergative   → upstairs 3

(The absolutive is the nuclear argument of an intransitive
predicate and the 2 of a transitive one. The ergative is the 1 of a
transitive predicate.)
   This is echoed in Comrie's treatment. He points out that if we
consider the following relational hierarchy:

[19] subject–direct object–indirect object–other oblique constituent

then the embedded subject is shifted to the first available position (1976:263). Checking this against the Turkish examples we see the embedded subject becoming a 2 with an intransitive [14], 3 with a transitive [15], and an 'oblique' with a ditransitive [16]. In RG the nominal marked by *tarafından* would be analysed as a chômeur, similarly the nominal marked by *da* in the Italian example [17b].

Radford (1977:252–3), writing in favour of an RG analysis, points out that while the downstairs subject needs to be revalued in Clause Union, the other dependents of the downstairs clause come to bear the same relation to the upstairs clause. He proposes a revaluation principle similar to Comrie's. However, the Union Law of Perlmutter and Postal and the similar revaluation principles of Comrie and Radford have been found not to be universally valid. Gibson (1980) demonstrates that in Chamorro the downstairs 1 always revalues to 2 in Clause Union. When a transitive verb is causativized the downstairs 2 is put en chômage. The following examples also appear in Gibson and Raposo (1986):

[20a] Maipi i   kafe.
      hot   the coffee
      'The coffee is hot.'
[20b] In taitai esti na lebblu.
      we read this lk book
      'We read the book.'

[21a] Hu na'-maipi i   kafe.
      I   cau-hot   the coffee
      'I heated the coffee.'
[21b] Ha na'-taitai häm i   ma'estru ni esti na lebblu.
      3sg cau-read us the teacher obl this lk book
      'The teacher made us read the book.'

In Chamorro final non-pronominal nuclear terms are unmarked for case relation. An absolutive is represented by pronominal forms enclitic to the verb (zero for third singular) and the ergative by a proclitic. In [21a] the downstairs 1 revalues to 2 and appears as an unmarked NP immediately after the verb. In [21b] the downstairs ergative 1 also shows up as a 2 and the downstairs 2 is marked by the oblique marking preposition *ni* which suggests it is a chômeur.

Gibson and Raposo (1986) have recently proposed a general treatment of causatives that allows for languages like Chamorro that are not susceptible of an ergative/absolutive analysis as per the Union Law [18]. They suggest the following principles:

Clause Union

(i) *Clause Union revaluation parameter*
The downstairs 1 must become a 2 or a 3.
Language particular rules specify which and under what conditions.
(ii) *Inheritance principle*
All other nominals inherit their downstairs relation subject to the Stratal Uniqueness Law and the Motivated Chômage Law. (Fauconnier puts forward a similar principle (1983:14).)

In languages like Turkish, Italian, and French language-particular rules will specify that the 1 of an intransitive downstairs verb will be revalued as a 2 and that the 1 of a transitive downstairs verb will be revalued as a 3, as in Perlmutter and Postal's Union Law, but in Chamorro there will be a rule stipulating that a downstairs 1 always becomes an upstairs 2.

Gibson and Raposo present an analysis of French causatives and attempt to account for types of downstairs clause other than one-place intransitives and two-place transitives. They note, for instance, that if the downstairs verb is an unergative verb that is subcategorized for a complement (e.g. *téléphoner à quelqu'un* 'to telephone to somone') then the downstairs 1 is revalued to a 3 which may advance to 2. Consider the following examples.

[22a] Paul téléphone à Marie.
     1   3
'Paul telephones (to) Mary.'
[22b] Paul lui téléphone.
'Paul telephones (to) her.'
[22c] Je ferai téléphoner Paul à Marie.
    1   2   Cho
'I'll get Paul to phone (to) Mary.'
[22d] Je le/lui ferai téléphoner à Marie.
   1 2/3   Cho
'I'll get him to phone (to) Mary.'

In [22a] *Marie* is an initial/final 3 and its status as a final 3 can be confirmed by the substitution of an indirect object proclitic [22b]. In the causative of *téléphoner* the initial/final 3 of the downstairs clause cannot be represented by any proclitic, but the downstairs 1 can be represented by an indirect object (*lui*) or direct object clitic (*le* or *la*) as in [22d]. This suggests that the downstairs 1 has been revalued to 3 in the Union stratum (like the 1 of a transitive complement) forcing the initial 3 into chômage (hence no possibility of clitic representation). The downstairs 1/Union 3 may revalue to 2.

Legendre (1987) presents an analysis of French causatives in which the downstairs 1 always revalues to 3 in the Union stratum and sometimes revalues to 2 in a subsequent stratum, regularly with intransitives.

Gibson and Raposo assume that revaluations to 1 such as unaccusative advancement and passive occur in the downstairs clause of a Union construction. However, Legendre demonstrates that this is not the case. Legendre's arguments are French parallels of arguments put forward for Italian in Rosen (1983).

As noted in Chapter 4 (section 4.3.1), Legendre has established that the only objects that can participate in object-to-subject raising in French are nominals that hold only the 2 relation. This rules out advancees to and from 2 and demotees to and from 2. Consider the contrast between [23] and [24] (Legendre 1987:29ff.):

[23] *La glace est facile à fondre au soleil.
'The ice is easy to melt in the sun.'

[24] La glace est facile à faire fondre au soleil.
'The ice is easy to make melt in the sun.'

In [23] *la glace* would be analysed as an initial 2 of *fondre* which would advance to 1 in the lower clause in accordance with the Final 1 Law. This advancement, it is argued, renders *la glace* ineligible to undergo object-to-subject raising. In [24] *la glace* is successfully raised. Legendre argues that this reflects the fact that the Final 1 Law does not operate in the complement of a causative predicate so *la glace* remains a 2 and is eligible for raising:

[25]

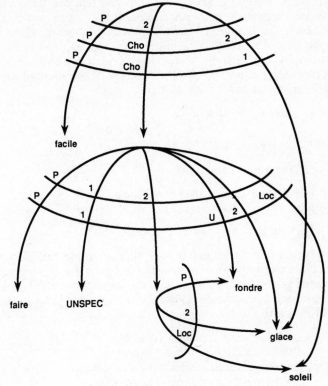

Another interesting contrast occurs when reflexive unaccusatives appear under raising and causative predicates. A verb like *se taire* 'to keep quiet' is analysed as having an initial 2 which advances to 1 with retroherent multiattachment which is resolved in the final stratum by cancellation of the lower relation. The form *se* is interpreted as a marker of the resolution of the multiattachment (as described in section 3.1.2):

[26] Les enfants se taisent.

2	P
1,2	P
1	P

'The children keep quiet.'

The initial 2 of a verb like *se taire* cannot be raised, because, Legendre argues, it is not just a 2 at all levels:

[27] *Les enfants sont faciles à se taire.

However, when a verb like *se taire* appears in the complement of the causative predicate *faire*, which is in turn in the complement of a raising predicate like *facile*, then the initial 2 can raise provided the reflexive marker *se* does not appear. Compare [28a] without *se* and [28b] with *se*:

[28a] Les enfants sont faciles à faire taire.
     'Children are easy to make keep quiet.'
[28b] *Les enfants sont faciles à faire se taire.
     'Children are easy to make keep quiet.'

This makes sense under an analysis which takes *se* to be a concomitant of unaccusative advancement and which claims that only 'just 2s' can raise. The absence of *se* in [28a] can be interpreted as indicating that there is no 2–1 in the lowest clause, hence leaving the initial 2 eligible for raising.

An argument parallel to the preceding ones can be mounted to show that spontaneous chômage is possible in the complement of a causative predicate. As noted above a downstairs initial 1 in a transitive stratum can appear in the Union stratum marked like the chômeur of a passive, but there is no passive morphology (see [16b], [17b]):

[29] Il fera dire la vérité par les enfants.
     'He will have the truth told by the children.'

The initial downstairs 2 in [29] can be raised as in [30] (Legendre 1987:31):

[30] La vérité est facile à faire dire par les enfants.
      'Truth is easy to have told by children.'

Under the hypothesis that only 'just 2s' can be raised, *la vérité* can
be raised because it has not advanced to 1 in the complement of
faire. The initial 1 demotes to chômeur spontaneously. This
hypothesis also accounts for the absence of passive morphology:

[31]

5.3 Uniclausal analysis

Davies and Rosen (1988) have recently proposed a new analysis of
Unions. They take them to be multipredicate uniclausal con-
structions. We will consider in the next two subsections modal
Unions and then causative Unions.

5.3.1 *Modal Union*

The following examples were previously presented as [3b] and [4b] with their biclausal analysis as [5a] and [5b] respectively:

[32] Ugo te   lo deve invidiare.
     Ugo thee it must envy
     'Ugo must envy you it.'

[33] Ugo te   lo deve spiegare.
     Ugo thee it must explain
     'Ugo must explain it to you.'

[32] will be interpreted in an epistemic sense and [33] in a root sense. The new monoclausal analyses are shown in [34]. As can be seen the stratal diagram is the same for both:

[34a]

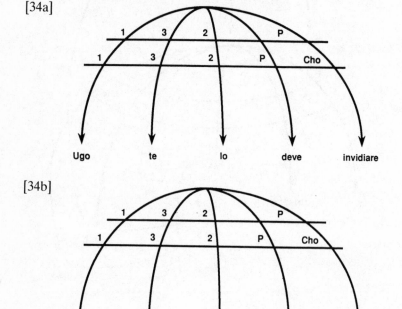

[34b]

In each case there is only one clause node and the inner clause occupies the first stratum. A second predicate starts in the second stratum which puts the inner P in chômage. The second predicate will have its own valency. An epistemic modal will initialize only

118

the complement clause (it has a termless valency); a root modal will initialize a 1 as well. *Ugo* in [33] is initialized twice, once by *spiegare* and once by *dovere*. Thus there is a difference between the analysis of [32] and the analysis of [33], but it is only apparent from the lexicon not from the stratal diagram.

There is one striking advantage to this analysis in Italian. In Chapter 3 (section 3.1.2) it was pointed out that one could frame a rule for auxiliary selection to the effect that *essere* 'to be' is used in any clause containing a 1-arc and a 2-arc with the same tail. In other cases *avere* 'to have' is used. This covers unaccusatives, passives, true reflexives, and false reflexives (analysed as having unaccusative advancement with retroherent multiattachment). But consider the following pair with the modal *dovere* (Davies and Rosen 1988:64):

[35a] Ugo ha dovuto intervenir-ci.
     Ugo has had   intervene-in:it
     'Ugo had to intervene in it.'
[35b] Ugo ci è dovuto intervenire.
     Ugo in:it is had   intervene
     'Ugo had to intervene in it.'

Example [35a] presents no problem for the auxiliary selection rule. The conditions for choosing *essere* are not met in the main clause so, by default as it were, *avere* is used. In [35b] *essere* is chosen, apparently in response to the presence of *intervenire*, an unaccusative predicate that takes *essere* (*Ci è intervenuto* 'He intervened in it'). The auxiliary selection rule will not account for *essere* under a biclausal analysis, but, as we can see from the following, the choice falls out under the monoclausal analysis. [36] presents the stratal diagram for [35b]:

[36]

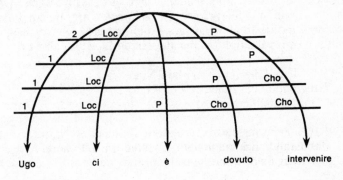

As can be seen we now have a single clause containing a 1-arc and a 2-arc with the same tail and it is this clause that is relevant to the selection of the auxiliary.

Note in [36] that the auxiliary is shown as a P which puts the P *dovere* in chômage and this P puts *intervenire* in chômage. The last P to be introduced remains a P. It is finite; it agrees with the final 1, and it hosts clitics. In Italian Ps linearize in the reverse order of their introduction. The initial P comes last in the sequence and the last P to be introduced comes first (Davies and Rosen 1988:66).

This analysis of 'verb words' implies that the perfect and the passive are Union constructions. Clauses with a copula and a non-verbal predicate are also taken to be Unions. In the following example *un eroe* 'a hero' is the initial predicate and like all non-verbal intransitive predicates it is unaccusative. The unaccusative advancement accounts for the selection of *essere* as a copula. In this instance the copula is perfect (*stato*) and requires a finite form of *essere* (*è*) to support it. Note that as each P is introduced it pushes the previous P into chômage (Rosen 1987b:452):

[37a] Leo è stato un eroe.
     Leo is been a hero
     'Leo was a hero.'

[37b]

		P	2
		P	1
	P	Cho	1
P	Cho	Cho	1
PERF	COP	eroe	Leo

5.3.2 Causative Union

Davies and Rosen's monoclausal analysis of Causative Clause Union is illustrated in [40] below. The examples are Italian but the analysis applies to all languages exhibiting the ergative/absolutive pattern of revaluation (as per the Union Law [18] above):

[38] Il babbo ha fatto parlare Nino.
     the daddy has made talk   Nino
     'Father made Nino talk.'

[39] Il babbo ha fatto accendere il fuoco a Nino.
     the daddy has made light   the fire   to Nino
     'Father made Nino light the fire.'

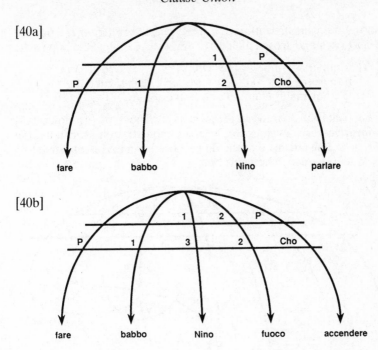

[40a]

fare   babbo   Nino   parlare

[40b]

fare   babbo   Nino   fuoco   accendere

As can be seen there is only one clause node. There are two predicates. The inner predicate and its dependents occupy the initial stratum. The Union predicate and the causer 1 are introduced in a subsequent stratum which forces revaluation of the inner 1.

The monoclausal analysis of causatives represents a spectacular advance over the biclausal analysis:

(i) As noted in section 5.3.1 there is no longer any need for the notion of a Union predicate. The inner predicate is forced into chômage. The Stratal Uniqueness Law needs to be extended from covering the term relations (1, 2, 3) to include P as well so that the pushing of the inner P into chômage follows from the law.

(ii) The Inheritance Principle can be eliminated. Relations of the inner clause simply continue in the union stratum by default, i.e. by not being revalued.[1]

(iii) No special provision is needed for chômeurs that arise in the union stratum. These simply arise in response to the Stratal Uniqueness Law. In fact, under the biclausal analysis Union chômeurs were illegal as far as the Motivated Chômage Law was concerned. Consider the following example from Georgian which

121

shows the causativization of a three-place verb (from Harris 1981 via Davies and Rosen 1988:71):

[41] Mamam   Ninos   miacemina   țorți čemtvis.
     father:erg Nino:dat he:caused:give:her:it cake me:for
     'Father made Nino give the cake to me.'

The biclausal analysis is given in [42]. The 1 of the downstairs transitive verb revalues to 3 in the Union stratum as in Italian or French. This means that the downstairs 3 cannot be inherited as a 3 so it becomes a chômeur:

[42]

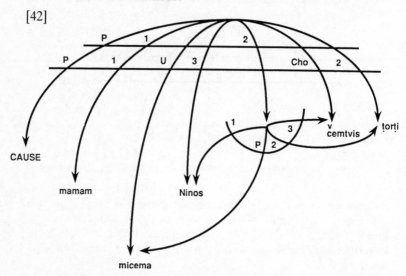

The chômeur *čem* 'me' violates the Motivated Chômage Law because it does not head a term arc in an earlier stratum with the same tail, i.e. in the same clause. Now compare the monoclausal analysis given in [43] in tabular notation. As can be seen the chômeur now has a 'local predecessor', i.e. *čem* heads a term arc in an earlier stratum of the same clause:

[43]

		P	1	2	3
P	1	Cho	3	2	Cho
CAUSE	mama	micema	Nino	țorți	čem

(iv) As was pointed out in section 5.3.1 revaluations to 1 seem not to occur in the downstairs clause of a causative construction. The Final 1 Law does not operate, although it does operate in ordinary subordinate clauses. Under the monoclausal analysis the complement clause of causatives is not an exception to the Final 1 Law. The inner clause occupies the initial stratum of a clause (and possibly other early strata if there are revaluations to 2 or 3) but is never the final stratum of a clause.

(v) With the biclausal analysis there is an asymmetry between Union and ascension. In ascension the ascendee usurps the relation of its host (the Relational Succession Law) pushing the host or the remnant thereof into chômage. However, where chômeurs arise in Unions, it is the raised nominal that is put en chômage. Compare the examples of raising given in Chapter 4 with the following example of a no-revaluation union (adapted from Davies and Rosen 1988:83):

[44] Maria farà   accompagnare il   gruppo da un interprete.
     Maria make:fut accompany   the group by an interpreter
     'Maria will have an interpreter accompany the group.'

Un interprete is the initial 1 of the inner predicate *accompagnare*. In a biclausal analysis it is interpreted as a chômeur that arises when it ascends into the upstairs clause and finds itself the victim of the Stratal Uniqueness Law. Unlike an ascendee it fails to force a demotion in the upstairs clause. In the monoclausal analysis it becomes a chômeur under the Stratal Uniqueness Law, but the asymmetry between raised nominals in unions and ascensions disappears:

[45]			P	2	1
	1	P	Cho	2	Cho

| Maria | farà | accompagnare | il gruppo | da un | interprete |

5.3.3 Nominal Union

Recently Rosen has suggested that what was previously described as possessor ascension (section 4.3.2) could be better described in terms of **Nominal Union**.[2] She hypothesizes that a noun has a relational substructure of the form shown in [46] with the noun multiattached as a 2 and as a P:

[46]

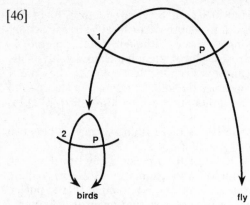

birds   fly

The ascribing of P status to a noun reflects the fact that a noun not only refers but predicates something of its referent. The idea of the noun having a 2-relation to the hypothesized predicate makes sense in terms of the Universal Alignment Hypothesis (even if it is not universal). The argument of a predicate of existence is normally taken to be a 2, and the hypothesis involves taking a noun to incorporate a downgraded predication. Moreover, the hypothesis fits in with the fact that the head of a noun phrase can be the scope of a local phrase (*the sonagram on the cover of Ladefoged*). In clauses the scope of a local phrase is either a predication or an initial 2.

Rosen also suggests that a noun predicate can initialize a 1 with the semantic role of possessor:

[47]

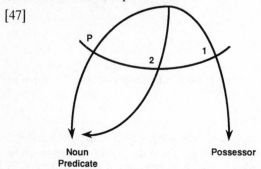

Noun   Possessor
Predicate

Rosen illustrates this hypothesis from Tzotzil. In this language pronominal possessors are cross-referenced on the possessed noun by the same series of forms as is used on the verb to mark a transitive subject. Many languages mark pronominal possessors with subject forms, but in the Mayan languages we have the unusual situation of the cross-referencing pronominal forms

operating on an ergative/absolutive basis. The choice of the
ergative series for marking possessors is positive evidence for the
notion that the possessor–possessum relation is transitive:

[48] L-i-bat.
      asp-I-go
      'I went.'

[49] J-man-oj.
      I-buy-perf
      'I bought it.'

[50] J-tot.
      my-father
      'my father.'

As pointed out in section 4.3.2 one of the problems with the
possessor ascension analysis is that in many languages the
possessor shows up as a 3 contrary to the Relational Succession
Law. This is the case in Tzotzil:

[51] L-a-j-nup-be   ta be l-a-tot-e
      asp-thee-I-meet-adv   on road the-2:erg-father-cl
      'I met your father on the road.'

The presence of the possessor in the clause proper is indicated by
the absolutive proclitic *a-*. Tzotzil has obligatory 3–2 advancement
registered by *-be*, so *a-* must be interpreted as a 2 that is the
successor of a 3. A pronominal possessor is not normally expressed
by a pronoun but by a pronominal prefix attached to the head
noun. In [51] the form is *a-* and it is retained where the possessor is
also expressed in the clause proper as here. In the second person
there is neutralization of ergative *a-* and absolutive *a-*. Under a
Union analysis the 1 of the noun predicate can revalue. Under
Rosen's analysis of Tzotzil it revalues to 3. This fits in with
Causative Clause Union in this language where ergatives revalue
to 3. If the construction illustrated in [51] is interpreted as
involving Union rather than Possessor Ascension, then the
problem of there being an exception to the Relational Succession
Law evaporates. Here is Rosen's analysis of [51] in tabular form:

[52]

		2,P	1		
	P	2	3	1	Loc
	P	Cho	2	1	Loc
	nup	tot	2nd pers.	1st pers.	be
	'meet'	'father'			'road'

I am not certain why the initial P is erased. One would have expected it to become a P-chômeur. Rosen enumerates other advantages of the Nominal Union analysis, including the fact that it explains why the host must be a noun (pronouns do not have an internal 2-arc) and why the host must be an initial 2 (the internal 2-arc falls through to the next P, i.e. the clausal P).

The Rosen analysis will work for the Lardil and Stoney examples presented in Chapter 4, assuming that the 1 of the possessor phrase revalues to 2 (see [25] and [26]). It is not clear, however, how the analysis would apply where the host is an oblique. See the Kalkatungu example given as [28] in Chapter 4.

Nominal Union apart, there are interesting questions concerning grammatical relations within noun phrases. Discussions of examples such as the celebrated *the enemy's destruction of the city* within the Chomskian tradition would suggest that in English the genitive phrase encodes 1s and the *of*-phrase 2s.[3] However, there are numerous problems with such an analysis including the possibility that the head of the phrase is a 2, following Rosen, and the *of*-phrase a 2-chômeur. The investigation of relations within the noun phrase has less to go on than the investigation of relations within the clause since there is little sign of revaluation and little interaction with the clause.

5.4 Review

The RG contribution to the typology of union constructions has been substantial. Relational Grammarians have identified several types of construction which they analyse as single clauses with more than one predicate and they have produced elegant descriptions of the underlying relational networks. However, the price of this elegance is power and the practice of setting up predicates that are not realized as words, plus the use of the **extended valence** convention, has the potential to allow a great number of possible analyses. RG needs to make clear what kind of principles are to be used, particularly in the matter of establishing underlying abstract predicates. The following paragraph presents a typical argument for taking a morphological causative to be an underlying predicate. The rest of this section describes some implications of a Union analysis for multiple role assignment and concludes with an example of the kind of novel analysis that seems to be available if one exploits the system to its full potential.

There would probably be widespread agreement among linguists of various persuasions that Union constructions are single clauses in surface structure even where the predicates involved are non-adjacent, but the notion of analysing a morphological causative as having an underlying bipredicate structure is controversial. A number of conservative theories such as Lexical Functional Grammar (Bresnan (ed.) 1982), Functional Grammar (Hoekstra *et al.* (eds) 1981), and Lexicase (Starosta 1988) use valency-increasing word formation rules for morphological causatives. The RG challenge to these lexical analyses is to point to examples like the following from Turkish (Ozkaragöz 1986:136) (compare [13] above):

[53] Ben Hasan-a   ekmek almağ-ı unut-tur-du-m.
     I   Hasan-dat bread buy-acc forget-caus-past-1sg
     'I made Hasan forget to buy bread.'

Here the dative-marked 3, *Hasana*, controls the deleted subject of *almağ* 'to buy'. The controller of Equi is normally a 1. In a multipredicate analysis Equi can be stated with reference to the biclausal initial stratum in which *Hasan* is multiattached as a 1 of *unut* 'forget' and of *almağ* 'buy'. This example is raised by Ozkaragöz in the context of arguing against a proposal by Aissen and Hankamer for a lexical derivational analysis. Aissen and Hankamer (1980) suggest that control rules can make reference to basic lexical entries, in this instance to the valency of *unut* 'forget'.

In section 5.3 the following sentences were used to illustrate Unions involving an epistemic modal and a root modal (see [32], [33], and the analysis in [34a,b]):

[54] Ugo te lo deve invidiare.
     1   3 2   P
     1   3 2 P   Cho
     'Ugo must envy you it.'

[55] Ugo te lo deve spiegare.
     1   3 2   P
     1   3 2 P   Cho
     'Ugo must explain it to you.'

As was pointed out there an epistemic modal has a termless valency, but a root modal initializes a 1. Thus in an 'Equi Union' like [55] *Ugo* is initialized twice, once by the inner predicate and once by the modal. With each initialization there is an assignment of semantic role, so *Ugo* in [55] is an EXPLAINER and OBLIGATEE (Davies and Rosen 1988:61, but the role labels are my own *ad hoc* inventions).

Dubinsky (1985, 1987) notes that in Causative Union the causative predicate introduces and initializes an argument which is an initial 1 of the causative and which bears the role of CAUSER. He suggests that in Japanese *-rare*, when it is used in the 'indirect passive', introduces an argument that is an initial 2 with the role of AFFECTEE. In this construction *-rare* marks the addition of an argument to the valency of the uninflected verb and this argument appears as a final 1. Here is Dubinsky's union analysis of an indirect passive (1987:7–8):

[56]	Taroo	wa	Ziroo	ni	saihu	o	nusum-are-ta.
	Taroo	topic	Ziroo	dat	wallet	acc	steal-pass-perf
			1		2		P
	2		1		Cho		Cho P
	1		Cho		Cho		Cho P

'Taroo suffered Ziroo stealing (his) wallet.'

As we can see, *Taroo* is an initial 2 of *-rare* which advances to 1. The introduction of *Taroo* as a 2 in the Union stratum accounts for the chômage of the initial 2 of the lexical predicate (*saihu* 'wallet'). The fact that *Taroo* advances to 1 accounts for the chômage of the initial 1, *Ziroo*. The fact that *Taroo* is an initial 2 means that there is a normal alignment of role and initial relation, since affected patients are normally 2s.

Dubinsky also extends this kind of analysis to 'normal passives' (where *-rare* does not introduce an extra argument) providing the sense is 'affective':

[57]	Otooto	wa	sensei	ni	sikar-are-ta.
	brother	top	teacher	dat	scold-pass-perf
	2		1		P
	2		1		Cho P
	1		Cho		Cho P

'(My little) brother was scolded by the teacher.'

Here *-rare* initializes a 2 which it has inherited from the inner predicate and assigns the AFFECTEE role. Passive occurs after the Union stratum. This is not the analysis for any Japanese passive nor for passives in general only for the subset interpreted as 'affective'.

The practice of treating morphemes as predicates combined with the notion of extended valence opens up a great range of possible analyses. Consider, for example, advancements to 2. What is to prevent an analysis in which the marker of the advancement is taken as a predicate with a valency that specifies that it takes a 2, assigning the role of AFFECTEE, and that this 2 must be the successor of whatever oblique is to be advanced? Such an analysis suggests itself strongly in languages where the same marker signals causative and advancement. If causatives are to be analysed as predicates that introduce a 1, why not analyse another function of the same form as introducing a 2? Consider the following examples from Kalkatungu where *-nti* marks causative and the advancement of locative, instrumental, and causal obliques. Example [58] illustrates the standard causative relation and [59] illustrates the advancement of an instrumental (an example of locative advancement in this language was given as [85] in Chapter 2):

[58a] Wampa iti.
      1   P
      girl   return
      'The girl returns.'

[58b] Marapai-thu wampa iti-nti-nytyaaya.
                       1   P
      1   2   Cho P
      woman-erg girl   return-cause-purp
      'The woman is going to send the girl back.'

[59a] Marapai-thu wampa karri-mi thupu-ngku.
      1   2   P   Instr
      woman-erg girl   wash-fut soap-erg (INSTR)
      'The woman will wash the girl with soap.'

[59b] Marapai-thu thupu wampa-a karri-nti-mi.
      1   Instr   2   P
      1   2   3   Cho   P
      'The woman will use the soap for washing the girl.'

RG has the apparatus to take *-nti* to be a predicate not only in [58] but also in [59]. The valency of the instrumental advancement marker could be expressed as follows:

[60] $P(nti,b)c_j \rightarrow 2(a,b)c_j$
                    Instr $(a,b)c_j$-1

This states that a predicate *nti* heading an arc with tail *b* must have a neighbouring 2-arc and that this arc must be the successor of an instrumental arc in the previous (j-1) stratum. As the theory now stands, only a 1 can be revalued to a term in a Union (Gibson and Raposo 1986; Davies and Rosen 1988:86). (Dubinsky's example [56] shows a 2 being put en chômage in a Union.) It so happens that the advancement of an instrumental to 2 in Kalkatungu involves the revaluation of a 2 to a 3 (see the discussion in the last part of section 2.5). To accommodate examples like [59b] in a Union analysis would require a relaxation of the Union revaluation principle, but this seems a small step and in any case in other languages a common fate of an ousted 2 is chômage.

This analysis has a certain interest quite apart from RG, since there is evidence to suggest that causative markers, advancement markers, and indeed most verbal affixes apart from person and number markers, derive historically from free-form predicates, but there is a price for such an abstract model of syntactic description.[4] The number of potential analyses that now arise is increased enormously and there needs to be a new assessment of what constitutes an example of Union and what constitutes an advancement. Moreover, positing predicates that are not instantiated as words adds to the burden of describing the relationship between final strata and surface structures. For every deviation from surface structure that is made to capture a generalization at a non-surface level, the cost is a more elaborate reconciliation of the abstract level with the surface level. RG is in danger of becoming like Generative Semantics where there was ever increasing complexity of abstract underlying semantic structure with little attempt to make explicit the details of realization.

Chapter 6

Relations and strata

6.1 Introduction

Relational Grammar analyses involve the positing of grammatical relations at various levels or strata. This chapter presents a summary of the type of reference that is made to strata in writing universal laws and language particular rules. RG is a powerful theory which allows rules relating to case marking, agreement, control, etc. to be based on strata other than the final stratum. Rules of this type, i.e. rules that refer back to earlier underlying levels, have become known in the grammatical literature as global rules (Lakoff 1970) and are generally considered excessively powerful. Although Relational Grammarians are clearly aware of the inadequacy of an overstrong theory and regularly seek to constrain possible revaluations, they never attack the multistratal nature of the theory nor the use of global rules. On the contrary they are fond of adducing examples which in their estimation demand global treatment.

The treatment will proceed as follows. The following sections will give instances of analyses where RG makes reference to non-final strata. Two notions not previously introduced will be presented, the notion of the **working 1** and the notion of the **acting term**. The final section deals with some alternatives in other theories, notably the use of derivational rules for predicate formation and the use of macroroles.

6.2 Final relations

Naturally RG makes reference to final relations. It could hardly do otherwise. The level of final relations is common to all theories, though this level has a different significance in theories such as Lexical Functional Grammar (Bresnan (ed.) 1982), Functional Grammar (Dik 1978), and Generalized Phrase Structure Grammar

(Gazdar *et al.* 1985) where it is the only level. Moreover, different theories can posit different sets of final relations. For instance, no theory recognizes the chômeur relation of RG and few theories recognize the ergative and absolutive which in RG overlap with subject and direct object and cross-classify the nuclear relations. These are not exclusive to final strata of course. RG also posits overlay relations such as Topic and Focus which can be held in addition to the final central relations.

The level of final relations is not the same as surface structure. The former is the set of relations held after all revaluations. These relations are not necessarily held by words. They may be held by morphemes (like the CAUSATIVE (see [43] in Chapter 5) or PERFECT (see [37b] in Chapter 5)). Relational Grammar has remained vague about how the final stratum is to be transformed (?) into surface structure.

The notion of final relations is the basis for most rules of order, case and adpositional marking, agreement, Equi NP deletion, control, and raising.

6.3 Initial relations

Rules referring to initial terms are common in the RG literature. A number of these rules refer to Inversion clauses and distinguish Inversion nominals (initial 1/final 3) from 'ordinary indirect objects' (initial/final 3). Although agreement marking on the verb is usually based on final relations there are some instances where it is sensitive to initial relations. In the Caucasian language Udi the initial subject triggers agreement, i.e. the initial/final 1 of normal constructions and the initial 1/final 3 of Inversion constructions (Harris 1984a). In another Caucasian language, Georgian, the initial 1/final 3 in Inversion clauses triggers number agreement where both arguments of the verb are third person (Harris 1984b). This was illustrated in [48] and [49] in Chapter 2.[1]

A clear case of reference to initial relations is provided by some Australian languages which detransitivize purpose clauses to show co-reference between the initial ergative of the purpose clause and the initial absolutive of the governing clause. The following examples are from Kalkatungu where the case marking schemas are as follows:

[1]	1	2	3
intransitive	ø		
transitive	-tu	-ø	
2–3 retreat	-ø		-ku

The detransitivization is usually marked on the verb by *-yi*, but some verbs are marked by *-li* or *-ti*. In [2] the initial downstairs ergative is co-referent with the upstairs initial/final 1 of an intransitive clause, so the downstairs clause undergoes 2–3 retreat. The detransitivization is apparent from *-yi* on the verb and the dative marking on the initial 2/final 3. The subject is represented by *-i* enclitic to the future-purpose auxiliary particle *a-*. The clitic system marks subject and sometimes object, not ergative and absolutive, and thus a form like *-i* does not give any indication of transitivity. *Ngarrkunku* is the first word of the downstairs clause. It is placed first in its clause under a focus first rule.

[2] Kalpin ingka ngarrkun-ku a-i   lha-yi.
   man   go   wallaroo-dat aux-3s kill-detrans
   'The man went to get walloroos.'

In the next example detransitivization occurs because the downstairs initial ergative is co-referent with the upstairs initial/final 2:

[3] Kalpin-tu unpiyi-nha nhaurr mangarnaan-ku a-i   nanyi-yi
   man-erg take-past child   doctor-dat   aux-3s
                                          see-detrans

   'The man took the kid to see the doctor.'

Where the downstairs initial ergative is co-referent with an upstairs initial 3, upstairs oblique, or an upstairs initial ergative, there is no 2–3 retreat. In [4] the downstairs initial ergative is co-referent with the upstairs initial ergative:

[4] Kalpin-tu yaraman yuunti pulaka a-i   ngaimi.
   man-erg horse   ride   bullock aux-3s chase
   'The man mounted a horse to chase the bullock.'

In [4] *ngaimi* is in its normal transitive form; the detransitivized form would have been *ngaima-yi*. If 2–3 had been used, it would have indicated that the horse was to do the chasing.

The examples above are not critical with respect to an initial/non-initial distinction, but if we consider the case where a purpose clause is governed by a purpose clause which is itself detransitivized, we see that the use of 2–3 retreat is sensitive to initial relations.

In the second clause of [5] there is detransitivization because the initial ergative is co-referent with the initial/final 2 of the first clause. Note that there is also detransitivization in the third clause where its initial ergative is co-referent with a nominal that is initial 2 but final 3:

[5] Nga-thu nyini pati-nha kalpin-ku a-ni   pati-yi   uytan-ku
a-i   mani-yi.

   I-erg   you   tell-past   man-dat   aux-2s   tell-detr   wood-dat
aux-3s   get-detrans
   'I told you to tell the man to get the wood.'

There is no space here to provide a full range of examples, but the
use of 2–3 retreat in the third clause of [5] would appear to
indicate that the co-reference system operates on the basis of
initial stratum relations.

Allen and Frantz (1983a) claim that in Southern Tiwa the cross-
referencing system encodes an initial 2, as well as a final 1 and final
2. Example [6a] includes an initial 1, 2, and 3. The prefix *ti-*
encodes the first person subject and third singular direct object.
Compare this with [6b], which illustrates 3–2 advancement and
where *ka-* encodes the first person subject and second person
direct object:

[6a] ti-khwien-wia-ban i-'ay.
     I:it-dog-give-past   you-to
     'I gave the dog to you.'
[6b] ka-khwien-wia-ban.
     I:you:it-dog-give-past
     'I gave you the dog.'

In the next pair we see the effect of varying the number of the
nominal that is the initial 2 and final 2-chômeur. Note that when it
is plural, the verb prefix *ka-* (compare [6b] above) is augmented by
an element *-m-*:

[7a] ka-'u'u-wia-ban.
     I:you:it-baby-give-past
     'I gave you the baby.'
[7b] kam-'u'u-wia-ban.
     I:you:them-baby-give-past
     'I gave you the babies.'

Allen and Frantz argue that the pronominal prefix system is
sensitive to the initial 2 as well as the final 1 and 2. Note also that
the initial 2 is incorporated in the verb both in [6a] where it is a
final 2 and [6b], [7a], and [7b] where it is a final 2-chômeur.

There are, however, alternative interpretations of the Southern
Tiwa data. Dryer (1986a:826) would take [6b] to be monostratal
with the second person as indirect object and *khwien* 'dog' as
direct object. Example [6a], on the other hand, would be
interpreted as reflecting **antidative**. This notion was introduced in

section 2.7.3. It involves the cross-classification of objects into primary object (PO) and secondary object (SO). Example [6a] would be allotted the following multistratal interpretation with the initial DO(SO) (*khwien*) advancing to DO(PO) and pushing the initial IO(PO) into chômage (compare [75] in Chapter 2), this revaluation being named antidative:

| [8] | 1 | DO(SO) | IO(PO) | P |
| | 1 | DO(PO) | Cho | P |

| 1st pers. | khwien | 2nd pers. | wia |

Recently, Rosen (n.d.) has proposed an analysis of Southern Tiwa in conventional RG notions. Like Dryer, she would take a sentence like [6b] to be monostratal, with *khwien* to be 2 and the second person to be 3. However, she would interpret a sentence like [6a] to be monostratal, with the second person encoded as an oblique:

[9a]	1	2	3	P (for [6b])
	1st pers.	khwien	2nd pers.	wia
[9b]	1	2	Obl	P (for [6a])
	1st pers.	khwien	2nd pers.	wia

Apart from the fact that it means that Southern Tiwa is no longer an indisputable example of the need to refer to initial relations, this analysis is interesting with respect to the Universal Alignment Hypothesis and the identification of indirect objects. Note that Rosen does not take the recipient in sentences like [6a] to be an initial 3 and she does not relate the synonymous pair [6a,b] via revaluation. As I pointed out in section 2.3, recipients that look like obliques may well be simply obliques. One needs to be careful not to assume a recipient is a 3 because of considerations of typical alignment of role and relation, and one needs to be careful of underdetermined analyses which ascribe term status to nominals for which evidence of term status is lacking.[2]

6.4 Terms unspecified for level

RG posits a number of rules that refer to terms without any specification of level. Thus a rule referring simply to 1 would cover say initial 1/final 1, initial 1/final chômeur, initial 1/final 3, initial 2/final 1. The following example concerns control of reflexive forms in Russian (Perlmutter 1982; see also Perlmutter 1984a:28–9).

In Russian only an initial or final 1 can antecede a reflexive.

Relational Grammar

Consider first of all an active sentence [10] and two passives [11] and [12] (all the Russian examples are from Perlmutter 1982: 302–4):

[10] Anna otpravila rebenka k svoim roditeljam.
Anna sent   child:acc to refl's parents
'Anna sent the child to her parents.'

[11] Rebenok byl otpravlen k svoim roditeljam.
child   was sent   to refl's parents
'The child was sent to his parents.'

[12] Eta kniga byla kuplena Borisom   dlja sebja.
this book was bought Boris:instr for refl
'This book was bought by Boris for himself.'

In [10] the initial/final 1 antecedes the reflexive. In [11] the initial 2/final 1 antecedes the reflexive. At this point we could say that only a final 1 antecedes a reflexive, but in [12] we see that the passive chômeur antecedes the reflexive which rules out the possibility of basing the generalization on final 1. Apparently in passives the final 1 (as in [11]) or the 1-chômeur (as in [12]) can serve as an antecedent so that a sentence like [13] is ambiguous:

[13] Rebenok byl otpravlen Annoj   k svoim roditeljam.
child   was sent   Anna:instr to refl's parents
'The child was sent by Anna to his/her parents.'

In Inversion clauses the initial 1/final 3 can antecede the reflexive [14] and so can an initial 2/final 1 [15]:

[14] Mne   nužna bolee udobnaja   kvartira   ne dlja sebja
me: dat needs more comfortable apartment not for refl
a   dlja svoej semi'i.
but for refl's family
'I need a more comfortable apartment not for myself, but for my family.'

[15] Boris ne nužen svoim detjam.
Boris not needs refl's children:dat
'Boris's children don't need him.'

In [15] *Boris*, the initial 2, advances to the 1 relation vacated by *detj* which demotes to 3.

It seems from the examples that a reflexive can be anteceded by an initial/final 1 [10], initial 2/final 1 [11], initial 1/final chômeur [12], initial 1/final 3 [14], and initial 2/final 1 [15], but not an initial/final 2 [10].

Perlmutter considers two ways of capturing the required generalization:

(a) Only a nominal heading a 1-arc can serve as antecedent of a reflexive.

(b) Only a nominal that heads either an initial or final 1-arc can serve as antecedent of a reflexive.

He claims that the single statement (a) is preferable since there is no reason to state the condition as a disjunction, as in (b), but one could consider (a) a disguised disjunction.

Davies (1981b) argues that the notion 'nominal heading a 1-arc' (i.e. without any specification of level) is needed in Choctaw in stating the rules for antecedents of reflexives, nominative case marking, nominative agreement marking, and same subject marking. He also claims that accusative agreement is on the basis of 'nominal heading a 2-arc', that dative agreement is on the basis of 'nominal heading a 3-arc', and that possessor ascension occurs with 'nominals heading an absolutive arc'.

6.5 Acting terms

The notion **acting** term covers a final term and its corresponding chômeur, e.g. a final 1 and a final 1-chômeur. The full range of possibilities is as follows:

[16a] acting 1: 1 & 1̂
[16b] acting 2: 2 & 2̂
[16c] acting 3: 3 & 3̂

The notion of an acting term finds scope in the frequently encountered phenomenon of terms not assuming new marking when pushed into chômage. This gives rise to a need to be able to state generalizations about marking over a particular term and its corresponding chômeur. The notion of acting 2, for instance, will be useful for covering the distribution of accusative case in some languages that are like English in having 3–2 advancement and 2–1 advancement. Accusative will occur on a final 2 and a 2-chômeur (assuming no new marking), but since a 2 can advance to 1, there will be no possibility of stating the generalization in terms of 'nominal heading a 2-arc'. Perlmutter gives an example from Latin citing *docere* 'to teach' which takes two accusative complements, one for the 'pupil' and one for the 'lesson'. RG analyses this and analogous verbs as exhibiting obligatory 3–2 advancement; the lesson is an initial 2 and the pupil an initial 3 (based on Perlmutter 1982:312):

[17] Magister pueros   grammaticam relationalem docet.
     master   boy:acc:pl grammar:acc relational:acc teach:3s
     1   3   2   P
     1   2   Cho   P
     'The master teaches the boys RG.'

In the passive the pupil can be advanced to 1 and the lesson retained in the accusative. The final 1 is marked by the nominative, hence, as noted above, the distribution of accusative cannot be stated in terms of 'nominal heading a 2-arc':[3]

[18] Pueri grammaticam relationalem a magistro   docentur.
     boys grammar:acc relational:acc by master:abl teach:pl:pass
     'The boys are taught RG by the teacher.'

6.6 Working 1

A working 1 must be a 1 at some level and a final term; hence it covers:
(a) The initial/final 1 of a monostratal clause.
(b) The initial 2/final 1 of a passive, or any other advancee to 1.
(c) The initial 1/final 3 or 2 of an Inversion clause.

   Perlmutter (1984b) argues that a number of rules in Italian, Japanese, and Quechua need to be described in terms of the notion **working 1**. In Italian it is the working 1 that controls the missing subject of the infinitive in 'consecutive *da* + infinitive' constructions and various other non-finite constructions. The following examples illustrate the consecutive *da* + infinitive construction:

[19] *the initial/final 1 of a monostratal clause*
     La mamma mi ha rimproverato tante volte da rompersi le scatole.
     'My mother scolded me so many times that she got fed up.'

In [19] *la mamma* controls the missing subject of the infinitive *rompere* but *mi*, the initial/final 2 of the main clause cannot. The missing subject of the second clause controls the reflexive *si* in the idiomatic phrase *romper-si le scatole* (literally, 'to break to oneself the boxes'). If *mi* in the main clause controlled the missing subject, this subject would be reflected as *mi*, but *da rompermi le scatole* cannot be used here to mean 'that I got fed up' (compare the next example):

[20] *initial 2/final 1 of a passive*
Sono stato rimproverato dalla mamma tante volte da rompermi
le scatole.
'I was scolded by mother so many times that I got fed up.'

Here *mamma*, which is an initial 1 but a final chômeur, cannot
control the subject of the infinitive, so *da rompersi le scatole* would
be impossible (compare the preceding example):

[21] *initial 1/final 3 of an Inversion clause*
Gli sono mancate vitamine tanto da ammalarsi.
'He lacked vitamins to such an extent that he got sick.'
('To him were lacking vitamins so much . . .')

As noted in section 2.6, verbs like *mancare a* 'to lack' and *piacere a*
'to please', which have an experiencer expressed as indirect object
and the neutral entity or phenomenon expressed as subject, are
analysed in RG with the experiencer as an initial 1 and the
phenomenon as initial 2. The initial 1 (experiencer) that retreats to
final 3, the Inversion nominal, can control the missing subject of
the *da* + infinitive construction as can be seen in [21] where the
Inversion nominal is third singular, represented by *gli* in the main
clause. Another example of the Inversion nominal controlling the
missing subject appeared as [58] in Chapter 2.
    This behaviour of the Inversion nominal contrasts with that of
an initial 3/final 3 which cannot be a controller in this construction.
In [22] there is a finite consecutive clause where the subject is co-
referent with the initial/final 3 of the governing clause:

[22] Ho telefonato a Giorgio tanta volte che si è arrabbiato.
'I telephoned (to) George so many times that he got angry.'

One cannot substitute *da arrabbiarsi* in [22] to express George's
becoming angry (such a string was presented as a starred example
[59] in Chapter 2).
    In an Inversion clause both the final 1 and the Inversion nominal
are working 1s, so that there are two potential controllers. In [23]
the final 1 controls the infinitival clause, but in [24] the Inversion
nominal does so:

[23] Alla mamma Giorgio pareva talmente nervoso da non poter
dormire.
'To his mother George seemed so nervous as not to be able to
sleep.'

[24] Alla mamma Giorgio pareva talmente nervoso da volerlo far
visitare da un specialista.
'To his mother George seemed so nervous that she wanted to
have him examined by a specialist.'

Perlmutter's Japanese and Quechua examples also involve
Inversion nominals. In Japanese an initial/final 1, a final 1 in a
passive clause, and an Inversion nominal can antecede a reflexive.
Equi in *-nagara* constructions is controlled by the same set of
relations. In Quechua Inversion nominals behave like final 1s in
that they can be Equi victims.[4]

6.7 Review

As pointed out at the beginning of this chapter, Relational
Grammarians are fond of arguing that there is a need for the
specification of grammatical relations at various levels. They claim
that theories that recognize only one level of grammatical relations
are inadequate when it comes to handling data of the type
presented in this chapter. Perlmutter (1982:327ff.), for instance,
compares RG with theories such as Fillmore's Case Grammar
(1968, 1977) and Dik's Functional Grammar (1978) and claims
that they are inadequate because they recognize only semantic
roles and surface grammatical relations.[5] However, some theories
that recognize only a single level of relations incorporate
macroroles and these have some potential for handling data such
as control of reflexives in Russian or missing subjects of infinitives
in Italian.

Foley and Van Valin's Role and Reference Grammar (1984) is a
single level theory but this single level is enriched by the use of
macroroles which cross-classify both syntactic structure and role
structure. These are two macroroles **actor** and **undergoer**. An
actor is the argument 'which expresses the participant which
performs, effects, instigates, or controls the situation denoted by
the predicate', and the undergoer is the argument 'which expresses
the participant which does not perform, initiate, or control any
situation but rather is affected by it in some way' (Foley and Van
Valin 1984:29). Actor and undergoer each subsume a number of
referential roles and are invariant across paraphrases such as
active–passive pairs. The actors in the following sentences are in
capitals and the undergoers in italics:

[25a] COLIN killed *the taipan*.
[25b] *The taipan* was killed by COLIN.

[26a] THE DOG sensed *the earthquake*.
[26b] *The earthquake* was sensed by THE DOG.

[27a] THE LAWYER received *a telegram*.
[27b] *A telegram* was received by THE LAWYER.

[28a] The ANNOUNCER presented *Mary* with the award.
[28b] *Mary* was presented with the award by the ANNOUNCER.

The usefulness of macroroles as an alternative to referring to initial relations can be illustrated on the basis of the Kalkatungu data presented in [2] to [5] above. As noted there, 2–3 retreat is used to signal co-reference between an initial 1 in a purpose clause and an initial absolutive in the governing clause. The rule cannot be stated neatly with reference to final relations or surface structure since 2–3 is also used in a purpose clause where the initial 2 in the governing clause is expressed as a 3 [5]. Since the macrorole undergoer remains constant under 2–3 retreat (and antipassive), the rule for co-reference can be based on this instead of initial 2. There are also instances where the co-reference system treats the 1 in a 2–3 retreat clause in the same way as a 1 in a transitive clause. Here the macrorole actor is useful, since it is unaffected by any detransitivization. For the purposes of the co-reference system the subject of any one-place predicate behaves like an undergoer. There does not seem to be any evidence of an unergative/unaccusative distinction in Kalkatungu. Where such a distinction is found in a language, it can be captured in terms of actor (initial 1) and undergoer (initial 2). (See section 7.2.)

Before confronting these macroroles with some of the data presented in earlier sections from the RG literature, it would be useful to look at a different conception of macroroles. Starosta's one-level theory of Lexicase incorporates two macroroles called **actor** and **undergoer**, but actor is somewhat different from the Foley and Van Valin actor. Starosta sees the actor as the entity to which the action of the verb (including happenings and conditions) is attributed (1988:145). It covers the ergative relation, the subject of an intransitive verb, and the inversion nominal of RG, but not the subject chômeur of a passive construction. Undergoer seems to cover only direct objects since demoted objects are treated as obliques:

[29a] Colin killed the taipan.
     actor   undergoer
[29b] The taipan was killed by Colin.
     actor

[30] Mir   ist kalt.
me:dat is cold
actor
'I'm cold.'

The generalization needed to cover the control of reflexives in Russian differs from the rule needed for the control of infinitives in Italian with respect to the status of subject chômeurs in the passive. These can control reflexives in Russian, but they cannot control the missing subject of infinitives in Italian. Here is a summary with the numbers of the examples presented in section 6.4 and section 6.6:

Russian	Italian
initial 1/final 1 [10]	initial 1/final 1 [19]
initial 2/final 1 [11]	initial 2/final 1 [20]
initial 1/final Cho [12]	
initial 1/final 3 [14]	initial 1/final 3 [21] [24]
initial 2/final 1 [15]	initial 2/final 1 [23]

The following is a summary of how the generalizations about controllers can be captured with the two versions of actor outlined above. I assume in both instances that the actor covers the inversion nominal. Inversion nominals would need to be distinguished from other indirect objects (see [21] and [22] above) by reference to roles (experiencer v. recipient) or syntagmatic opposition (opposed to neutral entity v. opposed to agent):

	Russian	Italian
Foley and Van Valin	subject or actor	subject or actor (less Î)
Starosta	actor (plus Î)	actor

On the basis of this body of data it would appear that the Foley and Van Valin actor is useful in capturing generalizations about control of reflexives in Russian and the Starosta actor is useful with respect to control of missing subjects in Italian. On the other hand the Foley and Van Valin actor cannot be used in connection with Italian infinitives without some qualification since it includes subject chômeurs. Similarly the Starosta actor cannot neatly capture a generalization about controllers of reflexives in Russian.

This comparison does not prove anything, but it does show one way in which an alternative to a multistratal theory can be formulated. Not surprisingly the alternatives require an enriched notion of surface relations to compensate for a lack of deep relations.

Chapter 7

Describing different nuclear types

7.1 Introduction

Almost all the grammatical models that have been proposed over the last thirty years (and there are over thirty of them!) have been based on English. This usually means that while they handle well languages with nuclear or core grammar in which subject and object figure prominently (often referred to as accusative languages), they are not well adapted to the description of grammars in which other schemes of organization are prominent, namely languages of the active or ergative type. Relational Grammar began with positing subject, direct object, and indirect object as primitives, but with the introduction of the Unaccusative Hypothesis and the recognition of absolute and ergative as derived relations it acquired a panoply sufficient to the task of describing these other treatments of nuclear grammar.

Philippines-type languages such as Tagalog and Cebuano are often typed as standing outside the accusative/ergative/active classification. Early RG treatments (mainly of Cebuano) take them to be essentially accusative, but there are strong reasons to take at least some of them to be ergative. Recently ergative RG analyses have been proposed for Ilokano by Gerdts and for Tagalog by De Guzman.

7.2 Active languages

Klimov (1973, 1979) introduced the term **active** for languages in which the sole argument of some one-place predicates is marked like the subject of a transitive verb while the sole argument of other one-place predicates is marked like the object of a transitive verb. These systems, which are sometimes referred to as **split-intransitive** (Dixon 1979), are found in the Caucasus among the Kartvelian languages (Svan, Laz, and Georgian (Harris 1985)) and in some American Indian languages such as Dakota, Arikara, and Seneca (Merlan 1985). The following illustrations are from Choctaw (Davies 1986), a language previously illustrated in section 2.4.

In Choctaw subjects, direct objects, indirect objects, beneficiaries and possessors can be represented by pronominal affixes on the verb. Examples [1] and [2] illustrate cross-referencing for subject and direct object in a transitive clause:

[1] Chi-bashli-li-tok
    thee-cut-I-past
    'I cut you.'

[2] Ano is-sa-hottopali-tok
    I   thou-me-hurt-past
    'You hurt me.'

In most intransitive clauses one finds either subject pronominal forms [3] or object pronominal forms [4]:

[3] Hilha-li-tok
    dance-I-past
    'I danced.'

[4] Sa-hohchafoh
    me-hungry
    'I am hungry.'

RG can handle this pattern of marking by assigning initial 2 status to those arguments that take object marking irrespective of transitivity. Thus the argument of *hohchafo* in [4] will be an initial 2. The arguments of one-place verbs like those in [3] and [4] behave like the subjects of transitive clauses as in [1] and [2] with respect to such properties as anteceding reflexives and taking nominative as opposed to oblique case marking. If the initial-2 of unaccusative predicates like *hohchafo* advances to 1 in conformity with the Final 1 Law, and if case is assigned on the basis of final stratum relations, then the system can be described simply and elegantly.

Labels such as accusative, ergative, and active are based on case marking and/or agreement and cannot be taken to indicate that the nuclear grammar consistently operates on the basis of subject versus object (accusative type), ergative versus absolutive (ergative type), or initial 1 versus initial 2 (active type). As we saw in section 2.4, Relational Grammarians have found that the unergative/ unaccusative distinction that is overt in languages like Choctaw is indirectly reflected in the grammar of numerous languages.

Active languages can also be described neatly in terms of the Foley and Van Valin macroroles, actor and undergoer, introduced in Chapter 6, actor corresponding to initial 1 and undergoer to initial 2. However, there is the further possibility that active-type marking is sensitive to the semantic class of the verb and/or aspect rather than reflecting underlying syntactic relations or macroroles. (See, for example, Van Valin 1987.)

7.3 Ergative languages

An ergative language is one in which the agent of a two-place verb is marked differently from the final subject of a one-place verb and the patient of a two-place verb. The difference can be in the form of case marking as in Warlpiri, an adposition as in Tongan (specifically a preposition in this instance), cross-referencing as in the Mayan languages, or case and cross-referencing as in Avar. Usually the patient of the transitive verb and the final 1 of the one-place verb are marked alike. Consider the following sentences from Avar (Tchekhoff 1979):

[5] Ḥama b-ač?-ila
    ass   it-come-future
    'The ass will come.'

[6] Ebel-aλ   ḥama b-ač?-ula
    mother-erg ass   it-come-pres
    'Mother leads the ass.'

[7] Ebel   y-es-ar-ula
    mother she-sew-imperf-pres
    'Mother sews.'

With a transitive verb the agent is marked [6] whereas the patient is unmarked, like the sole argument of a one-place verb. Note too that the patient of the transitive verb is cross-referenced (*b*- in [6]) like the sole argument of a one-place verb, whereas the agent is not cross-referenced.

In an accusative language the subject is typically the least marked relation and the relation most likely to control agreement (see the marking hierarchy in section 2.3). The subject, of course, embraces the agent of a transitive verb and the sole argument of a one-place verb, whereas the relation picked out by case marking and agreement in Avar covers the patient of a transitive verb and the sole argument of a one-place verb. As noted in section 2.3, RG handles such a treatment of nuclear relations by positing two derived relations **ergative** and **absolutive**. The ergative relation covers a 1 in a transitive stratum while the absolutive covers a 2 in a transitive stratum plus the nuclear relation (1 or 2) of an intransitive stratum.

In an accusative language it is the subject that is suppressed with non-finite verb forms and often the target of rules of control. In some ergative languages it is the absolutive that remains covert with non-finite verb forms. The following examples are from the Australian language Kalkatungu, which was used in Chapter 6 to illustrate rules based on initial ergative and initial absolutive. These sentences illustrate participial clauses modifying nominals. The covert head of the participial clause must be absolutive. In [8] it is the final 1 of an intransitive stratum and in [9] it is the final 2 of a transitive stratum:

[8] Nanya nga-thu kalpin thuni-nyin.
    saw   I-erg   man   run-part
    'I saw the man running.'

[9] Nyini kuntu yakapiyi kanimayinytyirtu parta-nyin.
    you   not   listen   policeman-erg   scold-part
    'You don't listen (when being) scolded by the policeman.'

Where the head of the participial clause is an initial 1 in a transitive stratum, the clause is detransitivized so that the head will be a final absolutive. In the second clause of [10] there is 2–3 retreat as evidenced by the *-yi* suffix on the verb and the dative marking on the patient.

[10] Nga-thu nanya marapai pilapila-a watinti-yi-tyin.
     I-erg   saw   woman baby-dat carry-detr-part
     'I saw the woman carrying a baby.'

Where the head of the participial clause is an initial 3 or an oblique, it is advanced to the absolutive:

[11a] Tyaa yurru arrkunaan-ati nga-thu nhitha-nytyama-tyin maa.
      this man angry-became I-erg steal-advan-part   food
      'This man got wild because I stole his food.' (robbed of his food by me).

In the second clause of [11a] the initial 3 *yurru* has been advanced to 2 and *maa* has been put in chômage. *-nytyama-* marks the advancement of 3 to 2. To clarify the construction in the second clause of [11a] the following are included. Example [11b] is a transitive clause with a dative-marked argument (interpretable as a 3, see section 2.5) and [11c] shows the effect of 3–2 advancement:

[11b] Nga-thu nhitha-mi maa yurr-ku.
I-erg   steal-fut   food man-dat
'I will steal the food of the man.'

[11c] Nga-thu nhitha-nytyama-mi yurru maa.
I-erg   steal-advan-fut   .man food
'I will rob the man of (his) food.'

Faced with the fact that the absolutive often behaves like a subject, one could consider defining subject as something like the most privileged grammatical relation and allow it to cover agents of transitive verbs in accusative languages and patients of transitive verbs in ergative languages. However, this proves unworkable for the simple reason that the nuclear relations can be treated on a subject/object basis and an absolutive/ergative basis within the same language. In fact it is difficult to find an ergative language where there are not some rules operating on a subject/object basis. Even in Kalkatungu, which has more than its fair share of ergative/absolutive based rules, the cross-referencing pronominal forms operate on a subject/object basis. In the following examples -*n* is the second person singular subject form and -*kin* the second person singular direct object form:

[12] Nyini yapatyarra-thati-nha-mpa-n?
you   will-become-past-perf-thou
'Are you well again?'

[13] Nyin-ti waku ithiti-mpa-n?
you-erg skin throw-perf-thou
'You threw away the skin?'

[14] Itya-nyin-kin nyini munthun-tu.
bite-ing-thee you bullant-erg
'The bullants are biting you.'

The RG system of overlapping nuclear relations can clearly cope with this or any other mixture of subject/object and ergative/absolutive rules. Perhaps it should be added that the absolutive regularly outranks ergative in terms of those characteristics that show up in the hierarchy of primitive term relations (see Dixon 1979, esp. 120ff.).

The view that the patient of a transitive verb is in fact the subject is still current in some quarters with respect to a subset of ergative languages that exhibit what is often referred to as 'ergative syntax'. The notion can be traced to Dixon's (1972) description of Dyirbal in which he showed that the language not only exhibited morphological ergativity (case marking) but also syntactic ergativity,

namely syntactic rules that operate on the basis of an ergative/
absolutive dichotomy. The rules involved in Dyirbal are much the
same as those illustrated above and in Chapter 6 from Kalkatungu.
Dyirbal essentially has a rule requiring detransitivization of
purpose clauses to show co-reference between an initial 1 of the
purpose clause and an initial absolutive of the governing clause
and a rule requiring the head of a relative clause to be a final
absolutive.

Dixon effectively took the patient to be the underlying or initial
subject of a transitive clause and also the final subject, though not
in those terms (Dixon 1972:150). Working in an *Aspects* based
framework (Chomsky 1965) he described clauses in terms of the
familiar NP VP dichotomy, but he took the patient to be the NP of
S (effectively the subject) and he took the agent to be the NP of
VP (effectively the object!):

[15]

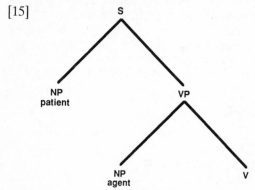

This analysis of a syntactically ergative language has been accepted
in principle in the framework of Montague Grammar (Dowty
1982) and in Marantz's (1984) variant of Chomsky's Government
and Binding (see also Levin 1987).

The patient-as-initial subject analysis has some startling consequences. Valency changing derivations such as 2–3 retreat and
antipassive are interpreted as passive. In fact the original
motivation for Silverstein's (1976) term **antipassive** was that it was
the analogue of passive in an accusative language since it was a
means of allowing an agent argument access to the privileged
grammatical relation just as the passive allowed the patient access
to the privileged relation in an accusative language (as noted in
section 2.5, the term antipassive outside the RG literature covers
2-Cho (antipassive) and 2–3 retreat).

If the patient is allowed to be an initial 1 in an RG description, then violations of 1AEX follow. In Kalkatungu it is normal for a clause to exhibit advancement to 2 and to be detransitivized. In Chapter 2 an example was given of a sentence exhibiting what appeared to be under normal RG assumptions the advancement of a recipient to 2 and 2–3 retreat. If the absolutive is interpreted as marking the initial/final subject, then such a clause would involve two advancements to 1, the recipient to 1 and the agent to 1 (see [77]).

The patient-as-subject analysis of syntactically ergative languages runs into the same difficulty as any attempt to equate absolutive with subject. The fact is that languages mix subject/object rules with ergative/absolutive ones. Languages that are designated ergative on the basis of case or adpositional marking always seem to be mixed in this respect. Kalkatungu and Dyirbal are syntactically as well as morphologically ergative, but, as pointed out above, bound pronouns in Kalkatungu operate on a subject/object basis and in Dyirbal first and second person free pronouns operate on a subject/object basis (there are no bound ones).

In Lexicase, mixtures of subject/object and ergative/absolutive rules are handled by positing two universal nuclear case relations, **Agent** and **Patient**. Agent corresponds to ergative and Patient to absolutive. Rules referring to subject are based on nominative case or the macrorole Actor (see section 6.7 of previous chapter).

7.4 Philippines-type languages

Typologies of nuclear relations recognize accusative, ergative, and active systems and sometimes present languages like Tagalog and Cebuano as standing outside this classification (e.g. Schachter 1976; Mallinson and Blake 1981:79). These languages are usually described as having a focus system in which one case marking preposition in a clause is replaced by a special focus marking preposition. For each case relation there is a verbal affix which is used when the case is focused. I will refer to such languages as Philippines-type languages.

In Tagalog, as described in conventional terms, the system operates in the following way. There is a set of prepositions that mark grammatical relations:

ng	Actor
ng	Patient
sa	Locative
para sa	Benefactive

In most clause types one grammatical relation is put in focus. The choice is indicated in two ways. First, a special focus preposition, *ang*, replaces the relational preposition, and second, an affix appears on the verb to indicate which relation is in focus. The sentences in the following set all have the same propositional content (apart from differences in definiteness which are commented on in connection with [28] below). They are said to differ in 'focus' (or sometimes 'topic'), but it would be more accurate to think of them differing in the same way as English sentences that differ in object selection (*provide X for Y, provide Y with X*):

[16] B*um*ili ng libro sa tindahan ang propesor.
    bought   book at shop   professor
    'The professor bought a book at a/the shop.'

[17] B*in*ili ng propesor ang libro sa tindahan.

[18] B*in*il*han* ng propesor ang tindahan ng libro.

In [16] the actor *propesor* is in focus and the verb is marked with the actor infix *-um-*. In [17] the patient *libro* is in focus and the verb is infixed with *-in-*. In [18] *tindahan* is in focus and the verb is marked by *-in-* and *-an* (the *-h-* is epenthetic). The normal word order is verb first. The order of the other constituents is not grammatically determined.

In order for the nuclear grammar to be classified as accusative or ergative, intransitive clauses need to be considered. Here are two intransitive clauses. The verb in [19] is infixed for actor focus and in [20] the predicate is stative and carries no focus marker:

[19] T*um*akbo ang propesor.
    ran:AF   professor
    'The professor ran.'

[20] Interesante ang libro.
    interesting   book
    'The book is interesting.'

The problem with classifying Tagalog on the basis of traditional descriptions is that all the focuses [16], [17], and [18] appear to be equally marked and it is not clear which one should be compared with the intransitive construction illustrated in [19] and [20] for the purposes of establishing the typology. More than typology is at stake. There is the question of interpreting these constructions in terms of familiar notions such as active/passive and transitive/intransitive.

In describing Cebuano, which is parallel with Tagalog in

relevant areas of morphology, Bell takes the actor focus to be active and the patient focus to be passive (1976, 1983). This is an accusative analysis. It in effect claims that the agent of a transitive verb is marked in the same way as the sole argument of a one-place verb, the two being marked by *ang* which is taken to be a marker of a final 1. Other Relational Grammarians have accepted this analysis, namely Johnson (1977b) and Perlmutter and Postal (1984a). Recently a number of linguists have suggested that Tagalog is in fact an ergative language. This means taking the patient focus to be active and the actor focus to be a detransitivized antipassive. Here is an actor focus version and a patient focus version of 'professor read book' in Tagalog (*basa propesor libro*) with the two opposed analyses:

[21] *Accusative analysis*
      Actor focus as active: patient focus as passive
[21a] bumasa ng libro ang propesor
      read:AF   book   professor
                   2   1
[21b] binasa   ng propesor ang libro
      read:PF   1   2
                    Cho   1

[22] *Ergative analysis*
      Patient focus as active: actor focus as antipassive
[22a] binasa   ng propesor ang libro
      read:PF   1   2
[22b] bumasa   ng libro   ang propesor[1]
      read:AF   2   1
                    Cho   1

If the patient focus is taken to be the normal, active, transitive, construction, then this means taking Tagalog to be ergative since the intransitive subject and the patient of a transitive verb are marked alike (by *ang*) and the agent of a transitive verb is marked differently (by *ng* (pronounced *nang*)). *Ang* is a marker of absolutive and *ng* is an oblique marker whose chief functions are to mark the ergative relation [22a] and a 2-chômeur [22b].

I believe the evidence in Tagalog clearly favours the ergative analysis and that this is probably true of Cebuano and a number of other Philippines-type languages. Cena (1979) supports the ergative analysis of Tagalog, though he does not use the term 'ergative'. De Guzman also supports it (1983, 1986). Both these writers make use of RG analyses. Gerdts, writing within the RG theoretical framework, supports an ergative analysis of Ilokano (to appear).

Other linguists who support the ergative analysis of Tagalog include Payne (1982), Cooreman, Fox, and Givón (1984), and Starosta (Lexicase framework) (1986, 1988).

A point missed by most analysts is that in the non-future tense-aspects, namely the perfective and imperfective, the patient focus is literally unmarked. Here is a paradigm for a typical verb *sulat* 'to write' showing the focus affixes in the three tense-aspects. Note that in the non-perfective the initial syllable of the base is reduplicated:

[23] | base | | actor | patient | benefactive | locative |
|---|---|---|---|---|---|
| sulat | fut | susulat | susulatin | isusulat | susulatan |
| 'write' | perf | sumulat | sinulat | isinulat | sinulatan |
| | imp | sumusulat | sinusulat | isinusulat | sinusulatan |

The critical point is that in the non-future *-in-* marks all non-actor focuses. In the standard analysis *-in-* is taken to be a marker of patient focus, but this cannot be since it is common to all non-actor focuses. In the future it is true that with simple verb stems the actor focus is unmarked and *-in-* (suffixed) is exclusive to the patient focus, but the future is not the unmarked tense-aspect. In any case with the large class of stems augmented with *pag-* (not illustrated here), the actor focus is marked by *mag-* (*-um-* plus *pag-*).[2]

In Cebuano, too, the patient focus appears to be literally unmarked (Bell 1983:205) since the forms that occur are common to the non-actor focuses:

[24] | | actor | patient | locative | instrumental |
|---|---|---|---|---|
| potential | naka- | na- | na- . . . -an | gika- |
| durative | nag(a)- | gi(na) | gi(na) . . . an | gi(pag(a))- |
| volitional | mi(ng)- | gi- | gi . . . an | gi- |
| | ni(ng)- | | | |

On the basis of the marking then one would have to take the patient focus to be unmarked providing there was no evidence to the contrary. In fact there is a good deal of evidence to support the morphology.

Cena (1979:21ff.) develops an argument within an RG framework that decides in favour of the ergative analysis for Tagalog. He notes that all nominals are accessible to the rules of movement processes of Inversion (not to be confused with Inversion nominals) with the exception of patient nominals marked by *ng*. If we look at [21] and [22] we see that the accusative analysis [21] predicts that *ng*-marked actors are chômeurs while the ergative analysis [22] predicts that *ng*-marked patients are chômeur. Cena's point suggests that *ng*-marked patients are at the bottom of a hierarchy of grammatical privilege. This would be consistent with the ergative analysis in which the actor focus is an intransitive antipassive and the *ng*-marked patient a 2-chômeur. Example [25a] is a patient focus construction. Example [25b] is the Inversion equivalent with the actor in front of the verb marked off by *ay*. Example [25c] is the Topicalized equivalent with the actor in front of the clause proper cross-referenced within the clause by *niya*. The form *niya* is the non-focus form for third person, *ni* is the non-focus form with personal names and *si* the focus form with personal names:

[25a] Binili ni John ang bigas.
     buy:PF John   rice
     'John bought the rice.'
[25b] Si John ay binili ang bigas.
[25c] Si John, binili niya ang bigas.

John can participate in these processes since it is a term, an ergative in fact, not a chômeur as the accusative (actor focus as active) analysis would predict.[3]

In her description of Cebuano, Bell makes the point that while an *ang-* marked nominal can precede the verb as can an indirect object and an oblique, the patient in an actor focus construction cannot (1983:175). This exception disappears under an ergative analysis. The appropriate generalization is that all non-chômeurs can precede the verb.[4]

If an actor-focus-as-active analysis of languages like Tagalog and Cebuano is accepted, they emerge as typologically bizarre. If on the other hand, they are accepted as ergative languages, all their oddities vanish. Consider the following points:

(a) the target of advancements
(b) reflexivization
(c) indefinite patients
(d) discourse frequency.

(a) the target of advancements

Many languages advance 3s and obliques to 2 and very often there is a passive which these advancements feed. Under the ergative analysis, Tagalog and Cebuano allow 3s and obliques to advance to 2 (marked by absolutive *ang*), but there is no passive as is the normal situation in ergative languages. As pointed out in section 7.3, the absolutive in an ergative/absolutive opposition occupies the topmost position in the hierarchy of grammatical privilege and the passive has no motivation. However, under the accusative analysis, Philippines-type languages are unusual in allowing 3s and obliques to advance directly to 1.

In these languages the head of a relative clause must be 'in focus' (Schachter 1976:500). The focused relation is the privileged relation. Under an ergative interpretation the head of a relative clause must be absolutive just as in Kalkatungu and various recognized ergative languages (see [8] and [11] above).

(b) reflexivization

In Philippines-type languages a reflexive pronoun can be in focus (marked by *ang*). Under an accusative analysis the focused nominal is the final 1. This means that a Cebuano sentence like the following has a reflexive form as final 1 controlled by a non-1 (Bell 1983:161):

[26] Tan'awon nako' ang akong ka'ugalingon sa salamin.
     look:at:PF I   my   self   loc mirror
     'I'll look at myself in the mirror.'

This is an odd arrangement. Final subjects usually control reflexives; they are not normally themselves reflexive controlled by a non-subject. Bell tries to explain examples like this in terms of control by initial 1, but the difficulty disappears under an ergative analysis. An *ang*-marked nominal in a transitive clause like [26] is a 2 (absolutive) and the reflexive is controlled by an ergative. Reflexive constructions like [26] are often commented on (see Schachter 1976:503–4 on Tagalog), but in a recognized ergative language a reflexive construction like the following from the Australian language Warluwara (Breen 1971:176) is considered unremarkable. Under the ergative analysis [26] and [27] are parallel:

[27] Warawurla-wiya-ku wula-pa tanma-rna.
     dog-dual-erg   they-self bite-past
     'The two dogs bit one another.'

(c) indefinite patients

If the patient is definite, the patient focus is normally used and an *ang*-marked nominal is interpreted as definite. If the patient is indefinite, the actor focus is normally used or one of the other non-patient focuses. Under the ergative analysis this is a normal alternation between transitive and intransitive (antipassive) with the transitive construction being used for a semantically full patient and the intransitive being used for a patient that is less than full, i.e. indefinite, non-specific, generic, or partitive (see Hopper and Thompson 1980).

[28a] B*in*asa ng propesor ang libro.
    PF:read   professor   book
    'A/the professor read the book.'
[28b] B*um*asa ng libro ang propesor.
    AF:read   book   professor
    'The professor read books.'

Under the accusative analysis the Philippines-type languages are glaring exceptions to an otherwise universal principle, since the 'direct object' must always be interpreted as indefinite.

(d) discourse frequency

The patient focus is the unmarked choice for the expression of a transitive proposition (providing the patient is definite). Patient focus constructions including patient focus imperatives predominate in discourse (see Cooreman, Fox, and Givón 1984). Under the accusative analysis, the Philippines-type languages are unusual in having the passive as their basic construction even in the imperative mood.

RG not only has the grammatical notions relevant to describing Philippines-type languages, it also has notions that make predictions about grammatical behaviour. Cena is able to exploit the notion of the hierarchy of grammatical relations and the concept of chômage to pick out the *ng*-marked patient as an unlikely 2 but a likely chômeur. This in turn leads to the ergative analysis, an analysis that is suggested by the distribution of the relational affix marking on the verb in Tagalog and Cebuano. Unfortunately the best known RG analysis of a Philippines-type language, namely Bell's analysis of Cebuano, seems to be misleading. This is a result of misapplication, not the result of a weakness in the theory.

Chapter 8

Overview

8.1 RG and rival theories

In *Syntactic Structures* (1957) and *Aspects of the Theory of Syntax* (1965) Chomsky introduced the notion of the formal, explicit, generative grammar. As indicated in Chapter 1 the *Aspects* model consisted of a syntactic deep structure and a surface structure. Deep structure formed the basis of semantic interpretation and surface structure was the basis for phonological representation. The two structures were mediated by transformations.

Developments of Chomsky's early work and reactions to it have between them given rise to something like thirty named varieties of grammatical theory including Chomsky's own Government and Binding model (Chomsky 1981). Early work in Transformational Grammar saw a proliferation of transformations and this lack of constraint obviously reduced the explanatory power of the theory. Some models that developed in the 1970s were partly a reaction to this lack of constraint. Dik's Functional Grammar (1978) and Bresnan's Lexical Functional Grammar (1978, 1982) banished deep syntactic structure and sought to describe languages in terms of a single syntactic level with grammatical relations defined independently of structure plus semantic roles. Generalized Phrase Structure Grammar (Gazdar *et al*. 1985) and Lexicase (Starosta 1978, 1988) are similarly restricted.

Relational Grammar represents a different kind of reaction to early Transformational Grammar. It is not a single level theory, but a multilevel one in which the initial stratum is analogous to deep structure, and revaluations to transformations. The principle difference between the two approaches is that RG conceives of a sentence in terms of labelled relations borne to a predicate. In TG the nuclear relations are not represented directly, but are derivable from a structural configuration, the subject being the relation held by the noun phrase immediately dominated by the sentence node and the direct object the relation held by the noun phrase immediately dominated by the verb phrase. To maintain these definitions universally TG must posit a verb phrase at some level for all languages including those where evidence is lacking for a surface VP. RG does not ascribe the structural properties of dominance and linear precedence to non-surface levels. Linear precedence is held to be a feature of surface structure and the only hierarchical structure is that which follows from the relational structure, hence there is no verb phrase. It is interesting to speculate how RG might capture the fact that the object is more closely related to the verb than the subject. Dependency grammars do not incorporate the notion of VP either. Hudson, describing his Word Grammar, which is a dependency based theory, suggests that the difference can be captured in terms of the difference in generality of the rules introducing objects and subjects as dependents of the verb (1984:96). This seems to capture a universal aspect of the asymmetry between subject–verb and object–verb (compare the remarks on Marantz in section 1.4), but some languages like English seem to have a structural unit VP which many languages lack.

Early Transformational Grammar was derivational or constructive in that it consisted of an algorithm for the generation of sentences starting with the expansion of the phrase structure rules (S = NP + VP, etc.) and followed by the application of transformations. Rules converted one structure into another. Early RG inherited this derivational approach, but Perlmutter and Postal (1983c orig. 1978; Postal 1977) soon began to see RG in terms of a set of conditions on well-formedness. These could be universal laws or language particular rules. They limit the possible relational networks. Postal, writing on Arc Pair Grammar, describes restrictions on the passive as follows (Postal 1982:343):

> . . . consider passivisation. Whatever this is, it is a possibility for some natural languages and therefore the structure of passives is such as to not violate any sentence laws. Thus passive clauses are a member of the set of *a priori* possible sentences. To the extent that a language has passive structures freely, no rules whatever are then needed to describe them. But limitations found in one language but not in another must result from language particular rules. The ultimate limitation in this domain would be a statement blocking all passivisation, which may exist in languages like, e.g. Walbiri.

Suppose we posit the following universal set of grammatical relations: 1, 2, 3, Benefactive, Locative, Instrumental, and

Chômeur and assume that there is no limit to revaluations. Obviously there would be an infinite number of possible networks. However, laws such as the Oblique Law, the Motivated Chômage Law, the Chômeur Advancement Ban and the 1 Advancement Exclusiveness Law serve to considerably reduce the number of possible networks. A particular language might have rules prohibiting 3–2 advancement or 2–3 demotion or both. In fact without language particular rules covering revaluations between 2 and 3 one could imagine the possibility of infinite alternation between the two over successive strata. Language particular rules can refer to specific predicates or specific classes of dependents. Consider the following illustration adapted from Postal (1982). In English 3–2 advancement is obligatory with verbs like *tell*, *show*, and *explain*, if the initial 2 is a clause, as can be seen from the following:

[1a] *I told to Graham that I would handle the first-years.
[1b] I told Graham that I would handle the first-years.

In the absence of any rules to the contrary both sentences with 3–2 advancement and those without are possible. If we add a rule along the following lines, we will prohibit sentences like [1a]:

[2] If A is a 3-arc with tail node *a* and B is a 2-arc with tail *a* and B is initial and has a head labelled Clause and if the predicate with tail *a* is *tell*, *show*, *inform*, etc. then there exists a 2-arc C which is the local successor of A.

This needs to be read in conjunction with a relational network:

[3]

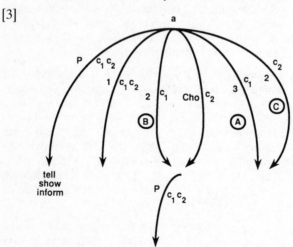

'Local successor' is the Arc Pair Grammar term for an arc with the same head and tail in the following stratum. Rule [2] has the effect of making 3–2 advancement compulsory with predicates like *tell* when the initial 2 is a clause.

It is natural to think of one revaluation feeding another, for instance, 3–2 advancement feeding 2–1 advancement, and this is indeed so, but it does not result from extrinsic ordering. In the absence of any restrictions there will be feeding and non-feeding. Consider a variety of English that allows the following:

[4a] The staff gave a case to the boss.
[4b] The staff gave the boss a case.
[4c] The boss was given a case by the staff.
[4d] A case was given to the boss by the staff.
[4e] A case was given the boss by the staff.

All of these constructions are possible in the absence of any restrictions on advancement of 2–1 and 3–2. For varieties of English that do not allow [4e], there would need to be a restriction of 3–2 advancement in a clause in which an initial 2 had advanced to 1. As pointed out in section 2.7.2, Bickford has in fact proposed such a principle, the Nuclear Novice Law.

In Postal's conception of Arc Pair Grammar there is no lexicon distinct from the grammar, only rules of different generality. Presumably rules will specify initial strata for predicates. Some rules will restrict initial relations to 1 (unergative), 2 (unaccusative), or 1 2 (transitive two-place) for large numbers of verbs, while others will restrict the initial relations of single predicates or small numbers of predicates (e.g. weather predicates with no initial relations beyond the predicate itself).

As noted in section 2.8, a number of leading Relational Grammarians conceive of a grammar as containing a conventional lexicon in addition to rules or conditions on well-formedness of relational networks. This is a more comfortable conception, but I am not certain that the difference is of much theoretical importance. Postal's conception has the advantage of grouping like predicates, and from the example just quoted it would appear that the notion of extended valence (see section 2.8) can be translated into Postal's system.

Obliques can be complements to particular predicates or classes of predicate or they can be adjuncts. In the latter instance there is no grammatical restriction on their co-occurrence with predicates. There has been practically no discussion in the RG literature of how many oblique relations there are or of how they are to be determined. In face there has been a lot of hedging, with the notation GR$_X$ being used for obliques that figure in examples. Ideally a universal set of obliques should be posited and this would presumably include Benefactive, Locative, and Instrumental. Establishing such a set will be no easy task. Languages with case systems provide an easily accessible system of classification for final relations and since there can be no revaluations to oblique relations, such a system provides a fairly direct guide to initial relations. However, experience shows that even closely related languages vary a good deal in the number of cases they employ and in the extension of particular cases.

If a universal set can be established, and this would be possible in intensional terms with allowance for extensional differences between languages, then the further questions arise of whether the whole set is instantiated in every language and whether the Stratal Uniqueness Law applies to obliques. The Stratal Uniqueness Law is a difficult criterion to apply non-circularly, and provision needs to be made for overlapping reference, particularly with locatives (*He buried the body in the back yard near the pig pen under the Red Gum*), for apposition, and for 'discontinuous NPs'. By that I mean cases where the translational equivalent of an English noun phrase appears as two or more separate phrases so that a sentence like 'I saw him hit it with a long stick' is rendered literally as 'With a long (one) I saw him hit it with stick.'

There is also the question of whether there needs to be a distinction between outer obliques that have a prediction as their scope and inner obliques that have the initial absolutive as their scope. The difference is clear in the following where the first locative phrase is outer and the second inner:

[5] In gaol Wilde had to sleep on a plank.

Inner obliques are normally candidates for advancement but not outer ones.

RG refers to atomic obliques, but consider local prepositions in English. Forms like *at*, *in*, *on*, *to*, *from*, and *through* all have a locative component, as can be seen in their ability to satisfy the valency of a verb like *put*. On the other hand there can be syntagmatic contrasts between them (*from A to B*) and paradigmatic oppositions (*recoil from* but *lean on*). This suggests some kind of hierarchical relationships between local forms.

As mentioned above, early TG developed a plethora of transformations and many theories that developed in the 1970s were concerned with the fact that TG was too powerful. In 1970 Lakoff introduced global rules, that is, rules that could make reference to earlier stages of a derivation. These were added to the panoply to account for long distance agreement in various languages including Ancient Greek and Modern Icelandic. Global rules represented a further increase in the power of TG and they were particularly anathema to those who were seeking to find ways to curb the range of descriptive devices in order to increase the explanatory power of linguistic theory. RG maintains global devices in the sense that rules can be sensitive to more than one stratum.

Consider a variety of English in which benefactives can advance to 2 but not advance further to 1:

[6a] John made a casserole for Fred.
[6b] John made Fred a casserole.
[6c] *Fred was made a casserole by John.

To rule out sentences like [6c] would require distinguishing those 2s that are successors of benefactives from other 2s. If one were to state that a 2 with a benefactive predecessor could not have a 1 as a successor, this would be clearly global. Alternatively, one could place conditions on the immediate and remote successors of the initial benefactive using the extended valence notation of Davies and Dubinsky (see section 2.8). This may not seem like a global rule in the accepted sense, but the power of the rule is the same. In a single level theory direct objects like the one in [6b] would have to be distinguished by reference to the benefactive role. Recognizing a benefactive role here is an alternative to referring to an initial stratum oblique.

Consider too the way RG distinguishes Inversion nominals from other indirect objects. Inversion nominals are superficially indirect objects, but they exhibit some subject-like properties such as controlling reflexives, missing subjects of non-finite verbs, or number marking. The RG way of distinguishing the two classes of indirect object and capturing what Inversion nominals have in common with subjects is to consider Inversion nominals to be initial subjects. The relevant control rules can then be based on subject (no level specified). A revaluation is required to relate the lexically specified class of initial 1s to final 3s. This is essentially a global strategy in that final 3s are distinguished on the basis of their initial stratum status. Postal claims that 'reference to properties of different "stages" is achieved naturally and directly with no extreme extensions of the character of rules by allowing reference to arcs with different co-ordinates . . . it is a real feature of natural languages that they involve constraints which refer at once to distinct levels' (1982:396).

Inversion nominals cannot be picked out on the basis of a

semantic role. In some languages we find some experiencers are treated as Inversion nominals while others are not (see the Italian examples [54], [55], and [56] in Chapter 2). In other languages the Inversion construction is determined by mode (see the Georgian examples [46], [48], and [49] in Chapter 2). A unilevel theory could capture the distinction among indirect objects by indirect reference to roles, for instance by distinguishing indirect objects syntagmatically opposed to agents from those opposed only to patients. As described in section 6.7 the use of the macroroles actor and undergoer is another alternative. An actor category can be established to cover agents and Inversion nominals. As expected the alternative to positing underlying levels involves the elaboration of surface structure.

A major difference between RG and its 'surfacist' competitors is that single level theories exploit derivational rules to handle revaluations such as passive, 3–2 advancement, etc. In RG these valency correspondences are treated as syntax and in some specific instances compelling evidence is adduced in favour of this approach. Two instances were given in Chapter 5 of the indirect object in a morphological causative construction controlling a missing subject of a non-finite verb (see [13] and [53]). In these causatives the indirect object (expressing the causee) behaves like a subject and the control rules fall out in a multiclause or multipredicate analysis of morphological causatives, where the indirect object is the initial subject of an embedded predicate. This point is similar to the one made in the previous two paragraphs about Inversion nominals, but here the point is that RG comes up with a neat analysis by undoing the morphology, as it were, i.e. by treating an internal word structure as part of the syntax.

RG gives the impression of being conceptually simpler than Transformational Grammar and other theories that make a lot of use of structure. In one respect this impression is justified. Since the theory does not demand any order among clausal dependents other than in surface structure, problems of deep ordering and reordering are avoided. However, part of the impression stems from the fact that RG simply ignores most questions of structure. It has hardly dealt with any of the substructures within clausal dependents, for instance. There is virtually no treatment of prepositions or postpositions, nor indeed of the internal structure of noun phrases. Aissen, who has published a number of papers in recent years on the structure of Tzotzil in an RG framework, has recently published a complete description. However, this analysis is formalized within the theory of Arc Pair Grammar (APG), because, says Aissen, 'ultimately RG was not a sufficiently articulated theory to support the kind of analysis developed here. Unlike RG, APG provides an explicit account of surface structure, of prepositions, of anaphora, of agreement, all of which figure centrally in the description' (1987:xv). As it stands at the moment, RG is a generative theory of relational networks that underlie surface structure.

Chomsky's aim has always been to account for knowledge of language rather than language *per se* and he has sought to explain the capacity of humans to learn language in terms of innate endowment. RG is not concerned with knowledge of language but with language itself. Questions of innate endowment, psychological reality, performance factors, etc. are irrelevant under the RG approach and are simply never raised. Postal (1986:1–4) makes it clear that language can be studied independently of language users and he points out that any study of linguistic knowledge presupposes an understanding of language.

8.2 RG, typology, and universals

Chomsky's early work not only provoked a proliferation of rival syntactic theories, it also stimulated interest in syntax generally. Chomsky is probably indirectly responsible for the huge amount of work published on comparative syntax by non-aligned linguists. I have in mind linguists like Comrie, Keenan, Thompson, and Givón, some of whom began their careers as disciples of some variety of generative grammar but who are no longer committed to any particular theory.[1] Their work makes an interesting comparison with work in RG for a number of reasons. Firstly, work on comparative syntax, more often referred to as typology and universals, took off in the early 1970s at the same time as RG was being developed. Secondly, the aims of RG seem to be the same as those of the non-aligned linguists, namely to characterize the essential properties of human language, to make precise the ways in which languages are the same and the ways in which they differ. This similarity of aims is reflected in the wide range of languages that have been studied in both camps. So far over forty languages have been investigated within the RG framework and a number of universals, implicational universals, and tendencies have been brought to light.[2]

One of the themes of the early 1970s was the establishment of implicational universals including hierarchies. A number of manifestations of the Great Chain of Being hierarchy were illustrated (Silverstein 1976 orig. 1973; Kuno 1976) and the Relational Hierarchy was developed both by Relational

Grammarians and others. Keenan and Comrie put forward the Accessibility to Relativization Hierarchy (1977, orig. 1972); Comrie wrote about the part the relational hierarchy plays in determining the fate of the causee in relative constructions (1976); and Johnson (1974), Keenan (1975), and Trithart (1975) proposed the Advancement Continuity Principle. This principle states that a continuous segment of the relational hierarchy can be advanced to subject, e.g. if benefactive can be advanced to subject then so can indirect object and direct object. Whatever the ultimate fate of RG, it would seem that the relational hierarchy and the associated notions of advancement or promotion and retreat or demotion will become part of a widely accepted way of looking at language. They are already in general use. See, for example, Hock's chapter on syntactic change in his monumental *Principles of Historical Linguistics* (Hock 1986).

An important difference between the non-aligned approach and the RG approach is that RG can posit for a particular language an analysis established on the basis of other languages in cases where internal support is lacking. It can do this providing there is no language internal evidence to the contrary. Consider, for instance, the analysis of double object constructions in a language that lacks the direct-plus-indirect object construction (*John gave the book to Fred*). Huichol, for instance, is such a language. The following sentences illustrate an intransitive and transitive clause (Comrie 1982:99ff.):

[7] Nee ne-nua.
    I   I-arrive
    'I arrived.'

[8] Nee eekie ne-meci-zeiya.
    I   you I-you-see
    'I see you.'

Word order does not provide any strong means of distinguishing grammatical relations and normally there is no case marking for the subject, the object, or the two objects of the double-object construction. As can be seen from the above examples the subject is cross-referenced in the first position on the verb with the object marking immediately preceding the stem. With a ditransitive verb the object agreement is with the recipient object (ibid. 107):

[9] Nee waakanaari ne-meci-tikiiti eeki.
    I   chickens   I-you-give   you
    'I gave the chickens to you.'

There is a passive construction and with ditransitive verbs the subject of the passive corresponds with the recipient object, never with the patient object. Thus the operation of the passive supports the evidence of the cross-referencing to indicate that the recipient object assumes the properties associated with the sole object of a transitive verb. This is handled in RG by positing obligatory advancement of the initial 3 to 2. There are also two-object constructions with a beneficiary object and a patient object. These parallel the behaviour with recipients: there is no alternative to the two-object construction; the agreement is with the beneficiary object, and it is the beneficiary that can appear as the subject of the corresponding passive. The only difference is the registration of the presence of a beneficiary object by means of a suffix on the verb (ibid. 110):

[10] Eeki nawazi tiiri pe-wa-rutinanairi.
      you knife kids you-them-buy:ben
      'You bought the knife for the children.'

In RG this will be described in terms of obligatory Benefactive–2 advancement. However, Comrie argues that there is no internal evidence for obligatory 3–2 advancement and Benefactive–2 advancement (1982:111):

> Within Huichol this analysis would have no motivation, as there is no way in which the noun phrase *waakanaari*, which would be the initial direct object, behaves like other direct objects, rather than like phrases that are neither subject nor direct object. In the absence of any reasonable paraphrase where the patient of a ditransitive verb shows up as a direct (prime) object, and in the absence of any properties that would treat such patients like clear instances of direct objects, the inescapable conclusion for Huichol is that they are not direct objects.

This throws into relief the essential difference between the theory neutral approach and the RG interpretation. If the only evidence available was the Huichol evidence, then the recipient and beneficiary objects would be direct objects. Comrie accepts this but suggests the term **prime object** to avoid confusion with languages where the patient object of a ditransitive verb is the direct object (ibid.:111). His objection to the RG analysis centres on the interpretation of the patient object. He points out that it does not behave like an object and is not a direct object, but RG would not claim it is a final direct object only that it would be an initial direct object. The basis for the RG analysis is ultimately semantic, namely the Universal Alignment Hypothesis. The patient object must be considered an initial direct object so that the analysis will be parallel with the analysis of double object constructions in languages like English that have the alternative. The RG analysis is underdetermined by the Huichol data, but there is nothing in the Huichol data that runs counter to it.[3]

The biggest difference between Relational Grammarians and the non-aligned group is that where RG is prepared to posit underlying strata and abstract elements such as a silent dummy, the non-aligned linguists as a whole are very conservative and accept only traditional categories and surface relations. The difference can have empirical consequences. Consider the following Italian sentence [11] and its French equivalent [12]:

[11] Passa un treno.
   'A train passes.' '(There) passes a train.'

[12] Il passe un train.

In the French example the pleonastic element *il* is clearly the surface subject. In Italian, however, no such element is required. In the conventional analysis *uno treno* in [11] would be taken to be the subject, partly because there is no competing nominal and partly because it controls person and number marking on the verb. The order in [11] is common particularly with unaccusative predicates (cf. Vincent 1987). In discussing word order typology it is conventional to say that Italian is an SVO (subject–verb–object) language and then to qualify this statement by mentioning the frequency and distribution of other orders such as VS (as in [11]). However, as we saw in section 3.2, the RG analysis of a sentence like [11] involves positing a silent dummy which puts the subject en chômage. Part of the evidence is that the post-verbal nominal in a sentence like [11] lacks the control properties that the corresponding pre-verbal nominal would have (see [31] in Chapter 3). Under this analysis the conventional description of word order is inaccurate since post-verbal nominals in sentences like [11] will be no more subjects than *train* is in an English sentence like 'There goes the train.'

The typology and universals literature is concerned with explanation, if only in a weak sense. It seeks to establish markedness (e.g. preferred word orders) and to suggest factors that motivate the bias, e.g. discourse strategies or processing constraints. Relational Grammarians retain a structuralist aloofness from all this. Just as it is not concerned with linguistic competence or linguistic knowledge, RG is not concerned with language use nor with speculations about how performance limitations or communicative needs could have shaped features of language design.

8.3 Conclusion

The future of a theory is determined partly by its intellectual strengths and partly by accidents of personality, changes in society, and other extraneous factors. RG developed in the early 1970s at a time when there was great dissatisfaction with the transformational model that had dominated the field for the preceding decade. It 'quickly won a sizeable number of adherents', as Newmeyer puts it, (1980:242), but it failed to capitalize on its early gains. No coherent account of the theory has ever appeared and the two collections of papers *Studies in Relational Grammar 1* and *Studies in Relational Grammar 2*, which are the best concentrated source of information at present available, are full of anachronistic inconsistencies.[4]

As I noted in the Preface, about 150 linguists have published in this framework. This sounds like a healthy enough figure, particularly when one notes that RG material is now appearing with increasing frequency in mainstream journals. However, given the large number of other theories available in the marketplace and given the resurgence of interest in what could be called the latest version of Transformational Grammar, namely Government and Binding, the future of RG is in the balance.

In the early years of RG most of the theoretical ideas came from Perlmutter and Postal themselves. Even now there are only half a dozen or so practitioners who are making a substantial contribution to the theory and Postal has broken away and developed, along with David Johnson, **Arc Pair Grammar** (APG) which Johnson and Postal describe as '95 percent new even to those familiar with work in RG' (1980:4), though unbiased observers will see APG and RG as much the same. As noted in section 1.6, APG is not exactly user friendly. In fact it has been a disaster from the point of view of acceptability. The relational graphs look like pieces of pre-Columbian art and are very difficult to read and reproduce, and the theory is couched in a terminology full of strange and somewhat humorous sounding terms like the following: Cho Arc Nonself-Sponsoring Theorem, Cho Arc Predecessor Local Assassination Theorem, Cosponsored Domestic Arc Theorem, Dead Arc Nonlogical Arc Theorem, No Vacuous Fall-Through Law, Domestic Cho Arc Graft Spawner Theorem, the No Infanticide Law, and the Parallel Assassin Law. This is hardly calculated to win hearts and minds which is a pity since Johnson and Postal's *Arc Pair Grammar* is rich in ideas and it does attempt to establish a precise, formalized account that makes testable claims.

If RG is to flourish, it needs to expand beyond its present area of concentration to encompass cross-referencing agreement, to establish principles of binding and control, to develop the notion of overlay relations, to deal with the substructure of clausal dependents, and so on. In short, to develop a more comprehensive theory that is comparable in range to that of its leading competitors.

Notes

Chapter 1 Outline

1 The indirect object is typically human or at least animate. Non-sentient destinations are probably to be considered a separate oblique relation sometimes referred to as **direction**:
[i] Bazza carried the bags to the car.
[ii] *Bazza carried the car the bags.
However, there are some inanimate indirect objects:
[iii] The feminist assigned a new interpretation to Ephesians 5:22.
[iv] The feminist assigned Ephesians 5:22 a new interpretation.

2 Bill Davies (personal communication) warns me that not all Relational Grammarians would accept the analysis I am attributing to them. The analysis presented here is almost inevitable if one accepts the Universal Alignment Hypothesis, but now that it is being abandoned (see section 2.2, especially the latter part), the way is open to accept that more than one of a set of paraphrases could be monostratal. An analysis of French *fournir* 'provide (with)' analogous with the one given in [17] is accepted among Relational Grammarians. The following example is from Fauconnier (1983:200), but see also Postal (1982) and Legendre (1987:21):
[v] On fournit des armes aux soldats.
     1   2   3
'One provides weapons for [lit. to] the soldiers.'
[vi] On fournit les soldats en armes.
     1   2   Cho
'One provides the soldiers with [lit. in] arms.'

3 Alert readers will wonder why the analysis offered in [8b] for *Power was given the people by Mao* is not available here. This point is discussed in section 2.7.2.
    Further information can be found in Sandra Chung's 1976 paper 'An object-creating rule in Bahasa Indonesia' (reprinted in Perlmutter (ed.) 1983), a classic exposition of advancements to 2 in Indonesian.

4 See references cited at the end of section 2.2.

5 In recent work by Davies and Rosen the SUL is extended to cover predicates in multipredicate clauses. The finite predicate is P and the others P-chômeurs. This is explained in section 5.3.1.

6 If the reader feels that I am being vague about just how surface structure is derived (?) from the relational network, all I can say is that RG has had practically nothing to say about surface structure.

7 Some redrafting of the Oblique Law has proved necessary, but the spirit of the original is still maintained. See note 2 in Chapter 3 and note 5 in Chapter 4.

8 Davies, Dubinsky, and Rosen accept the conventional notion of the lexicon, but Postal, writing in the Arc Pair framework, denies the distinction between grammar and lexicon. See section 8.1.

9 Bresnan disputes claims about there being a closer semantic relationship between object and verb than subject and verb (1982b:290–3).

10 In RG there is no underlying VP and it remains to be seen whether one will be posited in surface structure for languages like English which arguably have such a constituent. In Word Grammar, as in dependency grammars in general, there is no VP. Hudson (1984:96) points out that the distinction can be achieved by reference to the generality of the rules that introduce the modifiers of the verb. The subject is introduced by a more general rule than the one specifying objects and other complements. This is not *ad hoc*. It applies to phrases, for instance, and accounts for the fact that in *a student of linguistics with long hair* the first modifier phrase is more tightly bound to the head than the second modifier phrase and consequently comes closer to the head.

11 For an example of a nominal bearing a central relation and an overlay relation see [3b] in Chapter 4.

Pullum (1977) provides an interesting discussion of universals of linearization.

Chapter 2 Some clause-internal revaluations

1 I will use **patient** as a cover term for entities that are affected (*I cut the rope*), effected (*I wrote the song*), or neutral (*I like lamingtons*). Some linguists, following Gruber (1965), use **theme** to cover this range, but this is confusing since theme was well established earlier for a discourse function. Other linguists differentiate between a patient and a theme using the former for relatively more affected entities and the latter for less affected ones. I will use **neutral** for theme in the sense of unaffected entities, e.g. for the role of the object of verbs such as *know*, *like*, etc. This label corresponds, at least approximately, to Halliday's **phenomenon** (Halliday 1985).

2 [3b] is intransitive as can be seen from the absence of the ergative from *bunya* (compare [3c]). It should probably be analysed as an antipassive in the sense of Postal (1977). See section 2.5 for a discussion of antipassive and 2–3 retreat.

3 As noted in section 1.6 Arc Pair Grammar is an 'outgrowth' of RG developed by Johnson and Postal (1980). See also Postal (1982, 1986).

4 What is called agreement of subject, etc. with the verb is almost always cross-referencing, i.e. there is one reference in the verb (usually

obligatory) and one reference in the form of a noun phrase (usually optional). In Latin, for instance, the person and number of the subject is represented on the verb and in the absence of an NP as subject there is still a complete grammatical sentence. In the following examples *-t* represents third person singular subject:

[i] Caesar videt Calpurniam.
     'Caesar sees Calpurnia.'
[ii] Videt Calpurniam.
     'He/she/it sees Calpurnia.'

In the Germanic languages there is non-cross-referencing agreement. In English the *-s* in *Caesar sees Calpurnia* agrees with the subject, but does not represent it. *Caesar* cannot be omitted to leave a viable sentence.

Cross-referencing does not always involve an identical specification of the denotatum in the NP and on the verb. Often the specification on the verb is less precise. Discrepancies of number are common and occasionally there are discrepancies of person. This is a problem for any theory that involves copying features from an NP to the verb.

In some languages the cross-referencing forms are enclitic to the first constituent of the clause rather than on the verb. This happens in the Uto-Aztecan and Pama-Nyungan languages, for example. See also note 5.

5 The Australian Pama-Nyungan language Pintupi has five sets of enclitic pronominal forms: subject, object, indirect object, reflexive, and causal ('because of'). In this language and in some neighbouring languages sentient obliques tend to be cross-referenced or represented by enclitic pronouns. The cross-referencing forms are enclitic to the first dependent/constituent of the clause. The oblique forms in Pintupi bear transparent case marking and some of them are quite long (e.g. = *tyanampalura* 'because of them'), suggesting they are relatively new.

6 Absolutive could be defined as covering the 2 in a transitive stratum and the nuclear relations (1,2) in an intransitive stratum. As pointed out in section 2.4, a non-final stratum can contain a 2 but no 1.

7 See section 6.2 for examples from Kalkatungu where only the final absolutive can be relativized.

8 Shannon (1987:249) states that 1AEX is 'patently arbitrary and totally without motivation'. But whatever its ultimate fate in RG, 1AEX does have motivation in that advancements to 1 are to enable nominals to acquire grammatical privileges (e.g. to become topic and the like) and it is reasonable to expect on functional grounds that there will be only one advancement to 1 per clause.

9 The point depends on assuming the initial 2 advances to 1. See the discussion of apparent impersonal passives with unaccusatives in section 3.3.2.

10 It is a moot point whether the oblique in a pseudo-passive need advance to 2 before advancing to 1. RG allows direct advancement to 1, but since the pseudo-passive is typically possible only where there can be said to have been some effect on the oblique and since such

effect is commonly expressed by advancement to 2, it is tempting, on the grounds of semantic consistency, to interpret pseudo-passives as being based on an advancement of an oblique to 2.

11 This is probably to be taken to refer to one-place predicates such as *happy*, *sad*, etc., not to two-place ones such as *be suspicious of* where the suspect is a likely candidate for initial 2. This point comes up in connection with the Halkomelem examples [29] and [30] discussed later on in the section.

12 One could add that in English *die* is probably treated as unaccusative (normally) and unergative (in restricted contexts): *He died for his country* (note the benefactive adjunct), *Don't go and die on me after I've carried you all this way* (note the imperative and the adversative benefactive). There does not seem to be any pseudo-passive usage possible with the putative unergative 'die', but RG does not claim that there is always a pseudo-passive for every unergative predicate, only that there can never be a pseudo-passive with an unaccusative one.

13 Van Valin 1987 (see also Centineo 1986) claims that the unergative–unaccusative distinction in Italian and more generally can be captured semantically in terms of a classification of verbs into states, achievements, activities, and accomplishments. Unergative verbs are interpreted as intransitive activity verbs. When a verb like *correre* 'to run' is used with a goal as in *correre a casa* it becomes an accomplishment verb. Van Valin provides a battery of tests for distinguishing the four classes (derived from Vendler and Dowty; see also Foley and Van Valin 1984). However, in the absence of a comprehensive exposition the onus remains on him to account for a number of problematic cases. *Cadere* 'to fall' takes *essere* even when referring to deliberate falling, yet it seems to meet tests for activity verbs as opposed to state verbs. Bearing in mind that Rosen admits the basis of the distinction is 'NEARLY' semantic, the issue will be difficult to resolve.

One interesting point in Van Valin's paper is the claim that *ne* cannot be used with the *essere* itself:

[iii] Molti esperti sono buoni.   'Many experts are good.'
[iv] *Ne sono buoni molti.   'Many of them are good.'

This means that the alignment between the distribution of *ne* and of *essere* is defective.

Shannon (1987) provides a discussion of auxiliary selection in Dutch and German and notes apparent exceptions to the Unaccusative Hypothesis.

14 This is similar to the GB analysis of the passive. See [36] in Chapter 1.

15 Accusative languages (i.e. those whose nuclear grammar operates on the basis of a nominative–accusative or subject–object dichotomy) contrast with 'true' ergative languages. Marantz would take the agent to be within the VP in a language like Dyirbal and the patient to be the logical subject. This is discussed in section 7.3.

16 Matthew Dryer (personal communication) suggests formulating antipassive as ergative to absolutive. This puts the initial absolutive in chômage without violating the Motivated Chômage Law.

17 There is another characteristic that suggests that dative marked arguments are not obliques. They are like 1s and 2s and chômeurs in that if the nominal involved is PRO, the unspecified nominal, then there need be no overt realization.

18 Note that the term **inversion** is widely used for switches of word order so that, for instance, one talks of the inversion of subject and auxiliary in questions in English.

Note that [46b] is analysed by Harris as transitive, not as an example of 2–3 retreat as one might expect from the discussion in section 2.5.

19 Direct 3–1 advancement has been posited for Japanese and Quechua.

20 Perlmutter and Postal mention Pocomam and Dyirbal. Instrumentals advance to 2 in some other Australian languages besides Dyirbal, namely Yidiny, Nyawaygi, Wargamay, Kalkatungu, and Yalarnnga.

21 Bickford (1986) gives further support for this analysis with arguments based on possessor ascension.

22 Postal (1986:94) mentions the possibility of constructions like those in [71] being licit only where the initial 3 is a single word or perhaps a monosyllabic word.

Chapter 3 Reflexives and impersonals

1 In section 2.4 it was shown that only a single nuclear term can be expressed with the participle when it is used absolutely and this nuclear term must be an initial 2 which becomes a final 1 through unaccusative advancement or passive (see [20] and [21] in Chapter 2). With this in mind it is interesting to note the following contrast (Rosen 1981:69–70):
[i]   *Difesi-ci valorosamente i Frabiani, . . .
       'The Frabians having defended us gallantly, . . .
[ii]   Difesi-si valorosamente i Frabiani, . . .
       'The Frabians having defended themselves gallantly, . ..'
[ii] is grammatical, but [i] is not. This suggests that in [ii] *i Frabiani* is an initial 2 as well as being a 1.

2 See Rosen (1981) for arguments from Italian and Ozkaragöz (1986:73ff.) for arguments from Turkish. Both of these writers refer to the problem with the Oblique Law. Joseph (1982) and Davies (1985) have suggested reformulations of the Oblique Law that retain its spirit, but allow for non-initial obliques in certain instances. Joseph suggests a revised Oblique Law of the form: 'No oblique relation may be the target of a revaluation rule.' Such a formulation would allow oblique birth.

3 This will only be true if impersonal expressions with *si* are analysed as reflecting multiattachment. For such an analysis see [38], [39], and [40] in this chapter.

4 The reflexive forms in English are not always stressable, though they are usually analysed as pronouns rather than reflexive markers: *I always behave myself well*, *Peter expresses himself clearly*, *Claude hurt himself* (accidentally), *The baby's wet itself*. Expressions such as *to hurt oneself* give a clue to the way a reflexive can develop a passive sense. In the nature of things people do not normally deliberately hurt themselves so

the reflexive construction with *hurt* develops as its unmarked reference the common situation in which one suffers an accidental hurt.

5 There is a **Reflexive Rank Law** that stipulates that the antecedent must be higher than the reflexive in the stratum in which reflexive anaphora is stated (Bell 1983:159, quoting LSA lectures from Perlmutter and Postal 1974), but Hubbard provides evidence against it from Albanian (1982).

6 In the discussion in section 2.7.2 of passives such as *A book was given him* the Nuclear Novice Law proposed in Bickford (1987) was introduced. According to this law a nuclear novice arc begins before all nuclear experienced arcs with the same tail. Nuclear novice arcs do not have nuclear predecessors, nuclear experienced arcs do. The Nuclear Novice Law applies to impersonal constructions in the following way. A dummy birth must precede 2–1 advancement. In [49b] a dummy is introduced as a nuclear term (namely a 1) in the third stratum. It is a nuclear novice since it does not have a nuclear predecessor in an earlier stratum. The network in [49b] violates the Nuclear Novice Law because this dummy birth follows rather than precedes the nuclear experienced arc, namely the advancee to 1 (it is experienced since it has a 2 predecessor). Legendre, however, argues against the Nuclear Novice Law and in favour of networks like [49b]. She cites French examples such as the following (1987:216):

[iii] Il est arrivé   plusieurs femmes en pleurant.

    it is arrived several women in crying

    'There arrived several women while crying.'

This is an impersonal construction similar to the one cited in [37]. *Plusieurs femmes* is interpreted as an initial 2 (*arriver* is unaccusative; witness the auxiliary *est* (*<être*)) which advances to 1 and is put in chômage by the dummy. Legendre establishes that the nominal that controls the missing subject of *en*-phrases must be a 1 in some stratum. To accommodate [iii] it is necessary to assume that there is unaccusative advancement. Therefore Legendre argues against the Nuclear Novice Law and in favour of a network of the type in [49b] for sentences like [iii] (1987:194):

[iv]   P   2

              P   1

     1   P   Cho

---

     il   arriver plusieurs femmes

Perlmutter (1983b:172) rejects [49b] for Italian because there is evidence from the distribution of *ne* 'of it, of them' that the initial 2 in an unaccusative stratum does not become a 1 in a later stratum. Postal (1986:143ff.) rejects [49a] for Turkish on the basis of evidence from double passives.

7 There are impersonal inversion constructions in Latin such as the following with the gerundive:

[v] Mihi   dormiendum   est.

    me:dat sleep-gerundive be:3sg

    'I have to sleep.'

The appropriate analysis would appear to be one with the initial 1 demoting spontaneously to 3 and a dummy birth in a later stratum:

mihi	dormire	dummy
1	P	
3	P	(2?)
3	P	1

Such an analysis is provided by Berinstein (1986) for impersonal Inversion in K'echi. See also Davies (1986:130ff.) for impersonal Inversion in Choctaw.

8 Perlmutter and Postal (1984b:136) claim that there are personal reflexive passives in German, but the example they cite is rejected by all native speakers I have checked with. Steele (1986) discusses examples that are candidates for a reflexive passive analysis and decides they are all examples of retroherent unaccusative advancement. For this reason I have substituted an Italian example that Rosen analyses as reflexive passive (see [15]).

Chapter 4 Multinode networks

1 One problem with the Equi analysis is that a sentence like *Everybody wants to win* does not mean the same as *Everybody wants everybody to win*.

2 Lexical Functional Grammar adopts a non-movement approach. A verb like *seem* or *appear* is alloted a lexical entry indicating it takes a subject without a semantic role and a clausal complement and that its non-semantic subject is to be identified with the subject of the complement clause.

3 In Government and Binding a sentence such as *I expected the glass to fall* is not analysed as involving raising. *The glass* would be considered to be in the infinitival clause and to be the subject of that clause (van Remsdijk and Williams 1986:32).

4 It is clear what the analysis is where all arguments are expressed by noun phrases, but RG has remained vague about how cross-referencing is handled. This is not relevant to the possessor ascension analysis, but is a general problem. In Aissen's Arc Pair Grammar description of Tzotzil nominal arcs sponsor agreement arcs on the predicate (1987:54ff.). For 'sponsor' see section 1.6.

5 A possessor ascension analysis with an oblique host results in a new oblique contrary to the Oblique Law. However, as pointed out in note 2 in Chapter 3, there are suggested revisions of the Oblique Law that would allow this.

6 Tuggy (1980) argues against a possessor ascension analysis in Spanish and in favour of taking datives such as those in [30] and [31] to be examples of the 'ethical dative'.

7 A possessor ascension analysis was considered for the second member of pairs like the following (Klokeid 1977:28):
[i] Somebody kicked Bill's stomach.
[ii] Somebody kicked Bill in the stomach.

However, there are even further problems of semantic discrepancy here. To maintain the possessor ascension analysis for sentences like [ii] it is necessary to take phrases like *in the stomach* to be chômeurs. But such phrases are surely obliques and the choice of preposition is significant: *hit someone on/under the jaw*, *hit someone around/on the head*, etc.

Chapter 5 Clause Union

1 Dryer (1986b) suggests a biclausal analysis of causatives in which elements of the upstairs clause descend into the downstairs clause. His analysis of [i] is given in [ii].

[i] Enzo fa   pulire la casa   a Nino.
    Enzo make clean the house to Nino
    'Enzo makes Nino clean the house.'

[ii]

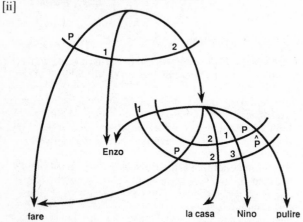

This analysis does away with the need for the Inheritance Principle since, as with the Davies and Rosen approach, the Union clause is a continuation of the lower clause.

2 The source for this section is a handout from Carol Rosen entitled 'Possessors and the internal structure of nominals'. The Tzotzil data is from Aissen (1987).

3 See Chomsky (1970) and discussions in secondary sources such as van Riemsdijk and Williams (1986:40) and Horrocks (1987:56ff.).

4 In Kalkatungu not only is the advancement marker for locative, instrumental, and causal identifiable with the causative, but the marker for benefactive advancement is also etymologically related to a causative *ma* (see [42] in Chapter 2).

Chapter 6 Relations and strata

1 Perlmutter (1982; see also 1984a) presents the following example from Achenese based on Lawler (1977). It purports to illustrate control of verb agreement by a subject chômeur in the passive, i.e. agreement sensitive to initial subject (1982:292):

[i] Lon lon-ja? u-pikan.
   I   I-go   to-market
   'I go to market.'

[ii] Gopnyan gi-ja? u-pikan.
   (s)he   3-go   to-market
   '(S)he goes to the market.'

[iii] Gopnyan ka gi-com lon.
   (s)he   perf 3-kiss me
   '(S)he kissed me.'

[iv] Lon ka gi-com le-gopnyan.
   I   perf 3-kiss by-he(r)
   'I've been kissed by her.'

These examples have always seemed suspect since chômeurs do not normally, if ever, control agreement. On the other hand ergatively marked subjects, like subjects in general, frequently control agreement. Moreover Austronesia is a hotbed of discovered and undiscovered ergativity (see section 7.4). Not surprisingly Durie (1987, 1988) claims that sentences like [iv] above are active, transitive sentences with an ergatively marked subject and therefore do not exhibit agreement with a subject chômeur (alterna, vely, with an initial 1). Durie spells the name of the language *Acehnese*.

2 See also my analysis of recipients in Kalkatungu (section 2.5).

3 *Docere* can also mean 'inform' and with this sense it takes an accusative informee with the information expressed in the ablative with the preposition *de*. This could perhaps be allotted a different initial stratum with the informee an initial 3 that advances to 2 and the information an oblique. The alternative is to take the information to be an initial 2 that is pushed into chômage by the advancing 2 and the ablative as marking the chômeur. Under this interpretation the notion 'acting term' will not cover the distribution of accusative, since some 2-chômeurs will be in the ablative. The construction is illustrated in the following sentence from Caesar (*De Bello Gallico* 7,10,3):

[v] Praemittit qui Boios de suo   adventu   doceant.
   send:3s   who Boii re his:abl coming:abl inform:subj:3pl
   'He sends forward men to inform the Boii of his arrival.'

Other Latin verbs that alternate between the double object construction and the one illustrated in [v] are *celare* 'to conceal' and *rogare* 'to ask'.

A similar problem arises in German which has the double object construction with a handful of verbs including *fragen* 'to ask' and *lehren* 'to teach':

[vi] Er lehrt unsere Kinder diesen Unsinn.
  he teach our:acc kids:acc this:acc nonsense:acc
  'He teaches our children this nonsense.'
Since German has the passive construction one cannot describe accusative in terms of the notion 'nominal heading a 2-arc', so the notion of acting 2 seems appropriate. However, Wilkinson (1983) presents the following pair and suggests that *in* in [viii] is marking a 2-chômeur arising from 3–2 advancement:
[vii] Er unterrichtet unsere Kinder die deutsche Sprache.
  'He teaches our children the German language.'
[viii] Er unterrichtet unsere Kinder in der deutschen Sprache.
  'He teaches our children in the German language.'
Under this analysis the construction in [viii] presents an exception to a generalization about accusative marking framed on the basis of acting 2. It is possible, however, that [vii] and [viii] are based on different initial strata and that *in* marks an oblique.

In both Latin and German the notion of acting 2 fails to capture the complete distribution of the accusative. In Latin the accusative marks the oblique relation of destination as in *Vado Romam* 'I am going to Rome', and it also marks extent or path. Similarly in German the accusative can mark extent: *jeden Tag* 'every day', *diesen Monat* 'this month'.

If one accepts that English has an accusative case, albeit marked distinctively only on some pronouns, then one could consider capturing part of its distribution in terms of acting 2; but there would appear to be a class of exceptions, namely 2-chômeurs marked by *with* as in *present with*, *furnish with*, *provide with*, *feed with*, etc.

4 Perlmutter (1984b) discusses the possibility of a working 2 and a working 3 and states that he knows of no empirical instances motivating these notions. Berinstein (1986:46) uses the notion of working nuclear term to describe the class of controllers of Equi in K'ekchi. To be a working nuclear term a nominal must be a 1 or 2 at some level and a final 1, 2, or 3. Essentially the notion covers Inversion nominals (1–3) and 2–3 retreatants as well as initial/final 1, initial/final 2, and initial 2/final 1.

5 Perlmutter (1982:327ff.) presents an argument against Functional Grammar as a representative of theories with a single level of grammatical relations plus semantic roles. The argument is based on Achenese/Acehnese and fails if one accepts the analysis of putative passives as ergative constructions (see note 1 above).

Chapter 7 Describing different nuclear types

1 In Postal's version of antipassive the initial 1 demotes to 2 pushing it into chômage. This satisfies the Motivated Chômage Law (no spontaneous demotion to chômeur). The 2 then advances back to 1 to satisfy the Final 1 Law (see section 2.5). Gerdts (to appear) accepts spontaneous chômage as represented in [22b].

2 Foley and Van Valin (1984:136) note that the patient focus is unmarked, but they see this point as counterbalanced by the distribution of *-um-* and *-in-*. They see *-in-* as marking all focuses except the actor focus and they see the actor focus as sharing marking with intransitives, namely *-um-*. However, if *-um-* two-place constructions are seen as intransitive antipassives, then *-in-* is common to all transitive focuses and its distribution does not suggest that the actor focus is unmarked.

3 Cena presents a large number of points indicating that the patient focus in Tagalog is unmarked. They include the fact that a number of verbs occur in patient focus but not in actor focus and the fact that with those verbs that take no focus marking at all the patient focus is obligatory in independent clauses.

4 An ergative can only precede the verb if pronominal.

Chapter 8 Overview

1 See Givón's confession in Chapter 1 of *On Understanding Grammar*. Thompson's early work was in a transformational framework.

2 Anna Siewierska reminds me that over sixty languages have been discussed within the framework of Dik's Functional Grammar.

3 Dryer's notion of primary and secondary object represent a way of reconciling Comrie's analysis with an RG one (see section 2.7.3).

4 See Perlmutter (ed.) (1983) *Studies in Relational Grammar 1*, and Perlmutter and Rosen (eds) *Studies in Relational Grammar 2*. A third collection, Joseph and Postal (eds) *Studies in Relational Grammar 3*, is due to appear in 1989 after the present work was completed.

Bibliography

BLS Berkeley Linguistics Society
CLS Chicago Linguistics Society
NELS Northeastern Linguistics Society
A fairly complete list of works on Relational Grammar is available in
S. Dubinsky and C. Rosen (eds) *A Bibliography on Relational Grammar
through May 1987 with Selected Titles on Lexical-Functional Grammar*,
Bloomington: Indiana University Linguistics Club.

Aissen, J. (1979) 'Possessor ascension in Tzotzil', in Laura Martin (ed.)
Papers in Mayan Linguistics, Columbia, Missouri: Lucas Bros Publishers.
Aissen, J. (1982a) 'Comments on "Grammatical Relations and Explanation
in Linguistic Theory" by Alec Marantz', in Annie Zaenen (ed.) *Subjects
and Other Subjects: Proceedings of the Harvard Conference on the
Representation of Grammatical Relations*, distributed by Indiana Uni-
versity Linguistics Club, Bloomington.
Aissen, J. (1982b) 'Valence and coreference', in P. Hopper and
S. Thompson (eds) *Syntax and Semantics 15: Studies in Transitivity*,
New York: Academic Press.
Aissen, J. (1983) 'Indirect object advancement in Tzotzil', in
D. Perlmutter (ed.) *Studies in Relational Grammar 1*, Chicago:
University of Chicago Press.
Aissen, J. (1984a) 'Control and command in Tzotzil purpose clauses',
BLS 10:559–71.
Aissen, J. (1984b) 'Themes and absolutives: some semantic rules in
Tzotzil', in E. D. Cook and D. Gerdts (eds) *Syntax and Semantics 16:
The Syntax of Native American Languages*, New York: Academic
Press.
Aissen, J. (1987) *Tzotzil Clause Structure*, Dordrecht: Reidel.
Aissen, J. (to appear) 'Toward a theory of agreement controllers', in
B. Joseph and P. Postal (eds) *Studies in Relational Grammar 3*.
Aissen, J. and Hankamer, J. (1980) 'Lexical extension and grammatical
transformations', *BLS* 6:238–49.
Aissen, J. and Perlmutter, D. (1983) 'Clause reduction in Spanish', in D.
Perlmutter (ed.) *Studies in Relational Grammar 1*, Chicago: University
of Chicago Press [earlier version in *BLS* 2:1–30].

Allen, B. and Frantz, D. (1983a) 'Advancements and verb agreement in Southern Tiwa', in D. Perlmutter (ed.) *Studies in Relational Grammar 1* Chicago: University of Chicago Press [original version in *BLS* 4:11–17].

Allen, B. and Frantz, D. (1983b). 'An impersonal passive in Southern Tiwa', *Workpapers of the Summer Institute of Linguistics* 27:1–9, North Dakota: University of North Dakota.

Allen, B., Franz, D., Gardiner, D., and Perlmutter, D. (to appear) 'Possessor ascension and syntactic levels in Southern Tiwa', in B. Joseph and P. Postal (eds) *Studies in Relational Grammar 3*.

Anderson, J. (1982) 'A disagreeable note on Relational Grammatical relations', in R. Dirven and G. Radden (eds) *Issues in the Theory of Universal Grammar*, Tübingen: Gunter Narr Verlag.

Bechert, J. (1977) 'Zur funktionalen Erklärung des Ergativsystems', *Papiere zur Linguistik* 12:57–86.

Bell, S. (1976) *Cebuano Subjects in Two Frameworks*, dissertation MIT. [Distributed by Indiana University Linguistics Club, Bloomington.]

Bell, S. (1981) 'Comparative restrictiveness of Relational Grammar and lexical syntax', *Lingua* 55:1–39.

Bell, S. (1983) 'Advancements and ascensions in Cebuano', in D. Perlmutter (ed.) *Studies in Relational Grammar 1*, Chicago: University of Chicago Press.

Bennett, P. (1980) 'English passives: a study in syntactic change and Relational Grammar', *Lingua* 51:101–14.

Berinstein, A. (1985) *Evidence for Multiattachment in K'ekchi (Mayan)*, New York: Garland.

Berinstein, A. (1986) 'Indirect object constructions and multiple levels of syntactic representation', *CLS* 22:36–50.

Bickford, J. A. (1982) 'Initial and non-initial indirect objects in Spanish', *Workpapers of the Summer Institute of Linguistics* 26:118–57, North Dakota: University of North Dakota.

Bickford, J. A. (1985) 'Spanish clitic doubling and levels of grammatical relations', *Lingua* 65:189–211.

Bickford, J. A. (1986) 'Possessor ascension in Kinyarwanda', *CLS* 22:129–43.

Bickford, J. A. (1987) *Universal Constraints on Relationally Complex Clauses*, dissertation, University of California at San Diego.

Bickford, J. A. (to appear) 'On tertiary passives', in B. Joseph and P. Postal (eds) *Studies in Relational Grammar 3*.

Blake, B. J. (1983) 'Structure and word order in Kalkatungu: the anatomy of a flat language', *Australian Journal of Linguistics*, 3.2, 143–76.

Blake, B. J. (1984) 'Problems for possessor ascension: some Australian examples', *Linguistics* 22:437–53.

Blake, B. J. (1987) *Australian Aboriginal Grammar*, London: Croom Helm.

Breen, J. G. (1971) *A Description of the Warluwara Language*, master's thesis, Monash University, Melbourne.

Bresnan, J. (1978) 'A realistic Transformational Grammar', in M. Halle,

J. Bresnan, and G. Miller (eds) *Linguistic Theory and Psychological Reality*, Cambridge, Mass.: MIT Press.

Bresnan, J. (1980) 'Polyadicity', in T. Hoekstra, H. van der Hulst, and M. Moortgat (eds) *Lexical Grammar*, Dordrecht: Foris Publications. [Revised version in J. Bresnan (ed.) 1982.]

Bresnan, J. (ed.) (1982) *The Mental Representation of Grammatical Relations*, Cambridge, Mass.: MIT Press.

Bresnan, J. (1982a) 'The passive in lexical theory', in J. Bresnan (ed.) 1982, 3–86.

Bresnan, J. (1982b) 'Control and complementation', in J. Bresnan (ed.) 1982, 282–390.

Burzio, L. (1986) *Italian Syntax*, Dordrecht: Reidel.

Cena, R. M. (1979) 'Patient primacy in Tagalog', paper read at LSA Winter Meeting.

Centineo, G. (1986) 'A lexical theory of auxiliary selection in Italian', *Davis Working Papers in Linguistics* 1:1–35, University of California, Davis.

Channon, R. (1982) '3–2 advancement, beneficiary advancement, and with', *BLS* 8:271–82.

Chomsky, N. (1957) *Syntactic Structures*, The Hague: Mouton.

Chomsky, N. (1965) *Aspects of the Theory of Syntax*, Cambridge, Mass.: MIT Press.

Chomsky, N. (1970) 'Remarks on nominalization', in R. Jacobs and P. Rosenbaum (eds) *Readings in English Transformational Grammar*, Waltham, Mass.: Ginn, 184–221.

Chomsky, N. (1981) *Lectures on Government and Binding*, Dordrecht: Foris Publications.

Chung, S. (1976) 'An object-creating rule in Bahasa Indonesia', *Linguistic Inquiry* 7:41–87. Reprinted in D. Perlmutter (ed.) 1983, *Studies in Relational Grammar 1*, Chicago: University of Chicago Press.

Cole, P. (1976) 'The interface of theory and description', *Language*, 53:563–83.

Comrie, B. (1976) 'The syntax of causative constructions: cross-language similarities and divergences', in M. Shibatani (ed.) *Syntax and Semantics 6: The Grammar of Causative Constructions*, New York: Academic Press, 261–312.

Comrie, B. (1977) 'In defence of spontaneous demotion: the impersonal passive', in P. Cole and J. Sadock (eds) *Syntax and Semantics 8: Grammatical Relations*, New York: Academic Press.

Comrie, B. (1981) *Language Universals and Linguistic Typology*, Oxford: Basil Blackwell.

Comrie, B. (1982) 'Grammatical relations in Huichol', in P. J. Hopper and S. A. Thompson (eds) *Syntax and Semantics 15: Studies in Transitivity*, New York: Academic Press, 95–116.

Comrie, B. (1986) 'Relational Grammar: whence, where, whether', *Linguistics* 24:773–89. [review article]

Cook, E. D. and Gerdts, D. (eds) (1984) *Syntax and Semantics 16: The Syntax of Native American Languages*, New York: Academic Press.

Bibliography

Cooreman, A., Fox, B., and Givón, T. (1984) 'The discourse definition of ergativity', *Studies in Language* 8.1:1–34.

Craig, C. (1977) *The Structure of Jacaltec*, Austin: University of Texas Press.

Crain, C. (1979) 'Advancement and ascension to direct object in Chamorro', *Linguistic Notes from La Jolla 6*, University of California at San Diego, La Jolla.

Dalgish, G. and Sheintuch, S. (1976) 'On the justification for language-specific sub-grammatical relations. *Studies in the Linguistic Sciences* 6:2.

Davies, W. (1981a) *Choctaw Clause Structure*, dissertation, University of California at San Diego.

Davies, W. (1981b) 'Choctaw subjects and multiple levels of syntax', in T. Hoekstra, H. van der Hulst, and M. Moortgat (eds.) *Perspectives on Functional Grammar*, Dordrecht: Foris Publications.

Davies, W. (1981c) 'Choctaw switch reference and levels of syntactic representation', *Linguistic Notes from La Jolla 9*, University of California at San Diego, La Jolla. Also in *Working Papers in Relational Grammar*, University of California at San Diego, La Jolla. Also in E. D. Cook and D. Gerdts (eds) (1984) *Syntax and Semantics 16: The Syntax of Native American Languages*, New York: Academic Press.

Davies, W. (1984) 'Antipassive: Choctaw evidence for a universal characterization', in D. Perlmutter and C. Rosen (eds) *Studies in Relational Grammar 2*, Chicago: University of Chicago Press.

Davies, W. (1985) 'A new formulation of the oblique law', typescript, University of Iowa.

Davies, W. (1986) *Choctaw Verb Agreement and Universal Grammar*, Dordrecht: Reidel.

Davies, W. (1987) 'Lexically governed rules and extended valence', typescript, University of Iowa.

Davies, W. and Dubinsky, S. (1988) 'Grammatical relations in lexical representations', typescript, University of Iowa.

Davies, W. and Rosen, C. (1988) 'Unions as multi-predicate clauses', *Language* 64:52–88.

Davies, W. and Sam-Colop, E. (1988) 'Regularizing K'iche' verb agreement', typescript, University of Iowa.

De Guzman, V. (1979) 'Morphological evidence for primacy of patient as subject in Tagalog', paper read at LSA Annual Meeting, Los Angeles.

De Guzman, V. (1983) 'Ergative analysis for Philippine languages', paper presented at the Third Eastern Conference on Austronesian Languages, Ohio University.

De Guzman, V. (1986) 'Some consequences of causative clause union in Tagalog', in G. Geraghty, L. Carrington, and S. A. Wurm (eds) *FOCAL 1: Papers from the Fourth International Conference on Austronesian Linguistics*, Pacific Linguistics, ANU, Canberra, 59–72.

Dik, S. (1978) *Functional Grammar*, Amsterdam: North-Holland.

Dixon, R. M. W. (1972) *The Dyirbal Language of North Queensland*, Cambridge: CUP.

Dixon, R. M. W. (1977) *A Grammar of Yidiny*, Cambridge: CUP.

Dixon, R. M. W. (1979) 'Ergativity', *Language*, 55:59–138.

Dowty, D. (1982) 'Grammatical relations and Montague Grammar' in P. Jacobson and G. Pullum (eds) *The Nature of Syntactic Representation*, Dordrecht: Reidel, 79–130.

Dryer, M. (1983) 'Indirect objects in Kinyarwanda revisited', in D. Perlmutter (ed.) *Studies in Relational Grammar 1*, Chicago: University of Chicago Press.

Dryer, M. (1986a) 'Primary objects, secondary objects, and antidative', *Language* 62:808–45.

Dryer, M. (1986b) 'Clause union as mass descension', typescript.

Dubinsky, S. (1985) *Union Constructions in Japanese: A Unified Analysis of '-sase' and '-rare'*, dissertation, Cornell.

Dubinsky, S. (1987) 'Extended valence and the assignment of thematic roles: Japanese affective union', typescript, University of Iowa.

Dubinsky, S. (to appear) 'Japanese object to indirect object demotion', in B. Joseph and P. Postal (eds) *Studies in Relational Grammar 3*.

Dubinsky, S. and Rosen, C. (eds) *A Bibliography on Relational Grammar through May 1987 with Selected Titles on Lexical-Functional Grammar*, Indiana University Linguistics Club, Bloomington.

Durie, M. (1988) 'The so-called passive of Acehnese', *Language* 64: 104–13.

Elson, B. and Marlett, S. (1983) 'Popoluca evidence for syntactic levels', *Workpapers of the Summer Institute of Linguistics* 27:107–34, University of North Dakota.

Fauconnier, G. (1983) 'Generalized union', *Communication and Cognition* 16.1–2:3–37. Also in L. Tasmowski and D. Willems (eds) *Problems in Syntax* (Studies in Language 2) New York: Plenum Press.

Fillmore, C. J. (1968) 'The case for case', in E. Bach and R. T. Harms (eds) *Universals in Linguistic Theory*, London: Holt, Rinehart & Winston, 1–88.

Fillmore, C. J. (1977) 'The case for case reopened', in P. Cole and J. Sadock (eds) *Syntax and Semantics 8: Grammatical Relations*, New York: Academic Press, 59–82.

Foley, W. and Van Valin, R., jr. (1984) *Functional Syntax and Universal Grammar*, Cambridge: CUP.

Frantz, D. (1979) 'Multiple dependency in Blackfoot: a counterexample to a law of Arc Pair Grammar', *BLS* 5:77–80.

Frantz, D. (1980) 'Ascensions to subject in Blackfoot', *BLS* 6:293–329.

Frantz, D. (1981) 'Grammatical relations in universal grammar', Indiana University Linguistics Club, Bloomington.

Frantz, D. (1984) 'A level-oriented constraint on agreement control in Chichewa', *CLS* 20:104–18.

Frantz, D. (1985a) 'Morphology in Relational Grammar', *CLS* 21: 107–21.

Frantz, D. (1985b) 'Syntactic constraints on noun incorporation in Southern Tiwa', *BLS* 11:107–16.

Gary, J. (1977) 'Object formation rules in several Bantu languages: questions and implications for universal grammar', *CLS* 12:125–36.

Bibliography

Gary, J. and Keenan, E. (1977) 'On collapsing grammatical relations in universal grammar', in P. Cole and J. Sadock (eds) *Syntax and Semantics 8: Grammatical Relations*, New York: Academic Press.

Gazdar, G., Klein, E., Pullum, G., and Sag, I. (1985) *Generalized Phrase Structure Grammar*, Cambridge, Mass.: Harvard UP.

George, L. (1974) 'Ergativity and Relational Grammar', *NELS* 5.

Gerdts, D. (1979) 'Out of control in Ilokano', *BLS* 5:81–93.

Gerdts, D. (1980a) 'Antipassives and causatives in Halkomelem', *BLS* 6:300–14.

Gerdts, D. (1980b) 'Causal to object advancement in Halkomelem', *CLS* 16:83–101.

Gerdts, D. (1984) 'A relational analysis of Halkomelem causals', in E. D. Cook and D. Gerdts (eds) *Syntax and Semantics 16: The Syntax of Native American Languages*, New York: Academic Press.

Gerdts, D. (to appear). 'Antipassives and causatives in Ilokano: evidence for an ergative analysis of Philippine languages', in R. McGinn (ed.) *Studies in Austronesian Linguistics*, Ohio: Ohio University Press.

Gibson, J. (1980) 'Clause Union in Chamorro and in Universal Grammar', dissertation, University of California at San Diego.

Gibson, J. (to appear) 'Categorial grammatical relations: The Chamorro evidence', in B. Joseph and P. Postal (eds) *Studies in Relational Grammar 3*.

Gibson, J. and Raposo, E. (1986) 'Clause union, the Stratal Uniqueness Law and the chômeur relation', *Natural Language and Linguistic Theory* 4:295–331.

Givón, T. (1979) *On Understanding Grammar*, New York: Academic Press.

Gonzalez, N. (to appear) 'The unaccusativity of Spanish raising predicates', in B. Joseph and P. Postal (eds) *Studies in Relational Grammar 3*. [preprint version entitled 'The unaccusativity of Chilean Spanish raising predicates']

Gruber, J. S. (1965) *Studies in Lexical Relations*, dissertation, MIT.

Halliday, M. A. K. (1985) *An Introduction to Functional Grammar*, London: Edward Arnold.

Harbert, W. (1977) 'Clause union and German accusative plus infinitive constructions', in P. Cole and J. Sadock (eds) *Syntax and Semantics 8: Grammatical Relations*, New York: Academic Press.

Harris, A. (1981) *Georgian Syntax: A Study in Relational Grammar*, Cambridge: CUP.

Harris, A. (1982) 'Georgian and the unaccusative hypothesis', *Language* 58:290–306.

Harris, A. (1984a) 'Case marking, verb agreement, and inversion in Udi', in D. Perlmutter and C. Rosen (eds) *Studies in Relational Grammar 2*, Chicago: University of Chicago Press, 243–58.

Harris, A. (1984b) 'Inversion as a rule of universal grammar: Georgian evidence', in D. Perlmutter and C. Rosen (eds) *Studies in Relational Grammar 2*, Chicago: University of Chicago Press, 259–91.

Harris, A. (1985) *Syntax and Semantics 18: Diachronic Syntax: The Kartvelian Case*, New York: Academic Press.

Bibliography

Hermon, Gabriella (1981) 'The relationship of meaning and underlying grammatical relations', *BLS* 7:68–81.

Hock, H. H. (1986) *Principles of Historical Linguistics*, Berlin: Mouton de Gruyter.

Hoekstra, T., van der Hulst, H., and Moorgat, M. (eds) (1981) *Perspectives on Functional Grammar*, Dordrecht: Foris Publications.

Hopper, P. and Thompson S. A. (1980) 'Transitivity in grammar and discourse', *Language* 56:251–99.

Horn, G. M. (1983) *Lexical-Functional Grammar*, Berlin: Mouton.

Horn, L. (1980) 'Affixation and the unaccusative Hypothesis', *CLS* 16.

Horrocks, G. (1987) *Generative Grammar*, London: Longman.

Hubbard, P. (1981) 'Dative clitics in Albanian: evidence for syntactic levels', *BLS* 7:82–92. Also in *Working Papers in Relational Grammar*, University of California at San Diego, La Jolla.

Hubbard, P. (1982) 'Albanian reflexives: violations of proposed universals', typescript, Ohio University, Athens.

Hudson, R. (1984) *Word Grammar*, Oxford: Blackwell.

Jackendoff, R. (1972) *Semantic Interpretation in Generative Grammar*, Cambridge, Mass.: MIT Press.

Johnson, D. (1974) 'On the role of grammatical relations in linguistic theory', *CLS* 10.

Johnson, D. (1977a) 'On Keenan's definition of *subject of*', *Linguistic Inquiry* 8:673–92.

Johnson, D. (1977b) 'On relational constraints on grammars', in P. Cole and J. Sadock (eds) *Syntax and Semantics 8: Grammatical Relations*, New York: Academic Press.

Johnson, D. (1979) *Toward a Theory of Relationally Based Grammar*, New York: Garland Publishing [dissertation, University of Illinois, Urbana (1974)].

Johnson, D. and Postal, P. (1980) *Arc Pair Grammar*, Princeton: Princeton University Press.

Johnson, M. (1980) 'Ergativity in Inuktitut (Eskimo) in Montague Grammar and in Relational Grammar'. [Distributed by Indiana University Linguistics Club, Bloomington.]

Joseph, B. (1979) 'Raising to oblique in Modern Greek', *BLS* 5:114–28.

Joseph, B. (1982) 'A note on the oblique law', *Ohio State University Working Papers in Linguistics* 26:93–101.

Joseph, B. and Postal, P. (to appear) *Studies in Relational Grammar 3*.

Kaplan, R. and Bresnan, J. (1982). 'Lexical Functional Grammar: a formal system for grammatical representation', in J. Bresnan (ed.) 1982, 173–281.

Katz, J. and Postal, P. (1964) *An Integrated Theory of Linguistic Descriptions*, Cambridge: Mass.: MIT Press.

Keenan, E. (1975) 'Some universals of passive in Relational Grammar', *CLS* 11:340–52.

Keenan, E. (1976) 'Towards a universal definition of "subject"', in C. Li (ed.) *Subject and Topic*, New York: Academic Press.

Bibliography

Keenan, E. and Comrie B. (1977) 'Noun phrase accessibility and universal grammar', *Linguistic Inquiry* 8:63–99.

Kimenyi, A. (1976) 'A relational grammar of Kinyarwanda', dissertation, UCLA.

Klimov, G., (1973) *Očerk Obščej Teorii Ergativnosti* (Outline of a General Theory of Ergativity), Moscow: Nauka.

Klimov, G., (1979) 'On the position of the ergative type in typological classification', in F. Plank (ed.) *Ergativity*, London: Academic Press, 327–32.

Klokeid, T. (1976) 'Topics in Lardil grammar', dissertation, MIT.

Klokeid, T. (1977) 'An outline of the framework of Relational Grammar', unpublished notes, University of Calgary.

Klokeid, T. (1978). 'Nominal inflection in Pamanyungan: a case study in Relational Grammar', in Werner Abraham (ed.) *Valence, Semantic Case and Grammatical Relations*, Amsterdam: John Benjamins.

Kuno, S. (1976) 'Subject, theme, and the speaker's empathy – a reexamination of relativization phenomena', in C. Li (ed.) *Subject and Topic*, New York: Academic Press.

Lakoff, G. (1970) 'Global rules', *Language* 46:627–39.

Lawler, J. (1977). '*A* agrees with *B* in Achenese: a problem for Relational Grammar', in P. Cole and J. Sadock (eds) *Syntax and Semantics 8: Grammatical Relations*, New York: Academic Press.

Legendre, G. (1986) 'Object raising in French', *Natural Language and Linguistic Theory*, 4:137–83.

Legendre, G. (1987) 'Topics in French syntax', dissertation, University of California at San Diego.

Lepschy, A. and Lepschy, G. (1977) *The Italian Language Today*, London: Hutchinson.

Levin, B. (1987) 'The middle construction and ergativity', *Lingua*, 71: 17–32.

Lightfoot, D. (1979) *Principles of Diachronic Syntax*, Cambridge: CUP.

Mallinson, G. and Blake, B. (1981) *Language Typology*, Amsterdam: North-Holland.

Marantz, Alec (1982) 'Grammatical relations and explanation in linguistics', in Annie Zaenen (ed.) *Subjects and Other Subjects: Proceedings of the Harvard Conference on the Representation of Grammatical Relations*. [Distributed by Indiana University Linguistics Club, Bloomington.]

Marantz, A. (1984) *On the Nature of Grammatical Relations*, Cambridge, Mass.: MIT Press.

Marlett, S. (1984) 'Personal and impersonal passives in Seri', in D. Perlmutter and C. Rosen (eds.) *Studies in Relational Grammar 2*, Chicago: University of Chicago Press.

Merlan, F. (1983) *Ngalakan Grammar, Texts and Vocabulary*, Pacific Linguistics, ANU Canberra.

Merlan, F. (1985) 'Split intransitivity: functional oppositions in intransitive inflection', in J. Nichols and A. C. Woodbury (eds) *Grammar Inside and Outside the Clause*, Cambridge: Cambridge University Press, 324–63.

Bibliography

Bibliography

Mulder, J. and Schwartz, A. (1981) 'On the subject of advancements in the Philippine languages', *Studies in Language* 5.2:227–68.

Newmeyer, F. (1976) 'Relational Grammar and autonomous syntax', *CLS* 12:506–15.

Newmeyer, F. (1980) *Linguistic Theory in America*, New York: Academic Press, [second edition 1986]

Ozkaragöz, Inci (1980) 'Evidence from Turkish for the unaccusative hypothesis', *BLS* 6:411–22.

Ozkaragöz, Inci (1982) 'Transitivity and the syntax of middle clauses in Turkish', in *Working Papers in Relational Grammar*, University of California at San Diego, La Jolla.

Ozkaragöz, Inci (1986) *The Relational Structure of Turkish Syntax*, dissertation, University of California at San Diego.

Pandharipande, R. and Kachru, Y. (1977) 'Relational Grammar, ergativity and Hindi-Urdu', *Lingua* 41:217–38.

Payne, T. E. (1982) 'Role and reference related subject properties and ergativity in Yup'ik Eskimo and Tagalog', *Studies in Language* 6.1:75–106.

Perlmutter, D. (1980) 'Relational Grammar', in E. Moravcsik and J. Wirth (eds) *Syntax and Semantics 13: Current Approaches to Syntax*, New York: Academic Press.

Perlmutter, D. (1981) 'Functional Grammar and Relational Grammar: points of convergence and divergence', in T. Hoekstra, H. van der Hulst, and M. Moortgat (eds) *Perspectives on Functional Grammar*, Dordrecht: Foris Publications.

Perlmutter, D. (1982) 'Syntactic representation, syntactic levels, and the notion of subject', in P. Jacobson and G. Pullum (eds) *The Nature of Syntatic Representation*, Dordrecht: Reidel.

Perlmutter, D. (1983a) 'Editor's afterword to the relational succession law', in D. Perlmutter (ed.) 1983, 53–73.

Perlmutter, D. (1983b) 'Personal versus impersonal constructions', *Natural Language and Linguistic Theory* 1:141–200.

Perlmutter, D. (ed.) (1983) *Studies in Relational Grammar 1*, Chicago: University of Chicago Press.

Perlmutter, D. (1984a) 'The inadequacy of some monostratal theories of passive', in D. Perlmutter and C. Rosen (eds) 1984, 3–37.

Perlmutter, D. (1984b) 'Working 1s and inversion in Italian, Japanese, and Quechua', in D. Perlmutter and C. Rosen (eds) 1984, 292–330. [original version in *BLS* 5, 1979]

Perlmutter, D. and Postal, P. (1983a) 'Toward a universal definition of the passive', in D. Perlmutter (ed.) 1983, 3–29. (original version in *BLS* 3, 1977]

Perlmutter, D. and Postal P. (1983b) 'The relational succession law', in D. Perlmutter (ed.) 1983, 30–80.

Perlmutter, D. and Postal P. (1983c) 'Some proposed laws of basic clause structure', in D. Perlmutter (ed.) 1983, 81–128.

Perlmutter, D. and Postal P. (1984a) 'The 1-Advancement Exclusiveness Law', in D. Perlmutter and C. Rosen (eds) 1984, 81–125.

Perlmutter, D. and Postal P. (1984b) 'Impersonal passives and some relational laws', in D. Perlmutter and C. Rosen (eds) 1984, 126–70.

Perlmutter, D. and Rosen, C. (eds) (1984) *Studies in Relational Grammar 2*, Chicago: University of Chicago Press.

Perlmutter, D. and Zaenen, A. (1984) 'The indefinite extraposition construction in Dutch and German', in D. Perlmutter and C. Rosen (eds) 1984, 171–216.

Postal, P (1977) 'Antipassive in French', *Lingvisticae Investigationes* 1:333–74.

Postal, P. (1982) 'Some Arc Pair Grammar descriptions', in P. Jacobson and G. Pullum (eds) *The Nature of Syntactic Representation*, Dordrecht: Reidel.

Postal, P. (1986) *Studies of Passive Clauses*, Albany: State University of New York Press.

Postal, P. (to appear) 'French indirect object demotion', in B. Joseph and P. Postal (eds) *Studies in Relational Grammar 3*.

Pullum, G. (1977) 'Word order universals and grammatical relations', in P. Cole and J. Sadock (eds) *Syntax and Semantics 8: Grammatical Relations*, New York: Academic Press, 249–78.

Radford, A. (1977) *Italian Syntax*, Cambridge: CUP.

Reed, I. *et al.* (1977) *Yup'ik Eskimo Grammar*, Alaska Native Languages Center, University of Alaska.

Rhodes, R. (1977) 'Semantics in a Relational Grammar', *CLS* 13: 503–14.

Rizzi (1978) 'A restructuring rule in Italian syntax', in S. Jay Keyser (ed.) *Recent Transformational Studies in European Languages*, Cambridge, Mass.: MIT Press.

Rosen, C. (1981) *The Relational Structure of Reflexive Clauses: Evidence from Italian*, dissertation, Harvard University.

Rosen, C. (1982) 'The unaccusative hypothesis and the "inherent clitic" phenomenon in Italian', *CLS* 18:530–41.

Rosen, C. (1983) 'Universals of causative union: a co-proposal to the Gibson–Raposo typology', *CLS* 19:338–52.

Rosen, C. (1984) 'The interface between semantic roles and initial grammatical relations', in D. Perlmutter and C. Rosen (eds) 1984, 38–80.

Rosen, C. (1987a) Review of A. Marantz, 'On the Nature of Grammatical Relations', *Journal of Linguistics* 23:435–45.

Rosen, C. (1987b) 'Star means bad: a syntactic divertimento for Italianists', *Italica*, 64:443–76.

Rosen, C. (n.d.) 'Southern Tiwa: another view of its morphosyntax', typescript, Cornell University.

Rosen, C. and Wali, K. (1988) 'Twin passives, inversion and multistratalism in Marathi', typescript, Cornell University.

Salih, M. H. (1985) 'Aspects of clause structure in standard Arabic: a study in Relational Grammar', dissertation, State University of New York at Buffalo.

Schachter, P. (1976) 'The subject in Philippines languages: topic, actor,

actor-topic, or none of the above', in C. Li (ed.) *Subject and Topic*, New York: Academic Press.

Scheintuch, G. (1976) 'On the syntactic motivation for a category "chômeur" in Relational Grammar', *Studies in the Linguistic Sciences* 6.1:49–56, University of Illinois, Urbana.

Seiter, W. (1978) 'Subject–direct object raising in Niuean', *BLS* 4:211–22. [Revised version in D. Perlmutter (ed.) (1983) *Studies in Relational Grammar 1*, Chicago: University of Chicago Press, 317–59.]

Sells, P. (1985) Lectures on contemporary syntactic theories, Center for the Study of Language and Information, Stanford.

Shannon, T. (1987) 'On some recent claims of Relational Grammar', *BLS* 13:247–62.

Siewierska, A. (1984) *The Passive: a Comparative Linguistic Analysis*, London: Croom Helm.

Silverstein, M. (1976) 'Hierarchy of features and ergativity', in R. M. W. Dixon (ed.) *Grammatical Categories in Australian Languages*, Australian Institute of Aboriginal Studies, Canberra and New Jersey: Humanities Press, 112–71.

Starosta, S. (1978) 'The one per sent solution', in W. Abraham (ed.) *Valence, Semantic Case and Grammatical Relations*, Amsterdam: John Benjamins, 459–576.

Starosta, S. (1986) 'Focus as recentralisation', in P. Geraghty, L. Carrington, and S. A. Wurm (eds) *FOCAL I: Papers from the Fourth International Conference on Austronesian Linguistics*, Pacific Linguistics, ANU, Canberra, 73–95.

Starosta, S. (1988) *The Case for Lexicase*, London: Pinter.

Steele, W. J. (1986) *Aspects of German Reflexivisation Within a Relational Grammar Framework*, master's thesis, Monash University, Melbourne.

Tchekhoff, C. (1979) *La Construction ergative en Avar et en Tongien*, Paris: Klincksiek.

Trithart, L. (1975) 'Relational Grammar and Chichewa subjectivization rules', *CLS* 11:615–24.

Tuggy, D. (1980) 'Ethical dative and possessor omission si, possessor ascension no!', *Workpapers of the Summer Institute of Linguistics* 24:97–141, University of North Dakota.

Van Riemsdijk, H. and Williams, E. (1986) *Introduction to the Theory of Grammar*, Cambridge, Mass.: MIT Press.

Van Valin, Jr, R. D. (1987) 'The unaccusative hypothesis vs semantic approaches to verb classification', *NELS* 17.

Van Valin, Jr, R. D. and Foley, W. (1980) 'Role and reference grammar' in E. Moravcsik and J. Wirth (eds) *Current Approaches to Syntax (Syntax and Semantics 13)*, New York: Academic Press.

Vincent, N. (1987) 'Italian' in M. Harris and N. Vincent (eds) *The Romance Languages*, London: Croom Helm.

Wierzbicka, A. (1980) *The Case for Surface Case*, Ann Arbor: Karoma.

Wilkinson, E. (1982) 'Indirect object advancement and constituent order in German', unpublished paper, Monash University.

Wilkinson, E. (1983) 'Indirect object advancement in German', *BLS* 9:281–91.

Wilkinson, E. (1987) Review article of *Studies in Relational Grammar I & II, Australian Journal of Linguistics* 7:257–86.

Zwicky, A. (1984) 'Welsh soft mutation and the case of object NPs', *CLS* 20:387–402.

Index of authors

Index of authors

Katz 62
Keenan 27, 51, 85, 163, 164
Klimov 143
Klokeid 43, 99, 175
Kuno 163

Lakoff 15, 131, 160
Lawler 177
Legendre 26, 98, 99, 114, 116, 169, 174
Lepschy 70
Levin 148
Lightfoot 50

Mallinson 149
Malory 50
Marantz 18, 40, 109, 148, 157, 172
Marlett 87
Merlan 144

Newmeyer 167

Ozkaragöz 10, 43, 59, 81, 83, 127, 173

Payne 152
Perlmutter 1, 3, 10, 12, 13, 14, 17, 20, 21, 23, 26, 29, 32, 33, 37, 42, 48, 49, 51, 52, 53, 66, 74, 75, 76, 77, 79, 81, 83, 84, 85, 86, 88, 92, 94, 96, 104, 105, 107, 108, 112, 113, 135, 136, 137, 138, 140, 151, 157, 167, 169, 170, 173, 174, 175, 177, 178, 179
Postal 1, 3, 10, 12, 13, 14, 17, 20, 21, 23, 25, 26, 33, 37, 41, 42, 49, 51, 52, 53, 55, 60, 61, 62, 66, 81, 83, 84, 85, 86, 88, 94, 96, 112, 113, 151, 157, 158, 159, 161, 163, 167, 168, 169, 170, 170, 173, 174, 175, 178, 179
Pullum 170

Radford 107, 112
Raposo 112, 113, 114, 129
Reed 41
Rizzi 107
Rosen 20, 26, 32, 34, 35, 36, 37, 45, 49, 59, 67, 68, 69, 71, 72, 75, 77, 78, 79, 88, 103, 105, 106, 110, 114, 117, 119, 120, 122, 123, 124, 125, 126, 127, 129, 135, 169, 170, 172, 173, 175, 176, 179

Schachter 149, 154
Shannon 81, 171, 172
Siewierska 85, 87, 179
Silverstein 42, 148, 163, 179
Starosta 19, 127, 141, 142, 152, 156
Steele 70

Tchekhoff 145
Thomson 41, 43, 155, 163, 179
Trithart 164
Tuggi 175
Tzotzil 17, 103, 124, 125, 175

Van Riemsdijk 19, 175, 176
Van Valin 140, 141, 142, 145, 172, 179
Vendler 172
Vincent 166

Wilde 54
Wilkinson 9, 178
Williams 19, 175, 176

Zaenen 74, 75, 92
Zwicky 86

Index of languages

Achenese, Acehnese 177, 178
Albanian 174
Ancient Greek 161
Arabic 59
Archi 59
Arikara 37, 144
Australian 25, 28, 43, 57, 67, 132, 154, 173
Austronesian 177
Avar 27, 145

Bantu 55, 58
Bats 37
Blackfoot 6

Caucasian 27, 37, 132
Cebuano 143, 149, 150, 151, 153, 154, 155
Celtic 18
Chamorro 37, 55, 112, 113
Choctaw 35, 36, 37, 42, 60, 137, 144, 175
Czech 111

Dakota 37, 144
Diyari 25
Djapu 25
Dutch 80, 92, 172
Dyirbal 18, 59, 147, 148, 149, 172, 173

English 5, 6, 7, 9, 10, 16, 17, 18, 19, 21, 24, 25, 26, 29, 31, 34, 36, 37, 47, 48, 49, 50, 54, 55, 56, 57, 58, 59, 63, 64, 68, 75, 81, 92, 103, 126, 137, 143, 150, 157, 158, 159, 160, 161, 166, 170, 171, 172, 173, 178
Eskimo 41, 44, 59

French 10, 26, 28, 32, 47, 59, 65, 77, 98, 111, 113, 114, 122, 166, 169, 174

Georgian 26, 45, 46, 59, 111, 121, 132, 162
German 9, 10, 47, 57, 59, 70, 80, 81, 88, 108, 171, 172, 175, 177, 178

Halkomelem 26, 37, 172
Hebrew 59
Hindi 111
Huichol 6, 164, 165, 166

Icelandic 161
Ilokano 143, 151
Indo-European 26
Indonesian 7, 8, 16, 55, 59, 169
Italian 32, 35, 36, 37, 39, 40, 47, 48, 59, 68, 69, 70, 75, 77, 78, 84, 88, 105, 107, 109, 110, 111, 112, 113, 114, 119, 120, 122, 138, 142, 162, 166, 172, 173, 174, 175

Jacaltec 108, 111
Japanese 58, 59, 128, 138, 140, 173

Subject index

Subject index